Value, Conflict, and Order

Value, Conflict, and Order

Berlin, Hampshire, Williams, and the
Realist Revival in Political Theory

EDWARD HALL

The University of Chicago Press
Chicago and London

The University of Chicago Press, Chicago 60637
The University of Chicago Press, Ltd., London
© 2020 by The University of Chicago
All rights reserved. No part of this book may be used or reproduced in any manner whatsoever without written permission, except in the case of brief quotations in critical articles and reviews. For more information, contact the University of Chicago Press, 1427 E. 60th St., Chicago, IL 60637.
Published 2020

29 28 27 26 25 24 23 22 21 20   1 2 3 4 5

ISBN-13: 978-0-226-71828-6 (cloth)
ISBN-13: 978-0-226-71831-6 (paper)
ISBN-13: 978-0-226-71845-3 (e-book)
DOI: https://doi.org/10.7208/chicago/9780226718453.001.0001

Library of Congress Cataloging-in-Publication Data

Names: Hall, Edward (Political scientist), author.
Title: Value, conflict, and order : Berlin, Hampshire, Williams, and the realist revival in political theory / Edward Hall.
Description: Chicago ; London : The University of Chicago Press, 2020. | Includes bibliographical references and index.
Identifiers: LCCN 2020001649 | ISBN 9780226718286 (cloth) | ISBN 9780226718316 (paperback) | ISBN 9780226718453 (ebook)
Subjects: LCSH: Berlin, Isaiah, 1909–1997. | Hampshire, Stuart, 1914–2004. | Williams, Bernard, 1929–2003. | Political science—Philosophy. | Political realism.
Classification: LCC JA71 .H258 2020 | DDC 320.092/2—dc23
LC record available at https://lccn.loc.gov/2020001649

For my parents

What is the quest to purify, if not *more* impurity?
PHILIP ROTH, *The Human Stain*

Contents

Abbreviations xi

Introduction 1

PART ONE Isaiah Berlin

1 Pluralism, Relativism, and the Human Horizon 21
2 The Sense of Reality 46

PART TWO Stuart Hampshire

3 The Vitality of Conflict 71
4 From Conflict to Compromise 90

PART THREE Bernard Williams

5 Standing Up to Reflection 117
6 Legitimacy and Liberalism 139

Conclusion 167

Acknowledgments 177
Notes 181
Bibliography 211
Index 223

Abbreviations

Works of Isaiah Berlin

A   *Affirming: Letters 1975–1997*. Edited by Henry Hardy and Mark Pottle. London: Chatto and Windus, 2015.
AC   *Against the Current: Essays in the History of Ideas*. Edited by Henry Hardy. 1979. Reprint, London: Pimlico, 1997.
CC   *Concepts and Categories: Philosophical Essays*. Edited by Henry Hardy and with an introduction by Bernard Williams. 1978. Reprint, London: Pimlico, 1999.
CIB   Ramin Jahanbegloo. *Conversations with Isaiah Berlin: Recollections of a Historian of Ideas*. 1991. Reprint, London: Orion, 1993.
CTH   *The Crooked Timber of Humanity: Chapters in the History of Ideas*. Edited by Henry Hardy. 1990. Reprint, Princeton, NJ: Princeton University Press, 2013.
FIB   *Freedom and Its Betrayal*. Edited by Henry Hardy. 2002. Reprint, London: Pimlico, 2003.
KM   *Karl Marx: His Life and Environment*. 1939. Reprint, Oxford: Oxford University Press, 1978.
L   *Liberty*. Edited by Henry Hardy. Oxford: Oxford University Press, 2002.
PI   *Personal Impressions*. Edited by Henry Hardy. London: Hogarth Press, 1980.
PIRA   *Political Ideas in the Romantic Age: Their Rise and Influence on Modern Thought*. Edited by Henry Hardy. London: Chatto and Windus, 2006.
POI   *The Power of Ideas*. Edited by Henry Hardy. 2000. Reprint, London: Pimlico, 2001.
RR   *The Roots of Romanticism*. Edited by Henry Hardy. London: Chatto and Windus, 1999.
RT   *Russian Thinkers*. Edited by Henry Hardy. 1978. Reprint, London: Penguin, 1988.
SR   *The Sense of Reality: Studies in Ideas and Their History*. Edited by Henry Hardy. London: Chatto and Windus, 1996.

TCE *Three Critics of the Enlightenment: Vico, Hamann, Herder.* Edited by Henry Hardy. London: Pimlico, 2000.
UD   *Unfinished Dialogue.* With Beata Polanowska-Sygulska. New York: Prometheus Books, 2006.

Works of Stuart Hampshire

FOM *Freedom of Mind: And Other Essays.* Oxford: Clarendon Press, 1972.
IE   *Innocence and Experience.* 1989. Reprint, London: Penguin, 1992.
JC   *Justice Is Conflict.* 1999. Reprint, Princeton, NJ: Princeton University Press, 2000.
MC   *Morality and Conflict.* Oxford: Basil Blackwell, 1983.
SS   *Spinoza and Spinozism.* Oxford: Clarendon Press, 2005.
TA   *Thought and Action.* London: Chatto and Windus, 1960.

Works of Bernard Williams

D   *Descartes: The Project of Pure Enquiry.* 1978. Reprint, London: Routledge, 2005.
ELP *Ethics and the Limits of Philosophy.* 1985. Reprint, London: Routledge, 2006.
IBWD *In the Beginning Was the Deed: Realism and Moralism in Political Argument.* Edited by Geoffrey Hawthorn. Princeton, NJ: Princeton University Press, 2005.
M   *Morality: An Introduction to Ethics.* 1972. Reprint, Cambridge: Cambridge University Press, 1993.
ML   *Moral Luck: Philosophical Papers 1973–1980.* 1981. Reprint, Cambridge: Cambridge University Press, 1999.
MSH *Making Sense of Humanity and Other Philosophical Papers 1982–1993.* 1995. Reprint, Cambridge: Cambridge University Press, 1998.
PHD *Philosophy as a Humanistic Discipline.* Edited by A. W. Moore. Princeton, NJ: Princeton University Press, 2006.
SN   *Shame and Necessity.* 1993. Reprint, Berkeley: University of California Press, 2008.
SP   *The Sense of the Past: Essays in the History of Philosophy.* Edited by Myles Burnyeat. Princeton, NJ: Princeton University Press, 2006.
TT   *Truth and Truthfulness: An Essay in Genealogy.* Princeton, NJ: Princeton University Press, 2002.
U   "A Critique of Utilitarianism." In *Utilitarianism: For and Against*, with J. C. C. Smart, 77–150. 1973. Reprint, Cambridge: Cambridge University Press, 2007.

Introduction

Dichotomies do something for us. Consider the staying power of the age-old contrasts we draw between true and false, good and evil, love and hate, nature and convention, pride and shame (among countless others). To be sure, the dichotomies in which we trade are often crude, and problems arise when we push them too far or take them too literally. But it is hard to shake the thought that certain dichotomies play a valuable role in helping us grasp a distinction of genuine significance, even if others do not. The kicker is that it is often hard to judge whether a given dichotomy has this salutary effect or if it stymies the attempt to make sense of something that puzzles us by deleteriously constraining our thoughts.

This book addresses the dichotomy between realism and moralism in political philosophy, around which a fraught methodological debate is raging. At the most basic level, the complaint that political realists make against their moralist opponents is striking and clear: that their work problematically "represents a desire to evade, displace, or escape from politics."[1] Realists claim that this shortcoming derives from the way that mainstream political philosophy, of the sort practiced by luminaries such as John Rawls, Robert Nozick, Ronald Dworkin, and G. A. Cohen, ultimately sees politics as a mere arena for applying a set of prior moral values and principles. That political philosophy is not just an especially important form of applied moral philosophy is the leitmotif of recent realist theorizing.

In methodological terms, this means that realists reject what Raymond Geuss refers to as the *ethics-first* approach, according to which "one can complete the work of ethics first, attaining an ideal theory of how we should act, and then in a second step, one can apply that ideal theory to the action of political agents."[2] On such views, many widely acknowledged features of politics—that much political activity is concerned with either pursuing or exercising power; that history amply reveals persistent fundamental disagreement among well-intentioned citizens on both the good life and principles of justice; and that severe conflicts of interest and principle often have to be coercively resolved before they become utterly destabilizing—are not believed to affect the philosophical theorization of the principles that ought to govern politics. These political realities only matter when we come to ask how fundamental principles might be realized or applied.

Of course, political moralists do not actually deny that real politics has these (in their view) grubby features; they just insist that this does not foreclose the attempt to theorize the moral values that politics would embody or realize if only it functioned as it *should*. Moreover, they assert that exercises in political philosophy that are too concessive to political realities compromise their claim to offer genuine normative guidance altogether. Among other defects, they are viewed as worryingly conservative, failing to appreciate the difference between how things are and how they ought to be. From the moralist perspective, political realism is thus morally and politically defeatist, and its proponents spectacularly fail to grasp the vital dichotomy between matters of fact and questions of value.

The central insight at the heart of the most thoughtful contributions to the recent revival of realism in political theory is that mainstream political philosophy's effacement of various commonplace features of real politics is itself the result of a profound misunderstanding of ethics and the role that "ethical" considerations play in political argument. For this reason, the most interesting realists reject the ethics-first approach not merely because it is often unable to conclusively guide practical judgments about which available, feasible courses of action ought to be pursued.[3] More troublingly, they allege that the ethics-first approach misidentifies the distinctive normative demands, and challenges, of politics. Thus understood, the problem with the mainstream view that political philosophy is a form of applied ethics is not that it generates impractical, utopian political recommendations but that it stops us from making sense of the distinctive goods of political life and the principles that are appropriate to it.

For this reason, supporters of the realist turn in political theory insist that when they refer to the contrast between seeing politics as politics, on the one hand, and seeing it as a form of applied ethics, on the other hand, they are addressing a distinction *with* a difference. Many commentators demur, arguing that advocates of realist political theory set up a false dichotomy between morality and politics at best or, at worst, endorse a series of philosophical claims that are rather obviously wrongheaded.[4] As I will show, there is no denying that the development of a realist approach faces genuine challenges, but these dismissals are easy and cheap. Political realism, in its most significant form, is grounded in a rejection of moral theory as standardly conceived and emerges from the adoption of a realistic spirit in ethics that problematizes traditional accounts of morality, as well as the assumed view of the relationship between morality and politics that such accounts explicitly or implicitly endorse.

To make my argument I examine the work of three postwar British thinkers—Isaiah Berlin (1909–97), Stuart Hampshire (1914–2004), and Bernard Williams (1929–2003)—who are often invoked to support such realist arguments but usually without any deep evaluation of how their scattered arguments in moral and political philosophy fit together. I argue that Berlin's, Hampshire's, and Williams's work suggests that rather than attempting to articulate normative political theories unsullied by realities of the political world as we experience it, political philosophy ignores such realities at its peril. In contrast to the Rawlsian view that "justice is the first virtue of social institutions, as truth is of systems of thought,"[5] they hold that order is the sine qua non of political life. Likewise, while the search for substantive principles of justice that could secure the compliance of rational citizens is the lodestar of much mainstream contemporary political philosophy, these three thinkers maintain that the conflicts that arise between many moral and political values or principles, and indeed entire ways of life, cannot be resolved by appeal to a supreme value or rationalistic decision procedure. As a result, they argue that the search for a set of principles that would secure the consent of all reasonable citizens is misguided. Moreover, rather than imagining political societies in which coercion is used only to protect the rights and entitlements of the (reasonable) majority from a small minority of recalcitrant (unreasonable) individuals, their work asks us to consider how power can rightly be exercised over subjects even when the ends it realizes cannot honestly be presented as the objective demands of impartial moral reasoning.

Consequently, I illustrate how their work suggests that rather than articulating the moral values that politics would realize or embody in a virtually perfect world, we ought to see politics as a response to the human condition that reflects the need to come to binding decisions on subjects considered to be of public concern, when deep disagreements exist on a host of things, including the requirements of morality.[6] In so doing, their work in moral and political philosophy contributes to our understanding of an array of political questions that mainstream political philosophy either obscures or says far too little about, such as the nature of moral and political conflict, the ethics of compromising with adversaries and opponents, and the character of political legitimacy.

Berlin, Hampshire, and Williams

Isaiah Berlin, Stuart Hampshire, and Bernard Williams were eminent figures in twentieth-century Anglo-American academia. They were each elected to Prize Fellowships at All Souls College, Oxford, at the start of their careers (Berlin in 1932, Hampshire in 1936, and Williams in 1951) and went on to occupy prominent positions at some of the most prestigious institutions in Britain and the United States.[7] They received numerous public honors and accolades, including knighthoods (Berlin in 1957, Hampshire in 1979, and Williams in 1999). Additionally, they had significant life experiences outside of the academy. For Berlin and Hampshire, like many other British philosophers of their generation, this was in large part due to the brute fact of the Second World War. Between 1940 and 1942, Berlin was stationed at the British Information Services in New York City, and then from 1942 to 1946 he worked at the British Embassy in Washington, where his primary role was to write weekly reports on American politics for readers back in London, including Churchill.[8] During the war, Hampshire worked for the British Intelligence Services, studying the operations of the Reichssicherheitshauptamt (Reich Main Security Office), and at the war's end he interrogated some leading Nazis—most notably Ernst Kaltenbrunner. He also continued in government service until 1947 in support of the nascent Labour administration under Clement Attlee. Williams spent his national service (1951–53) flying Spitfires for the RAF and was closely engaged in British politics throughout his life. In 1955, he married Shirley Brittain (later Shirley Williams), the leading female Labour—and later SDP and Liberal Democrat—parliamentarian, and subsequently he became well acquainted with a number of important figures in the British Labour Party.[9] In the following decades, he contributed to various royal commissions and policy committees.[10]

As I will illustrate, Berlin's, Hampshire's, and Williams's views in moral and political philosophy are not identical, but there are various shared aims and commonalities of perspective and attitude that enable one to discern a certain unity of purpose in their work. Most centrally, they each propound a deep account of the limitations of philosophical ethics that stands in contrast to those that many contemporary political philosophers implicitly, and sometimes explicitly, accept. In so doing, they offer powerful rejections of the view that moral conflict, disagreement, and tragedy can be overcome, in either theory or practice. Instead of trying to escape from these features of our lives, they insist that we must try to make philosophical sense of them and reflect on how to live with them. Their work consequently raises various questions

INTRODUCTION 5

that recent mainstream political philosophy has not adequately confronted and addresses some common features of politics about which it says too little.

There are various reasons behind Berlin's, Hampshire's, and Williams's shared skepticism about the power of philosophical ethics and insistence on the ineliminability of moral conflict and tragedy. First, their work begins from the view that human nature drastically underdetermines answers to the question of the best life for human beings as there is not a determinate enough conception of human well-being that can underwrite such judgments. Second, they repudiate the idea that our moral intuitions can be systematized in order to deliver a moral or political theory that can satisfactorily guide our judgments and direct our behavior. Third, they insist that moral philosophy must start with and show genuine fidelity to our moral experience, and this leads them to stress that there are many fundamental values that conflict and are incommensurable. To this end, they insist that we must negotiate between different moral claims that pull on us and make compromises between different goods and ways of life even though these compromises cannot receive any kind of absolute, external validation in philosophical theory. This also leads them to affirm that conflict and disagreement are integral aspects of morality and politics and that political theory needs to try and make sense of these in principled terms, rather than merely imagining them away or trying to overcome them.

If one sees things in this way, the very point of reimagining politics according to a specific conception of the ideally just society is called into question. This is surely a large part of the reason why Berlin, Hampshire, and Williams have not been more thoroughly engaged with in mainstream political philosophy. Most contemporary moral and political philosophers simply do not think that the world is as resistant to philosophical righting as Berlin, Hampshire, and Williams maintain.

With these shared aims and positions in mind, scholars routinely consider Berlin, Hampshire, and Williams to be among the foremost value pluralists of the twentieth century.[11] Indeed, an anonymous review of Stuart Hampshire's *Justice Is Conflict* in the *Daily Telegraph* regards Berlin, Hampshire, and Williams—noting the similarities between the three—as the kernel of a group of "Oxford Pessimists" who gave "a new direction, or at least a new mood, to moral and political thought."[12] "Pessimism" has multiple resonances, many of which do not obviously fit the work of Berlin, Hampshire, and Williams or, indeed, capture the impressions one gleams about them as people when reading the remembrances of their friends and colleagues. Nonetheless, as they each powerfully and persistently insisted that philosophy cannot definitively answer the question of how we should live, nor can philosophy identify a timeless moral solution to the question of how political societies should be organized, calling them "pessimistic" is not wholly inaccurate.[13]

Crucially, however, Berlin, Hampshire, and Williams did not think that their understanding of the limits of philosophical ethics inexorably leads to political nihilism: Berlin and Williams vocally self-identified as liberals, while Hampshire referred to himself as a democratic socialist. However, they recognized that their work generated disquieting questions about *how* a set of political convictions might be defended and supported against rivals. As I will show in the following chapters, their work demonstrates that putting conflict, disagreement, and tragedy at the heart of our understanding of ethics and politics has profound consequences for our view of what philosophical argument in ethics and politics might achieve. Certainly, it will not deliver a theory of an ideally just society that we can coherently hope reasonable and rational agents to concur on. Unlike mainstream contemporary political philosophy, which pays lip service to value conflict while seeking to offer a vision of politics in which it is overcome by the achievement of a moralized consensus on constitutional essentials (at least among right-minded members of society), their work convincingly suggests that if we are to take moral conflict seriously we must think about the ethics of politics in a different key.

This book principally sets out to do two things. First, I explore how Berlin's, Hampshire's, and Williams's work in ethics challenges the pretensions of moral philosophy. Second, I critically evaluate their distinct accounts of how we ought to think about politics in light of their own views about ethics. Put another way, I am interested in what Berlin, Hampshire, and Williams have to say about the limits of philosophical ethics and how we ought to think about politics as a result. While I am concerned with recovering and examining the central tenets of a specific strand of British postwar moral and political thought that is often overlooked in contemporary political theory, this is not a work of intellectual history. Instead of describing the development of these thinkers' ideas and paying particular attention to how their work was influenced by their intellectual and political contexts, I engage with their work in order to contribute to current ongoing debates in political theory. In this sense, this is an exercise in what Williams termed the history of philosophy rather than the history of ideas, a distinction constituted by the idea that "the history of ideas is history before it is philosophy, while with the history of philosophy it is the other way around." In the history of ideas, Williams claims that "the question about a work *what does it mean?* is centrally the question *what did it mean?*" For the history of philosophy, on the other hand, the primary objective is to articulate philosophical ideas by rationally reconstructing an author's arguments and then asking what they have to say to us (*D*, xiii–xiv).

In following Williams on this point, I do not intend to denigrate the history of ideas. There is no doubt that there would be great value in a book which, for example, painstakingly outlined the intellectual roots of Berlin's, Hampshire's, and Williams's thought; situated their work in the wider context of postwar analytic philosophy (paying particularly close attention to their personal interactions with each other); and explored the various ways that they contributed to public life in Britain. But I have chosen to focus on the elements of Berlin's, Hampshire's, and Williams's thought that I think have important implications for some pressing questions in contemporary political theory. The only way to prove that this is worthwhile is by demonstrating that it is so, which is what I hope to do here, while recognizing the unavoidable limitations of the exercise. One thing that can be said by way of exculpation is that my approach is, in a sense, in agreement with how Berlin, Hampshire, and Williams tended to treat the thinkers of the past who most interested them.

Political Moralism and Political Realism

By examining how Berlin's, Hampshire's, and Williams's work calls into question some of the basic assumptions of mainstream political philosophy and feeds into a set of political positions that contrast with prominent views in analytical political theory, this book is both a commentary on and a contribution to the recent realist turn in political theory. As its advocates have noted, realism is itself not a substantive political position.[14] Rather, the recent calls for realism in political theory are oppositional in nature: realists malign the tendency of mainstream political philosophers to treat political philosophy as a branch of applied moral philosophy. This shared hostility has enabled the grouping together of diverse political thinkers under the realist banner, even when they do not necessarily self-identify in these terms. Alongside Hampshire and Williams—as I discuss shortly, Berlin is not typically regarded as a realist thinker, though I contend that his work in fact is, in a sense, inadvertently realist—the most prominent members of the realist position in contemporary political theory are generally taken to be John Dunn, Raymond Geuss, John Gray, Bonnie Honig, Chantal Mouffe, Mark Philp, Andrew Sabl, and Judith Shklar.[15] The eclectic nature of the work of the thinkers grouped above is worth stressing. What is involved in theorizing realistically, rather than moralistically, about politics has been variously construed, and the strand of thought that I focus on in this book by no means exhausts the range of realist political positions in contemporary political theory. (Indeed, some fellow travelers consider it a tepid and uninspiring way of developing the realist position in political theory altogether.)[16] In many respects, the strain of realist thought I address is idiosyncratic: it is driven by a set of concerns in moral philosophy that feed into a set of political positions one can regard as realist, and more or less liberal or social democratic, in its political attitudes. In one way or another, this distinguishes it from other realist approaches in contemporary political theory, including the agonism of Bonnie Honig and Chantal Mouffe; Mark Philp's and Andrew Sabl's work in political ethics, which purposefully eschews engaging in discussions about deep philosophical foundations and a host of questions in moral philosophy and instead addresses political conduct in first-order terms; and the self-consciously antiliberal approach championed by Raymond Geuss, which often adopts a more Marxist view of the priority of politics to ethics.

In the academic study of politics, realism is most commonly associated with the field of international relations (IR). The most celebrated proponents of this form of realist thought are generally taken to be E. H. Carr, Hans Morgenthau, and Kenneth Waltz, though IR realists tend to present themselves as drawing on, and developing, the (in their view) venerable insights of canonical figures such as Thucydides, Machiavelli, and Hobbes. As Julian Korab-Karpowicz notes, IR realists generally "consider the principal actors in the international arena to be states, which are concerned with their own security, act in pursuit of their own national interests, and struggle for power. The negative side of the realists' emphasis on power and self-interest is often their skepticism regarding the relevance of ethical norms to relations among states. National politics is the realm of authority and law, whereas international politics, they sometimes claim, is a sphere without justice, characterized by active or potential conflict among states."[17] There is some overlap between this approach to international politics and the kind of political realism under examination in this book.[18] However, contrary to the typical (and rather caricatured) understanding of IR realism, realist political theorists are not committed to stressing the preeminence of self-interest or considerations of advantage in politics.[19] Rather, the defining feature of the political realism that I am referring to is the idea that political theory is not, fundamentally, a matter of applying a predetermined moral theory to the political world because the distinctive character of politics changes how we should think about political questions from a normative perspective.

Williams's way of rendering the distinction between "political moralism" and "political realism" is the most apposite entry point into the current debates about realism and moralism in contemporary political theory. For Williams, political moralism typically comes in two forms. *Enactment models*, like utilitarianism, formulate "principles, concepts, ideals, and values" and seek to "express these in political action." On the other hand, *structural models*, like Rawls's theory of justice, spell out the "moral conditions of co-existence under power, conditions in which power can be justly exercised" (*IBWD*, 1). Moralists, on this view, either see politics as a matter of enacting prior moral values or insist that political actions and decisions must be rigidly constrained by the deliverances of morality. As Enzo Rossi and Matt Sleat note, "The former consists in deriving political prescriptions from pre-political ethical ideals such as happiness, equality or autonomy. The latter amounts to specifying the limits of permissible political conduct through pre-political moral commitments such as a Kantian notion of autonomy or some conception of moral rights. Those ethical values are pre-political in two senses: they are taken to float free from the forces of politics, and they are assigned a foundational role insofar as they have antecedent authority over the political and determine or exhaust the appropriate ends and limits of politics."[20]

In contrast to moralist views that see politics as grounded in a particular moral conception (typically, nowadays, a moral conception of what justice demands), realists seek to give a "greater autonomy to distinctively political thought" (*IBWD*, 3). For realists, the normative standards employed in politics must be rooted in a realistic understanding of politics as a distinctive practice, one which moral considerations cannot unquestionably claim to legislate for. In this sense, many realists follow Williams in stressing that political philosophy should "use distinctively political concepts, such as power, and its normative relative, legitimation" (*IBWD*, 77).

There are various, purposefully underdetermined, correctives to the moralistic character of contemporary political theory that realists tend to endorse. Most centrally, realists are committed to the distinctiveness of politics as a separate domain of action. Seeing politics as a form of applied ethics not only misunderstands the nature of distinctively political goods—such as order and security—but also blinds us to the fact that political recommendations cannot be exhaustively determined by moral considerations made outside of politics, even though within politics some of these considerations might obviously have force.[21]

Second, realists typically stress that much contemporary political theory operates with misconceived—and typically overly idealized and optimistic—accounts of morality.[22] In this light, realist political theorists generally endorse what Raymond Geuss refers to as a "Thucydidean realism" that diagnoses much of the philosophical tradition as being "deeply optimistic." This optimism has several related features:

First of all, traditional philosophers assumed that the world could be made cognitively accessible to us without remainder. . . . Second, they assumed that when the world was correctly understood, it would make moral sense to us. Third, the kind of "moral sense" which the world made to us would be one that would show it to have *some* orientation toward the satisfaction of some basic, rational human desires or interests, that is, the world was not sheerly indifferent to or perversely frustrating of human happiness. Fourth, the world is set up so that for us to accumulate knowledge and use our reason as vigorously as possible will be good for us, and will contribute to making us happy. Finally, it was assumed that there was a natural fit between the exercise of reason, the conditions of healthy individual human development, the demands of individuals for the satisfaction of their needs, interests, and basic desires, and human sociability. Nature, reason, and all human goods, including human virtues, formed a potentially harmonious whole.[23]

On this understanding, I will show that Berlin, Hampshire, and Williams are exemplary Thucydidean realists.

Third, realists stress the agonistic or conflictual nature of politics. When addressing this theme, some realists resort to talking (rather opaquely) in heightened existential terms.[24] But just as often the reminders about the character of politics they highlight in this regard are more platitudinous but, in their view, still overlooked by much moralist thought.[25] As Alison McQueen notes, different realists attribute political disagreement to a number of discrete causes, including "human nature and the limits of rationality, competing identities and interests, and value pluralism." Regardless of how they explain conflict, the important point is that realists stress that "at their best, political institutions can channel and manage this disagreement. But they cannot eliminate it."[26]

Fourth, realists hold that much contemporary political theory has lost sight of, or failed to grasp the seriousness of, the fact that order and stability are fragile achievements and "preconditions for pursuing other political values, such as justice."[27] Thus, rather than seeing politics as a sphere for enacting prior moral values, realists tend to stress that, in the first instance, politics is a matter of ensuring order, trust, and social cooperation and that any further questions about which values or ends we should pursue in politics are secondary and must be theorized as such. In this regard, realists tend to agree that "preventing the worst is the first duty of political leaders, and striving for far-reaching social improvement makes sense only when doing so does not significantly increase the odds that some previous abated evil will reappear."[28] Theories and approaches that fail to take seriously the priority of order are

INTRODUCTION

dismissed as being idealistic and utopian in the pejorative sense; they are liable to be dangerous guides to what we should strive to achieve in politics.

Finally, nearly all realists warn of the perils of wishful thinking. This leads them to insist that theorists must "locate the levels of moral ambition which they espouse within their best causal understanding of the human world as this is," as this prevents them "from subordinating their understanding of how it really is to the importunities of their own projective desires."[29] This does not generate the fallacious thought that the possible is necessarily determined by the actual. But instead of endorsing a kind of Kantian faith that assumes an idealized and tractable human nature, postulating a hopeful account of how morally motivated democratic citizens *might* act in favorable situations,[30] realists insist that our beliefs about achievability be grounded in a resolutely historical and sociological understanding, drawing on the concrete lessons we have learned about how human beings are in fact *likely* to act in various institutional settings. This leads to a related commitment: the insistence that prescriptive political arguments must begin "from where a given political community is"[31] because we cannot illuminatingly determine how we should act by elaborating our favored utopian ideals, values, or virtues and simply imagining an empowered agent who can enact whatever we please (*IBWD*, 58).

In light of their endorsement of these correctives, realists reject the insistence that political philosophy must begin with the articulation of an "ideal theory." The term *ideal theory* is used in assorted ways in contemporary political theory.[32] For ease of exposition, one might summarize as follows: ideal theorists hold that we must inquire into the principles which would govern relevant institutions—and sometimes interpersonal interactions—in a society in which citizens were prepared to comply with the demands that justice made of them.[33] Purveyors of ideal theory hold that this serves both a practical and evaluative aim: it generates a vision of the political society we should aspire to create while also enabling us to determine how far our political societies currently fall short of being fully just.[34] Consequently, ideal theorists insist that if political philosophy does not begin with the articulation of such a theoretical ideal, we will not know how to reform existing political institutions or what kind of political arrangements we ought to strive for in the long run.[35] This is why they claim that ideal theory provides "a long-term goal of political endeavour."[36]

Realists do not think the articulation of such ideal theories is a good way to orient ourselves to politics or—relatedly, but also, importantly, differently—a good way to approach political philosophy. By stipulating citizens' full compliance with a set of moral principles, they argue, ideal theory fatally fails to speak to politics *as politics*; furthermore, they claim that imagining away moral disagreement, conflict, and a lack of compliance is problematic because one of the central purposes of politics is to manage such disagreement and conflict and to foster trust and cooperation despite the noncompliance of some members of society. On the realist view, this is not simply an empirical observation but something of direct relevance for the normative understanding of politics. In this regard, realists hold the kind of consensus and full compliance posited at the heart of ideal theory as akin to a category error. As Jacob Levy puts it, "The hope for a normative political theory that is ideal in some absolute sense is a conceptual mistake, the equivalent of taking the simplifying models of introductory physics ('frictionless movement in a vacuum') and trying to develop an ideal theory of aerodynamics. Like aerodynamics, political life is *about* friction."[37] Thus, realists claim that postulating full compliance is *not* the kind of "abstraction" that enables us "to focus on certain main questions free from distracting details."[38] Indeed, one of the most basic claims at the beating heart of realism is that "the principles appropriate to political and legal life are partly *constituted* by the problems and limitations of human social life; they are not imparted from a realm of moral truth and then applied to a more or less recalcitrant world."[39] If we wish away the friction that is constitutive of politics, we will often assume away many of the central problems that politics seeks to resolve.

Taking this idea seriously suggests that it is a mistake to see all realist approaches as being simply negative in orientation, even if some are. This point is worth highlighting. In his influential survey article, William Galston remarked that the majority of contributions to the realist turn in political theory have remained "essentially critical and cautionary, a warning against liberal utopianism, rather than a coherent affirmative alternative to it."[40] While this is not inaccurate, the body of work that I examine in this book has important first-order implications for political theory that do more than merely deliver the condemnatory methodological reminder that "some doctrines claiming to be political philosophy are nothing of the sort."[41] Though the alternative ways of thinking about politics developed by the thinkers I address do not form rival systematic theoretical accounts of the values that an ideally just political society would realize or the substantive principles that would structure its basic institutions, they are not merely critical repudiations of the work of others. In their own way, Berlin, Hampshire, and Williams offer constructive accounts of how we should theorize about politics, though their thought is grounded in a skeptical view of the power of philosophical argument to conclusively guide our moral and political judgments.

INTRODUCTION 13

A final comment on this matter. In his essay "The Hedgehog and the Fox," Isaiah Berlin famously drew on the Greek poet Archilochus's line, "The fox knows many things, but the hedgehog knows one big thing," to popularize the view—of which he was the twentieth century's most famed exponent—that this distinction may be one of the essential differences that separate human beings. Hedgehogs "relate everything to a single central vision, one system less or more coherent or articulate, in terms of which they understand, think and feel—a single, universal, organising principle in terms of which alone all that they are and say has significance." Foxes, on the other hand, "pursue many ends, often unrelated and even contradictory" and seize "upon the essence of a vast variety of experiences and objects for what they are in themselves, without, consciously or unconsciously, seeking to fit them into . . . any one unchanging, all embracing, sometimes self-contradictory and incomplete, at times fanatical, unitary inner vision" (*RT*, 22). Less well-remembered is Berlin's warning that "like all over simple classifications of this type," the hedgehog/fox distinction "becomes, if pressed, artificial, scholastic, and ultimately absurd." Still, Berlin insists it "offers a point of view from which to look and compare, a starting point for genuine investigation" (*RT*, 23).

These points are worth bearing in mind when considering the ongoing debates about realism and moralism in political theory. Despite their insistence that political theory is not a form of applied morality, realists unapologetically make ethical claims about politics. Some critics of realism, pressing the dichotomy too far, take this to reveal some kind of conceptual confusion at the heart of the position.[42] However, these complaints are very odd. Although realists are concerned with "recovering what is specifically political from the tendency to subsume politics into moral philosophy," no realist worth taking seriously seeks "a political theory cleansed of all moral content."[43]

In my view, the recent calls for realism in political theory should therefore not be seen as assertions that one must refrain from making any sort of ethical judgments about politics; nor should they be interpreted as defenses of a particular set of rigid methodological precepts. Instead, they are invitations to examine what it might mean to philosophize about politics if we accept that it is irreducible to morality. As a result, realism is perhaps best seen as a kind of sensibility, one that expresses disquiet with the character of contemporary moral and political philosophy. At the heart of political realism is the suggestion that we adopt a particular stance toward politics and "focus on the most salient dimensions of a given situation, whether or not they conform to our preferences or desires."[44] It is not obvious how this stance affects political theory. One of my aims is to show that Berlin, Hampshire, and Williams offer a rich and provocative account of how it might do so. The name that we give to this way of addressing questions of political value does not really matter, not least because the names we give to different "positions" often generate impressions that predispose some people to reject them out of hand. ("Realism" is itself a good case in point.) So whether we refer to these thinkers as realists, rather than something else, is not especially important to me in and of itself.[45] As ever, the only serious issue for any theoretical inquiry is whether we do, in fact, manage to make better sense of that which puzzles us.

The Argument of the Book

In part 1, I address the moral and political philosophy of Isaiah Berlin, asking what his thought can add to our understanding of how we might avoid theorizing about politics in moralistic terms. This is likely to elicit a degree of puzzlement, if not outright scorn. Berlin's inaugural address as Chichele Professor of Social and Political Theory at the University of Oxford, "Two Concepts of Liberty," remains his best-known work of political theory. Yet Berlin's distinction is largely orthogonal to my concerns: although I address it in chapter 2, I do so not in order to assess the acuity of the contrast between negative and positive conceptions of freedom per se but in order to examine what it reveals about Berlin's view of how we can think responsibly about political ideals. Moreover, Berlin's published comments about the nature of political theory are uniformly moralist in tone. He denies that there is a theoretically significant distinction between moral and political philosophy (*CIB*, 58) and frankly declares that political theory is "a branch of moral philosophy, which starts from the discovery, or application, of moral notions in the sphere of political relations" (*L*, 168; for similar iterations of this point, see *CIB*, 46, 57–58; *UD*, 140; *CTH*, 1–2). He even claimed that an early draft of Bernard Williams's "Realism and Moralism in Political Theory," which is treated as one of the canonical statements of contemporary political realism, did not greatly stimulate him precisely because he disagreed with Williams about the nature of political theory (*UD*, 93). If anyone is a political moralist, it seems that Berlin is.

Commentators tend to agree. According to Martha Nussbaum, Berlin derives political recommendations from "a set of controversial metaphysical and ethical doctrines concerning the nature of value and the good life, and then goes on to recommend political principles built on these values."[46] On this reading, Berlin's political thought is a striking example of the "enactment model" of political moralism that realists repudiate. Similarly, Jeremy Waldron lambastes Berlin for fixating on questions about the moral ends of politics while neglecting two concerns at the heart of "political" political theory:

the individual virtues that good governance requires and the issue of which sets of political institutions we ought to adopt, given the moral imperfections that human beings display.[47] Accordingly, Waldron claims that Berlin ignores the most salient political question that his work leaves us with: "the ways in which liberal or democratic political institutions might actually accommodate the pluralism and untidiness he thought so important in human life."[48]

If Nussbaum and Waldron are correct, realists should excoriate Berlin, rather than try to learn from him. There is consequently something quixotic about my attempt to examine what Berlin's thought has to add to our understanding of political realism. This is one of the reasons it is worth clarifying at the outset why I address Berlin's work. Explicitly: I do not think that Berlin *was* a realist (somehow, despite his clear protestations to the contrary), nor do I think that his oeuvre is necessarily best understood in realist terms. My aims are far more exegetically modest. Essentially, I want to show that certain elements of Berlin's thought—chiefly, but not exclusively, his value pluralism—open up a number of avenues of inquiry that are overlooked in much contemporary normative political theory, which in turn slant in a realist direction. Berlin, then, was not a realist, but he inadvertently gives us good reasons to consider that maybe we should be.

In chapter 1, I collect and reconstruct Berlin's disparate remarks on the nature of value pluralism and inquire into the ways in which value pluralism can be distinguished from moral relativism. Having elucidated the central features of Berlin's account of value pluralism, I argue that if pluralists want to reject moral relativism the best route is through endorsing a version of a minimum content of natural law. In making this point, I suggest that the considerations of mutual intelligibility and "normal" human behavior that Berlin's account of the "human horizon" highlights do not succeed in supporting pluralist accounts over relativist accounts. I also highlight some tensions inherent in Berlin's claim—frequently rehearsed by his exegetes—that value pluralism is compatible with a belief in the objectivity of values. This sustained examination of value pluralism paves the way for chapter 2, which argues that Berlin's work in ethics has several important implications for how we should think about politics from a philosophical perspective that resonate with and bolster a number of core realist commitments. In particular, Berlin endorses a view about the impurity of political theory and a chastened account of the authority of normative theory, both of which are congenial to the recent calls for realism in political theory. I also argue that by illustrating why it is futile to expect that conflicts among values can be resolved in a reasonable manner all citizens ought to accept, Berlin's value pluralism encourages us to conceive of politics in strikingly different terms to those employed by much contemporary political philosophy. It also affects the attempt to vindicate liberal politics in ways that are in turn revealing of the limitations of moralist approaches.

Thus, I do not attempt to extract a realist theory from Berlin, but I instead seek to show how some of his philosophical insights can be put into the service of a realist cause. Berlin might have enjoyed this treatment. He liked pointing out that intellectual positions often have obscure effects that their authors never intended. And just as Berlin claimed that Kant was a progenitor of nationalism despite his "liberal internationalism" (SR, 232–49), I think that Berlin's work pushes in the direction of political realism despite his avowedly moralistic understanding of the nature of political theory.

Stuart Hampshire is a largely neglected figure in contemporary political philosophy.[49] While it is unclear why this is so, I have some hunches. Chiefly, one is liable to become frustrated when trying to engage philosophically with Hampshire's moral and political work. Galen Strawson begins his review of *Innocence and Experience* by claiming, "This is a strangely wandering book. There is a tremendous floating unclarity underneath the fine movement of prose. Incomplete arguments stand suggestively like half-arches and broken pediments in a mild landscape of non-linear reflection, and the transitions of thought are often hard to grasp."[50] A less extreme, but related, judgment is made in the obituary of Hampshire that appeared in *The Times* on June 16, 2004, written by none other than Isaiah Berlin, his close friend.[51] One thing that Berlin says is particularly striking: Hampshire could not be classified as "one of the dominant philosophers of his age" because his work "was often found lacking in incisiveness, rigour and clarity."[52] As Strawson and Berlin suggest, Hampshire's work is often, at best, allusive. He does not explain in any real depth how the different elements of his thought cohere, nor does he spend much time clarifying the concrete implications of his moral and political philosophy. In this regard, his work is at odds with a lot of contemporary political philosophy that aspires toward theoretical systematicity and wears its practical implications on its sleeve.

Yet many of Hampshire's readers nonetheless insist that his work is worth persevering with. For example, despite his honest assessment of some of the limitations of Hampshire's work, Berlin claims it is rewarding precisely because it is "a great deal more suggestive and responsive to a wide range of human activity" than most philosophy tends to be.[53] Likewise, in his review of *Morality and Conflict*, William Frankena remarks that while Hampshire's work cannot be classed as "careful, clear, rigorous analytical philosophy," it "has global and historical scope and depth and richness of insight." Thus, Frankena claims that Hampshire articulates "an interesting and important kind of position," even if one wishes it had been "more clearly and professionally argued."[54]

In chapters 3 and 4, I show that although Hampshire can frustrate in the ways that Strawson, Berlin, and Frankena allude to, he nevertheless articulates a stimulating account of how we might think about the ethical demands of politics, provided we accept a particular view of the limits of moral philosophy. In chapter 3, I examine Hampshire's views that morality and conflict are inseparable and that searching for moral harmony and consensus is delusive. I argue that, for Hampshire, moral and political conflict is a sign of the proper functioning of the human imagination. His work, therefore, does not merely lead us to recognize, in a kind of resigned way, that the existence of conflict and disagreement must limit the feasible aims of any normative theory of politics. It more fundamentally affects our sense of what can coherently be regarded as *politically ideal* in the first place.

In chapter 4, I address Hampshire's consequent view that we must make considerations of basic procedural fairness and compromise, rather than more ambitious moral ideals, central to our understanding of politics. I argue, however, that Hampshire's account of basic procedural justice is either too thin to function as a robust standard of political evaluation or, if understood in thicker terms, in serious tension with many of his starting claims about the nature of ethics. I do, however, argue Hampshire's work in moral and political philosophy salutarily suggests that at its best politics will be a kind of decent settlement that can secure the acquiescence of different groups.

Bernard Williams's contributions to philosophy are more widely celebrated than Hampshire's, and perhaps even Berlin's. He produced notable work on the history of philosophy, metaphysics, and epistemology but is above all known for his work in ethics, where he is regarded as one of the most significant thinkers of the last century.[55] Until recently, Williams's contribution to the philosophical study of politics was thought to be much less significant, largely because there is not much of a sustained discussion to speak of, with the exception of his early paper "The Idea of Equality" and some parts of *Truth and Truthfulness*, in the works published before his death.[56] The posthumous publication of *In the Beginning Was the Deed: Realism and Moralism in Political Argument*, which contains a number of essays and lectures that he was planning to develop into a book on politics before he died, changed this. Williams has now come to be seen as a significant voice in contemporary political theory.

In part 3, I argue that there is an important continuity of purpose between Williams's work in ethics and his work in politics. Williams once remarked that his work in ethics was concerned with examining how we can "make *some* sense of the ethical as opposed to throwing out the whole thing because you can't have the idealized version of it."[57] In chapter 5, I address Williams's critique of "morality" and examine his account of what is required if we are to operate with a realistic view of the limited ability of philosophy to guide our ethical lives. Yet I also show that in his late work Williams is deeply concerned with thinking about how our moral and political commitments can "be something, despite their failures of self-understanding" and how some forms of philosophical reflection might contribute to this task (*SN*, 11). This sets up the argument of chapter 6, which focuses on Williams's political thought. Rather than seeing politics as a mere means for pursuing prior moral values, Williams argues that we must accept that the first question of politics is the question of order and make a resolutely realistic understanding of legitimacy central to our understanding of politics. I then show that, in a way that echoes his late work in ethics, Williams claims that this enables us to make some sense of how we might vindicate a commitment to liberal politics in spite of the fact that the idealized visions of liberalism offered by political moralists are impossible to affirm on both philosophical and political grounds.[58]

In the conclusion, I draw out the wider implications that my examination of the work of Berlin, Hampshire, and Williams has for the debates about realism and moralism in contemporary political theory. First, I address three shortcomings and limitations of the body of work that I have focused on that those who are attracted to the central elements of Berlin's, Hampshire's, and Williams's thought need to address going forward. Second, I argue that their work helps to illustrate the errors inherent in the view—endorsed by some realists and assumed by most of their moralist critics—that political realism requires us to assess politics in a way that is fully autonomous of moral or ethical considerations. Rather, I argue that Berlin, Hampshire, and Williams illustrate the need for realists to realistically consider what kinds of ethical claims about politics can be sensibly endorsed in a disenchanted world. Finally, I explain how my reading of Berlin, Hampshire, and Williams undermines the common refrain that the contemporary realist current is solely negative or critical in orientation.

PART ONE

Isaiah Berlin

1

Pluralism, Relativism, and the Human Horizon

Value pluralism is widely regarded to be Isaiah Berlin's "master idea."[1] However, working out precisely what Berlin's value pluralism consists of and grasping the implications that it has for moral and political theory are far from straightforward because Berlin refrained from offering a detailed, systematic account of the position. In this chapter, I employ the question "Is value pluralism a species of moral relativism?" as a vehicle for working out the central elements of the view. This is not merely due to the intrinsic interest of working out whether Berlin is a relativist and, if he is, deciding whether this is a "bad thing." Instead, I do so because this has two salutary results. First, examining how Berlin's value pluralism is distinct from versions of moral relativism requires philosophical reconstruction of his scattered remarks and arguments and elucidates many significant features of his thought that are still underappreciated. Second, realists are often accused of endorsing a kind of moral relativism by their opponents.[2] These critics allege that because realists deny the priority of morality to politics, they are unable to articulate any robust evaluative criteria that we can employ to assess the vagaries of real politics. The argument of this chapter shows that this line of criticism is inapt when directed at realists of a value pluralist stripe, provided they follow Berlin in endorsing some account of the minimum content of natural law.

I begin by examining the central theses of value pluralism. I then distinguish three different lines of argument that Berlin develops to support his claim that pluralism is not a species of relativism: his commitment to an empirically verifiable version of natural law, his claims about the "human horizon," and his view that some outlooks rest on obvious empirical falsehoods. In analyzing these claims, I argue that Berlin's invocation of the human horizon is extraneous to the issue at hand and that if pluralists want to reject relativism, they must focus on the minimum content of natural law and the basic needs and interests it highlights, rather than considerations about "normal" human behavior or mutual intelligibility. I also highlight some tensions in Berlin's claim that value pluralism is compatible with a belief in the objectivity of values.

Pluralism

Under the influence of Kant and Collingwood, Berlin held that one of the central purposes of philosophy is to examine the concepts and categories that mediate our experience of the world (*CC*, 10–11). He agrees with Kant that some of these concepts and categories are "permanent and unalterable" but holds that others, most notably the moral and aesthetic, vary a great deal across time and place. Berlin insists that thinking about moral and political concepts in this way—unearthing the implicit presuppositions of people's ways of making sense of the world and uncovering shifts in these concepts and categories—is one of the essential tasks of moral and political philosophy.

This is worth highlighting because Berlin's work is chiefly concerned with uncovering and examining the most basic presuppositions of the central tradition of Western political theory. As is well known, he claims that these presuppositions have not only distorted our experience in philosophically significant ways but also had harrowing political effects. Berlin diagnoses the central tradition of Western political and moral thought as *monistic*. Monism approaches ethics and politics rationalistically, holding that the domain of value is, at heart, a "harmonious whole" (*PIRA*, 54). What is meant by this is not immediately apparent, but the basic idea is that although we often talk about different values—freedom, equality, justice, kindness, efficiency, beauty, and so on—monists hold that these can, in the end, be either reduced to or regulated by a supreme value (e.g., utility) or principle of morality (e.g., the categorical imperative), or combined and realized without remainder in concrete circumstances. In this sense, monism holds that all the different values that constitute "the all-embracing idea of human society" can coexist (*PIRA*, 54). By thinking in this way, Berlin claims, monists embrace a "jigsaw puzzle" view, according to which, since it is possible for all genuine values to fit with another, the central task of ethics and politics is merely "to arrange the fragments . . . in the unique way in which they compose the total pattern that is the answer to all our wants and perplexities" (*L*, 292). On this view, then, conflict and tragedy are not "intrinsic to human life" (*CTH*, 196).

In theoretical terms, monism thus promises the possibility of rational inquiry uncovering a "total answer" of how human beings should live that solves "all questions, both of theory and of practice, once and for all" (*L*, 292). That is, monism offers the possibility of a description of "an ideal universe—a Utopia, if you like—which is simply that described by all true answers to all serious questions," and, saliently, even if we cannot hope to realize this utopia for practical reasons, it can function as an "ideal in terms of which we can measure off our own present imperfections" (*RR*, 22; see also *AC*, 68, and *CTH*, 6).

Rather than seeing value as "one big thing" (*RT*, 22), Berlin endorses a position now referred to as "value pluralism." The principal claim of value pluralism is reasonably straightforward: that there are many different values of *intrinsic* worth. Thus, different values are not merely means toward, or subservient to, more fundamental values or principles in the way that monist views suggest but must be understood in their own terms. Moreover, Berlin continually stresses that values are potentially incompatible and can conflict. Different values often cannot be achieved in concert, even in ideal circumstances, as the pursuit of some values conflicts with the pursuit of others. As Berlin puts it, "neither political equality nor efficient organisation nor social justice is compatible with more than a modicum of individual liberty," and "justice and generosity, public and private loyalties, the demands of genius and the claims of society can conflict violently with each other" (*L*, 213). This also suggests, in a way that is less immediately clear, that we can recognize different kinds of value (or, if one prefers, spheres of value), such as the moral, economic, and aesthetic, and that no one subset of values, such as the moral, necessarily trumps other kinds.

Developing these points, followers of Berlin hold that the values and virtues realized in different "styles of life," such as those associated with a life of action and a life of contemplation, are incompatible if "they cannot normally be exemplified in the same life."[3] Consequently, when an individual or group pursues a course of action in order to achieve some end, this often requires them to forgo other ends that a different course of action would realize. The implication is clear: "not all good things are compatible, still less the ideals of mankind" (*L*, 213).

Significantly, Berlin does not merely hold that values can conflict but also stresses that they are often incommensurable. Thus, conflicts between values cannot always be resolved by an uncontroversial rational standard, such as the conclusions of a particular ethical theory or decision procedure, or by agreement on a supreme principle or highest value, such as utility or rights. Put another way, there is no "infallible measuring rod" or "single universal overarching standard" (*AC*, 69–70) that we can appeal to in order to resolve value conflict in every case.[4] Thus, Berlinian pluralists deny that any particular value is overriding in the face of value conflict.[5]

For Berlin, and for those who endorse his claims about the plural nature of value, including Hampshire and Williams, there are many intrinsically valuable ends of human existence and styles of life that individuals can rationally pursue, but these often conflict with each other, with the result that there is no best life or set of ends on which we all have reason to settle.

The plurality and conflict of which Berlin speaks occurs at three levels.[6] First, at the level of goods and values. Berlin famously described liberty as having both negative ("How many doors are open?") and positive ("Who is master?") elements that do not cohere but are each ultimate values in their own right (*L*, 212). Hence, Berlinians insist that values are often "internally complex and can be inherently pluralistic, containing conflicting elements."[7]

Second, pluralism and conflict occur *within* what Berlin at one point calls a network of values, which he glosses as a "coherent vision of life" involving "patterns of behaviour and feeling and disposition and ideals . . . entire structures, entire ways of life, in which the values or ends or motives are interconnected in particular ways" (*A*, 207–8).[8] (I prefer the term *outlook* to the more cumbersome *network of values* and will employ it hereafter.) The point is that every outlook orders different values and ends in a particular way, but because values are multiple, potentially incompatible, and incommensurable, such ordering inevitably constrains the claims of some values in the pursuit of practical congruity. Consider liberalism with its commitment to freedom *and* equality (and many other values besides). If freedom and equality are intrinsically valuable, potentially conflicting, and incommensurable, then liberals must find a way of living with the tension between the intrinsic claims of these values, rather than imagining that such a tension does not exist or revising their understanding of these values in order to fool themselves into thinking that it does not exist.[9]

Third, conflict and incommensurability also apply *between* different outlooks. Outlooks differ according to the goods and values they promote or abhor, as well as by how they rank values. Consequently, distinct outlooks may pursue incommensurably valuable bundles of goods. In his work on Herder and Vico, Berlin stresses the realization that "more than one equally authentic, equally developed culture was possible, and that such cultures could be widely heterogeneous, could, indeed, be incompatible and incommensurable." This in turn entails a "genuine pluralism, and an explicit refutation of the belief that man everywhere, at all times, possessed an identical nature which, in its quest for self-fulfillment, sought after the same ends" (*TCE*, 164; for further statements, see *TCE*, 168, 176–77, and *AC*, 12). Subsequently, Berlin claims that the concept of an ideal state is incoherent: because realizing some values necessarily involves the forgoing or sacrificing of others, "the notion of total human fulfilment is a formal contradiction, a metaphysical chimera" (*L*, 213). This is one of the reasons why, for Berlin, tragedy is intrinsic to human life (*CTH*, 203). Significantly, this suggests that it is futile to grade different outlooks according to a transhistorical or perennial vision of how different values must coalesce (*CTH*, 68). Just as there is no one best life for man, there is no ideal form of society; in terms of value, each cultural, political, moral, and religious way of life has its own distinctive advantages and costs.

This points to a further element of Berlin's thought that readers and critics alike tend to overlook, or at least downplay, that I refer to as the *mutual dependence condition*. The basic idea is that historical and philosophical reflection reveals that the valuable elements of different outlooks cannot be freely combined and that it is often the case that the different constitutive features of an outlook are inexorably intertwined. As a crude example, we cannot isolate a favorable attitude toward samurai bravery from unfavorable attitudes toward *tsujigiri*, strict honor codes, and the hierarchical social relations that underpinned the samurai way of life.

According to the mutual dependence condition, the objectionable features of an outlook may be indispensable presuppositions of those features we praise. Pluralists who share Berlin's historical sensibility therefore stress that value is often not independent of disvalue, that virtue often coexists with vice, and that in many outlooks the bad may be a condition of the good. Consequently, they claim that life is tragic not only because values often conflict and are incommensurable, with the result that we cannot hope to achieve all good things at once, but also because justice, virtue, and value may be dependent on injustice, vice, and disvalue.[10]

As Stuart Hampshire notes, this historically informed style of thinking understands that such outlooks—which Hampshire calls *ways of life*—are "totalities of customs, attitudes, beliefs, institutions, which are interconnected and mutually dependent in patterns that are sometimes evident and sometimes subtle and concealed. One cannot easily abstract the activity or practice from its setting in a complete way of life, and make one-to-one comparisons between activities and practices which are part of different ways of life" (*MC*, 6). To this end, Hampshire endorses what he refers to as the "no-shopping principle": the claim that we cannot "pick and choose" aspects or elements of one outlook and combine them with aspects or elements of another outlook because the coherence of outlooks "comes from their distinct histories" (*MC*, 148). Value pluralists who endorse this consequently hold that trying to amalgamate the admirable features of different outlooks is an error because it is likely to be the case that they cannot, as a matter of empirical realism, be combined while retaining their vitality (AC, 124).[11] In some cases, the very attempt to do so can have terrifying political results.[12]

This way of thinking about value therefore repudiates a (pseudo-Hegelian) view of historical progress that holds that "nothing that is of permanent value need be lost irretrievably, for in some form it is preserved in the next higher stage" (AC, 123). Berlin insists that when some historical changes occur, "gains in one respect necessarily entail losses in another," and that, as a result, "some valuable forms of experience are doomed to disappearance, not always to be replaced by something necessarily more valuable than themselves" (AC, 123–24). Consider the distinction Berlin makes in his essay on Machiavelli between pagan morality and Christian morality. One does not have to be a full-blooded Nietzschean to believe that while the move from the former to the latter brings with it significant gains and benefits, it also imposes equally real losses to the values of pagan morality—"courage, vigour, fortitude and adversity, public achievement, order, discipline" (AC, 45).

Reasons for Pluralism

The last section cleared conceptual ground in order to outline the central features of the value pluralist position. In this section, I ask why value pluralists maintain we ought to endorse the above claims about the normative domain.

Two different kinds of considerations that Berlin isolates are relevant in this examination: historical and philosophical. Berlin emphasizes two historical turning points at which the central presuppositions of Western political theory were challenged. First, he claims that by acknowledging the sheer multiplicity of outlooks, and the distinctive ways of life they foster, the late Renaissance refuted "the belief that man everywhere, at all times, possessed an identical nature which, in its quest for self-fulfillment, sought after the same ends, and that this, indeed, was precisely what constituted man's human essence" (TCE, 164). This does not lead Berlin to abandon the concepts of human nature or natural law, but he insists our conceptions of both have to be more mutable (TCE, 164). In particular, ahistorical models of human nature must be rejected because the basic dispositions and capacities of mankind are revealed historically. This repudiates the idea that there is a "fixed order beneath the appearance of ordinary moral and political life" that reveals a "fixed hierarchy of needs and ends for human nature," one which could be mined to uncover specific laws of human nature and social development that our political systems should facilitate as best they can.[13]

The second, vital, historical turning point was Romanticism. Berlin claims that the Romantics followed Kant in denying that value judgments are descriptive propositions. However, contra Kant, they denied that morality is a matter of complying with the *categorical* demands of practical reason by radicalizing Kant's claims about the concepts and categories that order our experience, holding that many of the moral, political, and aesthetic concepts we employ are invented at particular historical junctures (*PIRA*, 10; *CTH*, 245–46; *SR*, 175; *POI*, 9–10). This Romanticist perspective appeals to Berlin's historical sensibility, causing him to reject the idea that moral values or ends exist in some mind-independent sense.[14] Many commentators deny or overlook this. I suspect that this is because they have been led astray by Berlin's insistence that his value pluralism is consistent with a belief in the objectivity of morality, and this leads them to impute ontological or metaphysical beliefs to Berlin that he did not in fact hold.[15] As we will see, Berlin endorses an account of human nature that grounds a minimal version of a kind of natural law alongside the Romantics' view of value creation. He acknowledges that this stretches the bounds of intellectual coherence but diagnoses it as our plight as heirs of two intellectual traditions we cannot repudiate in toto (*SR*, 193).

Berlin does not attempt an elaborate philosophical justification of his belief in value pluralism. This may seem a damaging omission, but it is not surprising because he consistently states that he is an empiricist who rejects all metaphysical and a priori approaches in ethics and politics (*POI*, 11; *CIB*, 114).[16] As far as he is concerned, "the ordinary resources of empirical observation" consistently reveal that values push in different directions and cannot be reconciled without remainder (*L*, 213). When value conflict arises, Berlin claims monists typically try to ignore it because they find it painful, pretend one of the values is "identical with its rival" (which merely ends in gross distortion), or artificially order values in light of some nonexistent "absolute criterion" in the attempt to evade it (*L*, 42, 151). In response to those who claim that such conflicts could be overcome in a perfect world, Berlin states: "The meanings they attach to the names which for us denote the conflicting values are not ours. We must say that the world in which what we see as incompatible values are not in conflict is a world altogether beyond our ken; that principles which are harmonised in this world are not the principles with which, in our daily lives, we are acquainted; if they are transformed, it is into conceptions not known to us on earth. But it is on earth that we live, and it is here that we must believe and act" (*CTH*, 13–14).

This point about prioritizing experience over the demands of theoretical parsimony unites Berlinian value pluralists.[17] They recognize that such arguments do not deliver decisive proof of their metaethical thesis.[18] Berlin's arguments in favor of pluralism should, accordingly, be seen as *provisional*—with the important proviso that from his point of view this provisional status does not weaken these claims because no set of philosophical claims in ethics and politics could ever hope to be anything else. The furthest most pluralists will go is to say that the burden of proof is on the monists to "show how the apparent diversity of values can be translated into a single vocabulary of value without loss of moral meaning."[19] Because countless philosophical attempts to conclusively establish the truth of monism have failed, pluralists argue that we have good reasons to endorse their provisional claim about the nature of value.[20]

As various theorists have pointed out, the claim that our experience supports value pluralism has trouble accounting for the fact that some people (such as the devoutly religious, political fanatics, or tedious public commentators who revel in passing immediate moral judgment over others) manifestly do not experience their lives in terms of value conflict, incommensurability, and tragedy.[21] It is not good enough for pluralists merely to claim that such people are myopic or morally insensitive, even if they often are. After all, if our experiences are the central reason why we should affirm value pluralism, pluralists must be able to explain why some people seem to experience life in monistic terms.

Although Berlin does not say a great deal about this, he makes some suggestive remarks. In particular, he regards the search for true certainty in normative matters, to avoid the discomfort that accompanies the recognition of value pluralism, as a "permanent need of mankind" (*CTH*, 250) and intimates that the a priori assumptions monists make lead people to ignore their ordinary experiences (*L*, 213). It is possible to see how pluralists could utilize these ideas to explain why many people are drawn to experience the world in monistic terms and how some of the most basic concepts and categories that mediate their experience have led them to do so.

Berlin's Attempt to Distinguish Pluralism and Relativism

Berlin strenuously denies that value pluralism inexorably leads to a version of moral relativism.[22] One of the difficulties with judging the veracity of this allegation lies in the fact that Berlin often equivocates between viewing relativism as a *metaethical* position that denies that there are any objective values and an *epistemological* position that claims that members of discrete cultures can "scarcely begin to understand what other civilisations lived by—can only describe their behaviour but not its purpose or meaning" (*CTH*, 85).[23]

Although the metaethical claim accords with ordinary understandings of moral relativism, Berlin's epistemological reading does not. Rather than endorsing claims about the limits of cross-cultural understanding per se, moral relativists are better understood as supporting the belief that we should refrain from making general judgments about the truth or falsity of moral claims because moral justification "is not absolute or universal, but is relative to the traditions, convictions, or practices of a group of persons."[24] This position is usually grounded in an awareness of moral diversity. The basic idea is that "in the moral domain the best explanation of diversity is relativity. Accordingly, there is a tendency to read moral relativism off the surface of foreign moral practices."[25]

As many thinkers have argued (Berlin included; see *CIB*, 107), some versions of relativism are self-refuting. Bernard Williams makes the point powerfully when he remarks that vulgar relativists endorse the following propositions:

1. "'Right' means (can only coherently be understood as meaning) 'right for a given society.'"
2. "'Right for a given society' is to be understood in a functionalist sense."
3. "Therefore, it is wrong for people in one society to condemn, interfere with, etc., the values of another society." (*M*, 20)

This argument is a nonstarter, however, because the third claim is nonrelative and the first supposedly rules out nonrelative judgments, revealing that it is logically fallacious to think that metaethical relativism leads to toleration in practice.

Yet the central intuition behind the relativist position can more plausibly be stated in the following terms: *Value commitment is an outcome of shared ways of life, and these differ enormously. Thus, the kinds of conduct that outlook X promotes and censures can be radically different from that which outlook Y promotes and censures, and we are unable to make general judgments about whether X or Y are correct, as all such judgments are relative to a particular tradition.* This is the understanding of moral relativism that I will be working with hereafter. In contrast, it is reasonably uncontroversial to hold that a belief in moral objectivity commits one to the view that "moral judgments are ordinarily true or false in an absolute or universal sense, that some of them are true, and that people sometimes are justified in accepting true moral judgments (and rejecting false ones) on the basis of evidence available to any reasonable and well-informed person."[26]

A number of Berlin's claims are hard to reconcile with such a view. For example, he remarks that if we acknowledge the truth of value pluralism, "we shall not distort the moral facts by artificially ordering them in terms of some one absolute criterion . . . and shall seek to comprehend the changing ideas of cultures, peoples, classes and individual human beings, without asking which are right, which wrong, at any rate not in terms of some simple home-made dogma" (*L*, 151). He also asserts that value pluralism reveals the incoherence of the search for a "single, unchanging, objective code of universal precepts" as it suggests that there are "many ways of living and thinking and feeling, each with its own 'centre of gravity,' self-validating, uncombinable, still less capable of being integrated into a seamless whole" (*TCE*, 15–16). Such quotations, which are representative of a certain strand of Berlin's thought, have an affinity with the basic idea that Leo Strauss (and others) find at the heart of relativism: "the assertion that all ends are relative to the chooser and hence equal."[27] Yet Berlin also repeatedly insists that pluralism is not relativism because "the multiple values are objective, part of the essence of humanity rather than the arbitrary creations of men's subjective fancies" (*POI*, 12). Moreover, he holds that value pluralism does not have subjectivist implications, rejecting the suggestion that "the judgement of a man or a group, since it is the expression or statement of a taste, or emotional attitude or outlook, is simply what it is, with no objective correlate which determines its truth or falsehood" (*CTH*, 83).

A lack of clarity bedevils many of Berlin's statements about the objectivity of values, and I will not proceed by trying to uncover a basic consistency between Berlin's different usages of the term.[28] Instead, I place Berlin's disparate remarks about the objectivity of morality and values in the context of the arguments he articulates against moral relativism, asking how Berlinian value pluralists can respond to the fundamental challenge moral relativism articulates: the claim that "there is no hope of finding a standpoint from which to assess objectively the validity of culturally diverse or conflicting moral claims."[29] This enables us to uncover the extent to which Berlinian value pluralists can rightly claim that their position is consistent with a belief in the objectivity of values.[30]

Berlin develops three different lines of argument to support his claim that pluralism is not a species of relativism, which I now address.

THE MINIMUM CONTENT OF NATURAL LAW

Berlin claims that we have good reason to endorse a minimal version of natural law on empirical grounds, self-consciously following H. L. A. Hart, who famously endeavors to demonstrate that

> Reflection on some very obvious generalizations—indeed truisms—concerning human nature and the world in which men live, show that as long as these hold good, there are certain rules of conduct which any social organization

must contain if it is to be viable. Such rules do in fact constitute a common element in the law and conventional morality of all societies which have progressed to the point where these are distinguished as different forms of social control. With them are found, both in law and in morals, much that is peculiar to a particular society and much that seems arbitrary or a mere matter of choice. Such universally recognised principles of conduct which have a basis in elementary truths concerning human beings, their natural environment, and aims, may be considered the *minimum content* of Natural Law, in contrast with the more grandiose and more challengeable constructions which have often been proffered under that name.[31]

Similarly, Berlin claims that there exists a "minimum of moral values accepted by all men without which human societies would disintegrate, and from which, for quasi-biological causes, men cannot depart without perishing" (*A*, 206). He disavows making this argument on theological or metaphysical grounds, claiming it has a resolutely empirical basis. Hart is clear that these minimal considerations can be classed as part of natural law because they respond to human beings' basic physiological needs and regulate the inevitable conflicts that arise when human beings live together. The fact that we share some basic physiological and psychological traits "dictates that some things will normally benefit all human beings, and, similarly, that some things will normally harm everyone."[32] Prohibitions that further the interest human beings have in enjoying such benefits and avoiding such harms enable us to live good lives, even if they cannot ensure that we do.

Berlin sometimes refers to the minimum content of natural law as the "common core" of morality, the idea being that a common set of prohibitions form part of genuine outlooks, and many commentators use this term accordingly. However, Berlin also invokes this idea of a core to explicate his belief that different outlooks share some common values, such as freedom, justice, and truth, as we will see when we turn to his claims about the human horizon. I will refrain from following him in this usage. Properly understood, Hart's and Berlin's accounts of the minimum content of natural law reflect a different idea: that all human beings share a set of basic needs and that respecting these needs is a genuinely universal moral demand.[33]

Cultural conventions determine the form that prohibitions directed at protecting people's basic needs take.[34] Moreover, it may be the case that we cannot fully explicate this set of needs.[35] But, drawing on Wittgenstein, Berlin claims that all genuine outlooks have a certain family resemblance as they seek to promote the basic interests that human beings share (*UD*, 41). This does not commit him to a static or fixed conception of human nature. Berlin insists that we can reject fixed conceptions without depriving the idea of human nature of all content. His defense of the idea that some basic needs are compatible with a commitment to value pluralism ought to be understood in these terms.

In his conversations with Ramin Jahanbegloo, Berlin draws on these ideas, claiming that a commitment to human rights rests on the belief that some goods "are in the interest of all human beings, as such" and that these interests must be respected, either by enabling them to be met or by protecting people from others who wish to frustrate them (*CIB*, 39). Jahanbegloo asks if this commitment contradicts "the spirit of nations." Berlin unequivocally replies that it does not because "every culture which has ever existed assumed that there exist such rights—or at least a minimum of them." Although he notes there is no universal agreement about to whom these rights apply—noting that in some social orders they have been denied to "helots, slaves, Jews, atheists, enemies, members of neighbouring tribes, barbarians, heretics"—he insists "that such rights exist and that they are an empirical pre-condition of the leading of full human lives—that has been recognized by every culture" (*CIB*, 39).

The minimum content of natural law is compatible with a wide range of different outlooks, including many nonliberal forms of politics.[36] Moreover, although protecting these needs is of first importance, every outlook pursues more expansive or thicker goals because its positive aspirations extend beyond merely respecting its denizens' basic needs and interests.

THE HUMAN HORIZON

The second way Berlin attempts to distance pluralism from relativism trades on the idea that only a finite number of outlooks, values, or ends make sense to us as outlooks, values, or ends that "normal" or "sane" human beings would pursue. He takes this to reveal that outlooks cannot be understood as entirely arbitrary or subjective creations; rather, they are constrained by some universal features of human nature. This has two important implications.

First, Berlin claims that if someone pursues an end that others simply cannot make sense of as *an end*, the individual is not considered a human being in the proper sense. So it is not the case that *any* set of values or end can motivate normal human behavior. In some passages, he employs nonmoralized examples to illustrate his point, claiming that if someone worships trees merely because they are made of wood, and not because of any divine powers they are supposed to possess or any significance they have in the historical memory of the group, we would find this unintelligible (*CTH*, 12). In other passages, Berlin employs more moralized examples, holding that if someone is indifferent to whether they should kick a pebble or kill their family because either would resolve their boredom, we would not be "disposed, like consistent relativists, to attribute to him merely a different code of morality from my own or that of most men, or declare that we disagree on essentials, but shall begin to speak of insanity and inhumanity" (CC, 166). The same point is made about people who cannot see anything wrong with torturing children, condemning the innocent without remorse, destroying the world to relieve minor bodily pain, or permitting the killing of blue-eyed men for no reason (CTH, 215–16; L, 24). Most evocatively, Berlin employs the example of a "pin-pusher" who enjoys pushing pins into resilient surfaces without discriminating between tennis balls and human skin.[37] Drawing on these more moralized examples, Berlin claims that accepting some minimum of values is one consideration in our judgment of whether someone is a normal human being (POI, 12; L, 24; for related claims, see CTH, 19).

Second, Berlin claims that we can understand different outlooks and communicate with people who endorse different ends because of the existence of common values (L, 24). Intercommunication and understanding between cultures are possible because "what makes men human is common to them, and acts as a bridge between them" (CTH, 11).[38] The question of which values are held in common is ultimately empirical (L, 45). In a letter to Stuart Hampshire, Berlin includes equality, justice, and the pursuit of knowledge and truth among his list of such common values, remarking that while the pursuit of these values is "mediated by local circumstances," they are pursued "in their own right, if anything is" (A, 423).

In the introduction to *Five Essays on Liberty*, Berlin declares that "we seem to distinguish subjective from objective appraisal by the degree to which the central values conveyed are those which are common to human beings as such, that is, for practical purposes, to the great majority of men in most places and times" (L, 25). If some values are anthropologically or historically attested to a sufficiently widespread degree, Berlin therefore suggests that we can refer to them as objective values, rather than mere subjective wants. The idea is that there are some values (liberty, equality, justice, social welfare, courage, truth) "that a great many human beings in the vast majority of places and situations, at almost all times, do in fact hold in common" (CIB, 37). Berlin claims this "common ground" is "correctly called objective" (L, 25). Thus,

> There are certain values, and only those values, which men, while remaining men, can pursue. If I am a man or woman with sufficient imagination (and this I do need), I can enter into a value system which is not my own, but which is nevertheless something I can conceive of men pursuing while

remaining human, while remaining creatures with whom I can communicate, with whom I have some common values—for all human beings must have some common values or they cease to be human, and also some different values else they cease to differ, as in fact they do. (*POI*, 12)

Therefore, Berlin claims to endorse an account of the objectivity of value and rejects the suggestion, which he takes to be at the beating heart of relativism, that values are arbitrary or subjective creations (*POI*, 12).

These considerations lead Berlin to declare that there are a finite number of outlooks compatible with our understanding of normal human behavior (*POI*, 12). Although values are plural, in order to remain comprehensible as values, they must fall within what Berlin calls the *human horizon* (*CTH*, 12, 136; *CIB*, 108). Values and ends are designated "objective" when they foster the pursuit of goals that we understand as being intelligible pursuits for human beings to embrace, given their nature and the situation in which they find themselves (*POI*, 12; *CTH*, 82–83, 86, 306–7). As George Crowder and Henry Hardy note, the values that fall within the human horizon "are called 'objective' by Berlin because they are not merely subjective, arbitrary, varying from person to person (as some relativists hold), but stable features of the world based in human nature, open to empirical view like the world's other contents."[39] While we do not have to *endorse* the values that fall within the human horizon, we can imaginatively "enter into" such outlooks and understand why people found value in, for example, being Roman soldiers, Jacobins, Chinese anti-imperialists, or American hippies (*CIB*, 37; *POI*, 12; *A*, 208).[40]

Berlin claims that this distinguishes pluralism from relativism (and other forms of subjectivism) because relativism "does *not* require the possibility of understanding other outlooks" in this way (*A*, 208). This remark is puzzling. After all, relativists may claim that they can gain insight into the distinctive practices of distinct outlooks and grasp the values and ends that animate their conduct in a number of ways: reading books, watching documentaries, visiting sites of historical interest, and so forth. To this end, it is hard to see why moral relativists cannot agree that normal human beings pursue a finite set of values or ends or claim to "understand" why people found value in these pursuits. The relativist seemingly has no more trouble than the pluralist in comprehending why the members of distinct outlooks acted as they did, but they do refrain from making general claims about the acceptability or justification of such practices.

Accordingly, the distinction between pluralism and relativism that Berlin is getting at must be explained in another way in order to remain sustainable. In my judgment, the best reconstruction of the underlying idea at work is thus the following: if we find an alien outlook comprehensible, this does not merely require us to understand it, in the same way that, for example, I *understand* why some people think that Zizzi is the best restaurant chain in the world despite the fact that the food there is terrible (maybe they have dire gastronomic judgment because there are very few restaurants where they live). Rather, for Berlin, one's comprehending an outlook is, in some sense, an exercise in *evaluation*.[41] For this to follow, it must be the case that when we comprehend an outlook in the way Berlin alludes to, this reveals that it *actually is valuable* by illustrating that it is of one of the many, but finite, ways that human nature can nonerroneously develop. This in turn enables us to class it as objective by Berlin's standards. In this regard, Berlin endorses the Herderian idea that a distinct outlook that reaches this threshold represents a "wonderful exfoliation of human potentialities in its own time and place" (*TCE*, 233).[42] This manifestly is not the case when I comprehend why people enjoy eating at Zizzi; comprehending this does not reveal that the food at that benighted chain is of objective gastronomic value.

Relativists cannot consistently think that an outlook represents a dimension along which human nature can valuably develop in the way that Berlin is alluding to. They have to refrain from making such claims as they hold that all such claims are *relative* to a particular evaluative frame of reference. This enables us to make sense of Berlin's important remark that, contrary to what subjectivist doctrines suggest, he renounces the idea that "anyone might be of any sort, pursue any end—everyone to his taste." Genuine outlooks are not invented ex nihilo: they are developments, or outgrowths, of distinctive human characteristics. This is the "bridge" that enables us to understand certain ways of life and forms of conduct as valuable expressions of human nature (*A*, 209).[43] This also suggests that we have to remain open to the idea that objective values and ends are yet to be discovered.[44] Thus, our sense of objectivity is constrained because some incomprehensible actions or commitments are ruled out. But it is also impossible to conclusively specify the character of these constraints because we cannot say which outlooks, values, and ends fall within the human horizon in advance of them coming about.

EMPIRICAL ERRORS

Berlin also suggests that we do not have to take a relativistic attitude toward doctrines which rest on certain empirical illusions. In particular, we can criticize views which rest on "evil fictions" that can be illustrated "by ordinary, rational argument, founded on empirical observation and common reasoning" (*UD*, 92). Berlin includes many examples of such demonstrably false beliefs: from *Untermenschen* to a Moloch demanding human sacrifice, burning people at the stake to better find salvation, or self-flagellating for spiritual enlightenment (*A*, 209; *UD*, 92). Once these errors are discounted, Berlin intimates that our understanding of the range of outlooks of objective worth is constrained.

Is Pluralism a Species of Relativism?

I now critically analyze Berlin's claims and offer a reconstruction of how value pluralists sympathetic to Berlin's insights ought to proceed if they wish to distinguish pluralism from relativism. In so doing, I illuminate some shortcomings and problematic features of Berlin's arguments. In particular, I contend that his claims about the human horizon do not serve to privilege pluralism over relativism in any deep sense. I also highlight some tensions in his claim that value pluralism is compatible with a belief in the objectivity of values.

THE MINIMUM CONTENT OF NATURAL LAW

The first concern likely to be raised about Berlin's defense of the minimum content of natural law is that he moves from asserting that all human beings share a set of basic needs to demanding that these needs be protected or promoted and thus violates the "fact/value distinction."

However, if one considers human nature a resource for moral and political thinking, then the implied understanding of the fact/value distinction that undergirds this complaint is mistaken. Here is how James Griffin puts the point when defending his attempt to derive human rights from considerations about the distinctive capacities we share as human agents:

> On the face of it, this looks like trying to derive values (human rights) from facts (human nature), which generations of philosophers have been taught cannot be done. However, it cannot be done only on a certain conception of nature: namely, the conception that sees nature as what scientists at the start of the modern era thought it was, as what the natural sciences, especially the physical sciences, describe. As such, nature excludes values. On this narrow conception of the natural, the conception of "human" that I am proposing is not natural. I single out functioning human agents via notions such as their autonomy and liberty, and I choose those features precisely because they are especially important human interests. It is only because they are especially important interests that rights can be derived from them; rights are strong protections, and so require something especially valuable to attract protection. So my notions of "human nature" and "human agent" are already well within the

normative circle, and there is no obvious fallacy involved in deriving rights from notions as evaluatively rich are they are.[45]

To be clear, Berlin is not committed to the same factual claims about human agency that Griffin is, but Griffin's response to the fact/value criticism works equally well in Berlin's case. Concepts such as "needs" and "interests" are, to use Bernard Williams's terminology, *thick* concepts that express "a union of fact and value." As Williams puts it, "The way these notions are applied is determined by what the world is like . . . and yet, at the same time, their application usually involves a certain valuation of the situation. . . . Moreover, they usually (though not necessarily) provide reasons for action" (*ELP*, 129–30).[46] Once we recognize that, in referring to *basic needs* or *fundamental interests* in order to explicate the minimum content of natural law, we are already enmeshed in evaluation, the worry that Berlin is crossing some watertight fact/value distinction is neutralized.

As noted earlier, recognizing the minimum content of natural law does not *resolve* the question of which outlook we should endorse because a wide range of such outlooks is compatible with respecting such needs. This is neither surprising nor, if one is a pluralist, lamentable. The important point is that recognizing these basic needs repudiates the claim that evaluation of different values, practices, and ends is *entirely* relative. To put it in the terms used earlier: *It may be the case that what outlook X promotes and censures differs from what outlook Y promotes and censures, but we can discriminate between X and Y to the extent that they censure, and do not promote, violations of the minimum content of natural law, even if the ways they do so will inevitably diverge.* Therefore, taking our shared needs seriously contradicts the relativist claim that there are *no* universal criteria we can employ to assess the validity of diverse and competing moral claims.

THE HUMAN HORIZON

I do not believe that Berlin's claims about the human horizon have the potential to undermine relativism in the way Berlin suggests. For one thing, some comprehensible and intelligible values, ends, and outlooks violate, or are inconsistent with, the minimum content of natural law.[47] For example, viewers of the television adaption of Philip K. Dick's *The Man in the High Castle* "enter into" the Nazi outlook—but it is implausible (to say the least) to hold that Nazism respects the minimum content of natural law. Similarly, consider Philipp Meyer's novel *The Son* or Jonathan Lear's *Radical Hope: Ethics in the Face of Cultural Devastation.*[48] Both of these books invite the reader to empathize with the lives of Comanche and Crow Native Americans by vividly expressing the constellation of values that sustained their conduct. This in turn enables one to appreciate (to a degree) the distinctive values the Comanche and Crow tribes realized and to perceive the passing of their traditional ways of life as a value loss of a sort. However, the Comanche and Crow outlooks were in some sense inextricably bound up with practices that routinely violated some human beings' basic needs (most generally by glorifying various forms of violence perpetrated against outsiders). If falling within the human horizon is the test of objectivity, as Berlin suggests, we therefore appear to be committed to saying that an outlook of *objective value* can violate the minimum content of natural law. This is contradictory, to say the least.

Second, I am skeptical that Berlin's insistence that we may label some values—justice, courage, equality, freedom, and so on—as objective because they are sufficiently anthropologically or historically widespread plausibly differentiates pluralism from relativism. Even if some values are so widely pursued, this does not enable us to evaluate the distinct, culturally specific practices and actions that express, or realize, these central values in order to judge their validity or reasonableness from a general standpoint.

Lear's account of Crow understandings of courage is informative in this regard. Lear describes the first coup of Plenty Coups (the last great chief of the Crow Nation) as such:

> His beloved older brother had been killed in an expedition against the Sioux. . . . [Plenty Coups] sought revenge. He waited a few years, until he was sixteen; then he and his partners sneaked up on a Sioux hunting party. As a Sioux warrior was chasing a wounded buffalo, young Plenty Coups waited until the warrior was almost upon him, sprang to his feet, jumped the Sioux, and scalped him alive. The author who recorded this incident comments: "Far more merciful to have sent an arrow down into his heart. Never could that scalped Sioux hope to become a warrior. He was disgraced; he would be ostracized by his tribe, forced to wear the dress of a squaw, and must henceforth crawl through life in utter ignominy. The mark of the coward was upon him."
>
> Young Plenty Coups inflicted on this wretched Sioux a fate worse than death. But the revenge goes beyond the humiliation of this warrior. For as the Crow tribe celebrated this coup, they would recognize that even the Sioux who mocked this man has to recognize—indeed, did recognize in the very act of mocking—that the Crow had made their mark. For as long as he lived, he would be a living witness to the reality of the Crows.[49]

Plenty Coups's actions are a comprehensible expression of a value—courage—that falls within the human horizon. Moreover, by paying attention to the thick concepts embedded in the Crow outlook, we can comprehend why their understanding of courageous behavior took the form it did.[50] However, understanding Plenty Coups's action as a paradigmatic expression of Crow bravery does not enable us to assess the *validity* of this culturally specific expression of courage. Yet it seems that this is exactly the kind of judgment we need to be able to make if invoking the "human horizon" is to succeed in distancing pluralism from relativism.

Third, though Berlin does show that there is a real distinction between the inferences that pluralists and relativists draw from their focus on moral diversity, it is not clear that the idea of a human horizon privileges the pluralist inference. After all, relativists do not deny that we can understand *why* people live according to different outlooks; they simply insist that we can do so without making any claims about the objectivity or general acceptability of those outlooks or the values they realize or express. In other words, it is question-begging to claim that an outlook, or the concrete expression of a common value to which an outlook gives rise, is objective because it is comprehensible in the sense Berlin alludes to.

As a result, I believe that pluralists should refrain from invoking the human horizon in order to differentiate their view from relativist accounts. The minimum content of natural law delivers some determinate criteria that can be employed to make judgments about the merits and demerits of values and practices that are not solely relative to a particular outlook. Berlin's claims about the human horizon do not.

In addition, one may accept that Berlin's minimal natural law view reveals that not all judgments are relative to a particular tradition while still questioning the aptness of using the term *objectivity* to characterize the claims about the normative domain that value pluralists endorse. Even if we accept that a finite number of ends and outlooks are compatible with "normal" human behavior, this merely reveals that our judgment of what counts as a genuine value or end is not wholly arbitrary; these judgments are constrained by our view of human nature and our sense of what different human beings, under the influence of different outlooks, may regard themselves as having reason to pursue. However, one might coherently hold that, even if an outlook or end falls within the human horizon, this merely shows us that its acceptance or pursuit is compatible with the most basic (value-laden) concepts and categories we employ to understand human conduct. With this in mind, it is hard to see how Berlin's claims about the human horizon serve to vindicate his use of the term *objectivity*. It is more apt for value pluralists to stress a different, more chastened claim: that a plurality of outlooks and values are expressive of the distinctive capacities and potentialities of human beings.[51]

A defender of Berlin may attempt to respond to these claims in one of three ways, which I now address.

THE EMPIRICAL ERRORS REJOINDER

First, defenders of Berlin may reply that outlooks that endorse violations of the minimum content of natural law rest on empirical falsehoods (for example, the belief that Jewish people are subhuman[52]), which enables us to comprehend why people in the grip of such outlooks acted as they did while retaining our judgment that they were objectively wrong to do so.

Berlin espouses this reading of Nazism at numerous points, explicitly stating that he does not regard the Nazis as "literally pathological or insane, only as wickedly wrong, totally misguided about the facts, for example in believing that some beings are subhuman, or that race is central, or that Nordic races alone are truly creative" (*POI*, 12–13). He is clear that doctrines propounding the view that some people are subhuman are empirically false, but given enough propaganda, we can understand how someone might endorse such views. In this sense, regarding such people as beyond the realm of human understanding is a mistake: "Persecution need not be insane: only spring from a conviction of the truth of appallingly false beliefs" (*CIB*, 38). At one point, Berlin even claims that Nazi-type denials of common humanity are new in human history as they deny "a premise upon which all previous humanism, religious and secular, has stood" (*CTH*, 190–91), implying that such empirical falsehoods distort universally recognized moral standards.

Claiming that all outlooks that violate the minimum content of natural law rest on demonstrable empirical errors would be a convenient way to escape the problem, but this is implausible. For one thing, Berlin's claim that the twentieth-century denial of common humanity is a perversion of universal sentiments is very hard to sustain, given the existence of institutions like slavery in the ancient world.[53] In addition, there is little reason to hold that outlooks that violate the minimum content of natural law do so only because they commit empirical errors. They just might value some goods (military glory, romantic self-assertion, etc.) over and above other kinds of value, like respecting people's basic needs.[54] In this spirit, Jan-Werner Müller objects to Berlin's reading of the Nazi case. As Müller sees it, "the idea that the Nazis simply had first looked at what they took to be the facts (just mistakenly) and then chosen their values, seems to be a complete failure of moral psychology: to put it simply, they chose values of racial struggle, the glorification of violence, etc., and then made the facts fit their particular moral picture."[55] These are the kind of reminders that value pluralists must confront head-on.[56]

In addition, making demonstrable empirical error a test of moral objectivity creates further problems because a host of outlooks have been intimately caught up in numerous false empirical beliefs, although these are not necessarily empirical errors about the bounds of humanity but more mundane and less morally troubling claims about, for example, the role of various divine powers in the universe. Given his historical sensibility, it is hard to believe that Berlin would be happy with the idea that outlooks that rest on these kinds of empirical errors are not genuinely valuable. Someone might reply that we should rule out only those that rest on morally egregious empirical errors, like a belief in subhumanity. But now all the work is being done by our sense of which empirical errors are morally grievous. I cannot see how we can make such judgments with reference to the horizon alone. However, they can be given by our endorsement of the minimum content of natural law.

THE VALUE-TWISTING REJOINDER

In a letter to Michael Ignatieff, Berlin hints at a second possible line of counterargument. He suggests that we can regard Nazis as "people trapped by emotions which are universal—namely, nationalism—driven to the point of pathological extreme" (*A*, 419). George Crowder develops this thought by arguing that we can distinguish between two senses of value. On the one hand, we can think of specific practices, such as "aggressive international expansionism," that we can understand without endorsing the idea that they meet the test of objectivity. However, on the other hand, Crowder claims that if this understanding is genuine in Berlin's sense, "then I necessarily appreciate the deeper purposes or goals which the practice serves. . . . It is these deeper values that I may then share, even if I strongly reject the particular way they are expressed in the practice confronting me." So even if I am repelled by Nazi expansionism, I can understand it as the *twisted* "expression of the deeper goal of national or cultural belonging," and Crowder claims, "it is this underlying value that I can identify with, and that implies a common horizon not only of understanding but of values."[57]

This is an ingenious way to save Berlin that has some textual support.[58] However, it is not the most convincing interpretation of Berlin's claims taken as a whole, and I do not find it has much independent plausibility. First, Berlin's conception of human nature leads him to declare that new values emerge at various historical junctures—for example, Berlin argues that values such as authenticity could not have made sense before the Romantic revolution (*RR*, passim)—and it is hard to regard such values as analogues of deeper, more universal values of the sort Crowder alludes to.[59] Moreover, new values are not merely created: some value commitments die out because we no longer think that they express anything of deep human significance (chastity, piety, or sportsmanship are perhaps recent examples). I fail to see how Crowder's position can account for either case. Second, Crowder's reconstruction of Berlin's position is contrary to the spirit of the central pluralist insight that a wide range of distinctive moral values and practices are of *intrinsic* worth. Crowder's position implies that the number of intrinsically valuable goods will be strictly delimited.[60] Most pluralists, including Berlin in most moods, disagree with the instrumentalist and reductive nature of this approach to understanding moral diversity.

Third, and most significantly, it is hard to see what criteria Crowder can employ to justify his claim that practices like "aggressive international expansionism" twist or corrupt the more generic universal values he claims they serve. Berlin's empiricism implies that history or the social sciences must be our guide to what counts as a typical or characteristic expression of these so-called deep values. But if we take history as our guide, aggressive international expansionism looks like a very common expression of nationalism, not a pathological corruption of it. The point multiplies. Consider practical expressions of values like familial intimacy or dignity. From a historical perspective, it would appear that gender equality twists the most basic values of family life and that considering microaggressions a source of humiliation is absurd. However, many liberal-pluralists, like Crowder, will not be happy with this conclusion as it undermines many of their contemporary moral and political convictions. With this in mind, it is hard to avoid the conclusion that Crowder's sense of which practices twist or corrupt the underlying universal values he speaks of is inevitably going to be determined by his first-order beliefs and commitments, rather than by some pristine understanding of a value's true nature that supposedly stands behind its particular concrete expression.

THE VALUES NOT OUTLOOKS REJOINDER

A third, related, response to my line of criticism might take the following form: *When we class an outlook, such as those endorsed by the Comanche or Crow tribes, as falling within the human horizon, we do not have to commit to making a claim about them being objectively valuable per se. Rather, we are recognizing that some practices or elements were valuable while others were not, and it is these practices and the values they realized that we judge as objective.*[61]

The basic problem with this view, however, is that it violates what I have called the *mutual dependence condition*. As I have said, historically informed thinkers like Berlin (and Hampshire and Williams) do not think that it makes sense to attempt to separate the things we find illustrative of value in an outlook from those we find illustrative of disvalue, as if ethical reflection enabled us to surgically cut away the bad in an attempt to preserve the good. Some moral customs and shared understandings are so intimately bound up in the evaluative practices at the heart of distinct outlooks that they should be considered partly constitutive of the outlook itself.[62] Implying that the admirable elements of these outlooks—bravery, daring, self-reliance, and so forth—could be sustained in the absence of these practices and customs violates the historical sensibility at play in Berlin's work. This is the point of Hampshire's no-shopping principle that I touched on earlier.

Given that, in my view, these three rejoinders fail, I reaffirm that if Berlinian value pluralists want to distance their position from relativist doctrines, they must focus on the minimum content of natural law and not the human horizon. As I have argued, an outlook can be one of the following: incomprehensible (pinpricking, praying to wood for being wood, etc.); comprehensible but morally abhorrent (Nazism); or comprehensible and not morally abhorrent (the life of an American hippy). On this basis, we can hold on to the thought that some outlooks are comprehensible but difficult to refer to as "objective" because some of their central features deny or fail to respect the minimum content of natural law.

This reveals that Berlin is in the grips of a trilemma and cannot concurrently believe in the following:

1. The minimum content of natural law
2. The mutual dependence condition
3. The claim that falling within the human horizon is the mark of moral objectivity

Value pluralists must forgo (1), (2), or (3). Relativists reject (1) and (3) and may, or may not, endorse (2). Commentators like Crowder imply that we should reject (2). In my view, Berlinian value pluralists should renounce (3) and, when responding to the relativist, focus on the conditions outlined in (1).

Yet Berlin is also skeptical of the idea that the minimum content of natural law can be considered a trumping consideration when we assess different outlooks:

> Clearly, an age in which there is a recognised standard of justice for all men, in which human sacrifice is not practised and rational methods of uncovering the facts of the past have superseded myth and legend, is in certain obvious respects superior to a culture in which Agamemnon causes his daughter to

> be slaughtered as an offering to the goddess, or men see the sky as a huge, animated body whose anger is expressed in thunder and lightning. But the increase in humanity and knowledge . . . is inevitably accompanied by a loss of primitive vigour, directness, imaginative force, beyond any made possible by the development of the critical intellect. . . . There is no need to compare and grade on some single scale of merit each cultural phase and its creations and forms of life and action; indeed, it is not possible to do so, for they are evidently incommensurable. (*AC*, 128)[63]

This comes from Berlin's essay on Vico. It is unclear, as it often is in such pieces, when exposition ends and Berlin's own commitments begin. The important point, however, is that if incommensurability runs this deep, we have to conclude that though the minimum content of natural law generates some universal criteria we can employ to assess different outlooks, such considerations do not necessarily play an *overriding role* in our assessment of these distinct outlooks. Some outlooks, such as those endorsed by the Comanche and Crow tribes, may, in part, be constituted by values and practices that violate some people's basic needs. Yet the above passage (and other similar sentiments of Berlin's) effectively suggests that we have reason to recognize that they are clearly not arbitrary or meaningless expressions of human nature and may represent valuable forms of human flourishing, even though their denizens engaged in wrongdoing.[64] If this is right, it suggests that the minimum content of natural law cannot play the decisive or overriding role in our judgment of the value of such outlooks.

In this regard, Berlin's value pluralism has some interesting pessimistic implications that are worth drawing out. In particular, it implies that many outlooks that represent comprehensible examples of how human nature can develop will, in some ways, fail to fully satisfy the demands of basic moral decency. This pessimism can have valuable effects by helping to guard against self-congratulation. After all, critics do not have a hard time pointing out the myriad ways in which people's basic needs are not met in the current liberal-capitalist system. The idea that this outlook may, therefore, be vulnerable on these grounds must be taken seriously and responded to, rather than simply dismissed.

Conclusion

In this chapter, I have offered an account of Berlin's value pluralism, outlining his central positions regarding the nature of value conflict and value incommensurability while also explicating the most important underlying presuppositions of his view, most notably a commitment to prioritizing our moral experience over the demands of theoretical parsimony and his endorsement of the mutual dependence condition. Although Hampshire's and Williams's accounts of ethics depart from Berlin's in various respects, both endorse many of these central claims.

In so doing, I examined whether pluralism is, in spite of Berlin's repeated protestations, a species of moral relativism. I have argued that Berlin's arguments about the human horizon are extraneous to the issue at hand and that if pluralists want to reject relativism they must focus on the minimum content of natural law and the basic needs and interests it highlights, rather than considerations about "normal" human behavior or mutual intelligibility. However, it is unclear that this vindicates Berlin's decision to employ the language of moral objectivity. In fact, discussing value pluralism in these terms is likely to obscure some of the position's most important skeptical insights about the limits of philosophical ethics.

I have not addressed a further concern that holds that recognizing the truth of value pluralism must undermine one's value commitments. The basic idea is as follows: *If I endorse outlook X but recognize that Y and Z are also minimally decent, incommensurable expressions of the distinctive capacities and potentialities of human beings, this recognition should undermine my endorsement of X because it reveals that the decision to endorse X rather than Y or Z is arbitrary.* I respond to this concern in the next chapter, arguing that it rests on a misunderstanding of Berlin's account of moral psychology and that his account of moral psychology vitiates the attempt to seamlessly derive moral and political recommendations from an appreciation of the truth of value pluralism alone (a derivation that a surprising number of Berlin scholars still mistakenly pursue). This is part of my broader examination of the political implications of Berlin's account of value pluralism. I argue that taking Berlinian value pluralism seriously reveals that a sense of realism is a central ingredient of good political judgment and requires us to think about the nature of political disagreement and the attractions of liberalism in strikingly different terms to those endorsed in most contemporary political theory.

2

The Sense of Reality

This chapter explores the upshots of Berlin's value pluralism for political theory, illustrating the ways in which it problematizes the idea that political theory is a kind of applied moral philosophy (in contrast to some of Berlin's own statements). Most centrally, I argue that, in a number of ways, value pluralism compromises a claim at the heart of Rawlsian, and much post-Rawlsian, political philosophy: that the first task of political theory is to articulate an ideal theory of political society before asking secondarily how our political institutions should be ordered, or political agents should act, in reference to this ideal. This is of direct relevance to the current dispute between realism and moralism because a number of prominent recent commentators have likewise noted the link between value pluralism and a rejection of Rawlsian ideal theory without elaborating on this in much detail.[1]

To make the case that Berlin's value pluralism supports a form of realism in political theory I address a number of elements of his thought, including his distinction between negative and positive conceptions of liberty and his remarks on anti-utopianism and political judgment, as well as the question of how value pluralists can have substantive political commitments. In a sense, this unsystematic way of proceeding is unfortunate because it ensures that this chapter does not take the form of a cumulative argument in defense of the realist approach in political theory. (It does, however, have the virtue of honestly representing its subject matter.) Relatedly, it is worth noting at the outset that this chapter does not attempt to offer a definitive defense of the realist approach. In large part, this is because the core philosophical views that underwrite the aspects of Berlin's thought that I focus on are in tension with the starting points of much moralist political philosophy. Instead of struggling to convert political moralists to the realist cause, I therefore attempt something more intellectually honest: to illustrate why realists of a value pluralist stripe can coherently dispute the idea that ideal theory must take priority in political theory.

I begin by arguing that Berlin's view of the dangers of monism and the distinction between negative and positive conceptions of liberty problematize the idea that political theory should be seen as a form of applied moral philosophy and, to this extent, inadvertently express a certain kind of realist orientation. I then turn to Berlin's critique of utopianism and his work on political judgment, demonstrating that his value pluralism endorses a very different understanding of the relationship between theory and judgment to that which is implicitly or explicitly affirmed in much moralist political philosophy. Following this, I explain how Berlinian value pluralism more directly buttresses a realist understanding of politics. I sketch an account of politics that is highly congenial to Berlin's account of value pluralism, even though he never develops it in any great detail, which stresses the ineliminability of disagreement and conflict and, therefore, suggests that questions of legitimacy and authority are of first importance in politics. I then clarify how such a view, in conjunction with an account of moral psychology that Berlin hints toward at various points in his essays and letters, makes sense of how value pluralists can commit to substantive political positions without having to implausibly claim that there is any kind of necessary or logical relation between pluralism as a metaethical theory and a particular substantive, first-order political position.

The Impurity of Political Theory

One of the distinguishing characteristics of recent realist thought is the insistence that political philosophy is "both normative and impure" in the sense that various nonphilosophical considerations—such as "an involvement with history, or the social sciences"—play a central role in guiding our political judgments (*PHD*, 155). In this section, I argue that Berlin's account of the political dangers of monist political theories and positive conceptions of liberty vividly demonstrates why value pluralist approaches to politics encourage us to reflect in these "impure" ways.

In chapter 1, I illustrated Berlin's philosophical reasons for rejecting monism, but it is important to note that he was also concerned with highlighting the "barbarous consequences" that monism can have in practice (*L*, 47–48). He claims that monism has authoritarian implications for two principal reasons: first, because it lends support to the idea that people who have knowledge of the ultimate ends we ought to pursue "should command those who do not" (*POI*, 14), and second, because it encourages making sacrifices for the sake of these ultimate ends. As Berlin sees it, if someone thinks that they have a grasp of the ultimate resolution to humanity's ills, they will be inclined to think that "no cost would be too high to obtain it" (*CTH*, 15–16; see also *CIB*, 143; *CTH*, 49).

As commentators have observed, these claims are far from conclusive. It simply does not follow that monists will necessarily hold that possession of the truth about how we should live justifies imposing this view on others or excuses the kinds of sacrifices that Berlin objects to.[2] After all, the ends or values that the monist seeks to realize may themselves rule out such sacrifices. The question whether a belief in monism will have the kind of disastrous political consequences that Berlin posits is, therefore, "more an empirical than a philosophical question, and is probably impossible to answer definitively."[3] The most it is reasonable to allege is that a belief in monism is *likely* to dispose one to authoritarianism by making it easier to justify, to oneself and one's supporters, the kind of coercion and sacrifices that Berlin has in mind.

One of the most important insights of Berlin's examination of the positive conceptions of liberty reaches something akin to this conclusion. As I noted in the last chapter, Berlin holds that the negative conception of liberty—focused on the question "Over what area am I master?"—and the positive conception—focused on the question "Who is master?"—both speak to genuine values. Negative freedom concerns the value of being able to do what one chooses without being obstructed or interfered with by others, while positive freedom highlights the value in being one's own master and in achieving a genuine degree of self-direction.[4] Berlin recognizes that both conceptions of liberty have a long political and philosophical pedigree and that it is often hard to fully disentangle one from the other. Indeed, many of Berlin's own claims concerning the value of liberty combine negative and positive elements.[5]

A great deal of ink has been spilled analyzing Berlin's distinction between negative and positive freedom. As is well known by anyone who has paid attention to these debates, a number of elements of Berlin's argument are—to put it mildly—problematic.[6] Scholars have also pointed out that Berlin's treatment of the figures in the history of political thought he associates with positive conceptions of liberty is very idiosyncratic.[7] But the philosophical acuity of Berlin's distinction is orthogonal to my concerns here. Berlin's work on liberty is relevant to the issues I am concerned with because his discussion of the dangers of positive conceptions of liberty expresses a stimulating view of what it means to theorize about values in a politically responsible manner that I think pushes in a realist direction. Indeed, Berlin effectively gives expression to the view that philosophical argument must be supplemented by the kind of "impure" considerations I alluded to earlier if we are to make sense of the attractions and dangers of these distinct views of liberty. Rather than merely counseling us to engage in conceptual analysis or to refine our moral intuitions, Berlin's work on liberty suggests that we need to keep in mind a host of practical and empirical questions about what acting in light of such views is likely to involve.

It is with such concerns in mind that Berlin argues that the positive conception of freedom lends itself to perversion. For Berlin, the positive conception of freedom has its basis in the idea that people can employ their rational capacities reflectively to determine how they should act in order to achieve ends they genuinely will. According to this understanding, "the free person is one who controls what they do or become."[8] Yet Berlin claims that thinking in these terms requires one to posit a metaphysical distinction between two "selves": a higher self that can direct the lower self. Adherents of the positive conception of freedom typically identify this dominant self with reason, in contrast to the lower, empirical self, which merely pursues what it happens to desire. By distinguishing between true desires or interests and merely empirical desires or interests in this way, Berlin claims, the positive conception of freedom is ripe for perversion because it encourages the thought that the lower self needs to be "rigidly disciplined if it is ever to rise to the full height of its 'real' nature" (L, 179). In some views, the real self is even conceived in corporate terms as a social "whole" of which the individual is simply one element. When this happens, the conclusion that freedom can be achieved by a collective imposing its will on "its recalcitrant 'members'" can arise (L, 179). But Berlin stresses that even less corporate views can indicate that by liberating people from their empirical selves, one merely enables them to free themselves from their baser desires and interests (L, 180).

Berlin objects to this way of thinking not because he thinks that coercing some people in the pursuit of some important goals is always impermissible. His point is rather that thinking in these terms encourages the thought that we coerce "others for their own sake, in their, not my, interest," and when this happens, "I am then claiming that I know what they truly need better than they know it themselves" (L, 179). It is this suggestion Berlin considers "monstrous" because it requires us to equate "what X would choose if he were something that he is not . . . with what X actually seeks and chooses," suggesting (he claims) that if someone is coerced in the name of a good, this does not limit their freedom because they implicitly will such ends even if their empirical-self does not recognize this (L, 180; see also PIRA, 124). Berlin claims that by following these steps, we end up in a paradoxical position according to which justified coercion cannot constrain one's freedom.

For Berlin, then, advocates of the positive conception of freedom often end up confusing freedom with entirely different values. According to the positive view, freedom is achieved by the realization of what we have *reason* to pursue. However, as we saw in the last chapter, Berlin thinks that we have reason to pursue a wide array of distinct goods and values. While it may be sensible to constrain people's freedom in order to promote other values, he stresses that when this happens "an absolute loss of liberty occurs." Indeed, Berlin is adamant that nothing is gained by blurring distinct values in this way: "Everything is what it is: liberty is liberty, not equality or fairness or justice or culture" (*L*, 172). In this sense, one of the central problems with positive conceptions of liberty is that they encourage us to think that the problem of how we might establish a political order that realizes freedom for all is soluble "by establishing a just order that would give each man all the freedom to which a rational being was entitled" (*L*, 191–92).

It is not hard to see why Berlin objects to this. For one thing, thinking in these terms is incompatible with the pluralist insight that we often have to sacrifice some values to realize others. Moreover, he claims that thinking in these terms can justify "some of the most frightful forms of oppression and enslavement in human history" (*POI*, 18). In contrast, the negative conception of liberty does not "deprive men in the name of some remote, or incoherent, ideal, of much that they have found to be indispensable to their life as unpredictably self-transforming beings" (*L*, 216–17).[9]

It is not my concern to critically evaluate Berlin's distinction in the way that so many scholars have done since 1958. For my purposes, what is most interesting about Berlin's work on liberty is his claim that positive conceptions of freedom are *historically* and *psychologically* predisposed to end up counseling political authoritarianism (*L*, 198). This suggests that focusing on what is likely to occur if agents attempt to realize a value, or act on a series of philosophical claims in the world as we know it, is itself of direct significance to our evaluation of the competing interpretations of political values. On this view, normative political argument is *not* corrupted by paying attention to various impure considerations. Indeed, it is only by focusing on such issues that we can actually make determinate judgments about what we should pursue here and now.

In this sense, Berlin's approach is at some distance from the growing trend in contemporary political philosophy to seek to uncover fundamental principles that are untouched by any nonphilosophical concerns. G. A. Cohen— a former student of Berlin's—offers the clearest expression of such a view when he claims that fundamental moral principles that lie "at the summit of our normative convictions" are not affected by the kinds of "practical considerations" to which Berlin draws our attention in his work on liberty because they are resolutely fact-independent.[10] Adam Swift similarly insists that it is "only by reference to philosophy—abstract, pure, context-free philosophy" that we can gain genuine insight into the nature of political values and, therefore, understand how to act in our current circumstances.[11] Cohen and Swift paint as an ethical requirement their refusal to accord a place to such impure considerations because they worry that if we focus on such impurities, we risk coming to accept the world as it is. This leads to a conception of political philosophy that distinguishes between the contingency and temporality of practice and fact and the realm of value and principle that supposedly transcends "the facts of the world."[12]

Berlin's work effectively suggests that such "an ascent to the a priori" ought to be regarded with deep skepticism.[13] As both the negative and positive conceptions speak to genuine human interests, it is hard to see why they cannot be classed as "ultimate values" of the sort Cohen has in mind. However, Berlin's analysis suggests that only if we pay attention to various impure considerations will we be able to grasp the merits and dangers of these competing ways of thinking about liberty and, therefore, work out which ultimate principle should guide our present political action.[14] To the extent that this way of approaching things will, inevitably, rest on a disputable interpretation of how things are likely to play out if we act in certain ways, Berlin's work also effectively suggests that our political judgments will be inherently messy and provisional in ways that much political philosophy, which seeks apodictic philosophical justification, simply fails to recognize.

Many of Berlin's comments regarding negative liberty subsequent to "Two Concepts" are revealing in this respect. He recognizes that unmitigated negative liberty generates its own social evils, as revealed by the "bloodstained story of economic individualism and unrestrained capitalist competition" (*L*, 37). He also claims that the New Deal was an admirable experiment in "promoting both justice and prosperity in a society without introducing the rather restrictive aspects of socialism."[15] Yet Berlin persisted with the political judgment that the positive conception of liberty was more liable to perversion, and had in fact been more dangerously perverted, than the negative conception (*L*, 37; *CIB*, 41). Left-leaning thinkers are likely to hold that the political context at the beginning of the twenty-first century is sufficiently different from Berlin's own that we should see things in a different light.[16] Leaving aside the substantive merits of this particular political judgment, what is important is that Berlin's work suggests that when we examine how an ultimate value is to be realized, these kinds of considerations—be they historical, psychological, or more directly political—do not matter only at a technical level. Rather, they are at the beating heart of any political philosophy that is actually going to be able to guide our political judgments and actions. To put it another way, it is precisely because values like liberty are internally pluralistic and potentially conflicting that philosophical argument, if it is to guide our judgments, must be impure.

Theory and Judgment

Berlin claims that the majority of utopian thinkers, like most adherents of positive conceptions of liberty, presuppose a "conception of a perfect world in which all the great values in light of which men have lived for so long can be realised together" (*POI*, 22). So for Berlin, utopian thinking is not misguided simply because it is impracticable; the problem is that most utopian visions of politics are incompatible with an appreciation of the core tenets of value pluralism.

Ideal theory's contemporary defenders, of various utopian hues, will point out that they are not committed to such a position. Rawls, for example, explicitly notes, "No society can include within itself all forms of life. We may indeed lament the limited space, as it were, of social worlds, and of ours in particular; and we may regret some of the inevitable effects of our culture and social structure. As Berlin has long maintained (it is one of his fundamental themes), there is no social world without loss: that is, no social world that does not exclude some ways of life that realize in special ways certain fundamental values."[17] On this basis, Rawls avers with Berlin that we are always "forced to select among cherished values" and holds that "when we hold several and must restrict each in view of the requirements of others, we face great difficulties in setting priorities and making adjustments."[18] So there is scant reason to think that ideal theorists necessarily endorse the kind of "conceptually incoherent" utopianism that Berlin objects to. On what grounds, then, might value pluralists object to the style of political theorizing that thinkers like Rawls endorse? Chiefly, I think, by rejecting the view of the necessity of "theory" to guide our political judgments that such positions affirm.

Contrary to the claims of some of his readers, Berlin's response to the theoretical approaches developed by some Enlightenment thinkers was not wholly negative.[19] Berlin explicitly claimed to be a "liberal rationalist" (*CIB*, 70) and held that the Enlightenment thinkers "rendered great service to mankind by the open war which they conducted against ignorance and obscurantism in every form, and in particular against brutality, stupidity, suppression of the truth, cynicism and disregard of human rights" (*AC*, 159; see also *CIB*, 70; *CTH*, 36). Yet he was sensitive to the potential dangers of approaching politics in an overly theoretical key. In a way redolent of Adam Smith's concerns about the "man of the system," Berlin states that theoretically minded political actors often attempt to make the word "conform to the symmetry and simplicity of the scheme" they propose. However, "the less the application of such formulae yield the expected results, the more exasperated the theorists become, the more they try to force the facts into some preconceived mould—the more resistance they encounter, the more violent are the efforts to overcome it, the greater the reaction, confusion, suffering untold, the more the original ends are lost sight of, until the consequences of the experiments are beyond what anybody had wished or planned or expected" (*SR*, 31). But, once again, even if some theoretically minded political agents in the twentieth century did act in the way Berlin describes, it is not clear that it is fair to impugn the attempt to construct a systematic normative theory of political society on this basis.

Nonetheless, Berlinian pluralists argue that the attempt to reorder politics in light of a predetermined "theory" can be challenged on other grounds. For example, William Galston claims that political philosophers who attempt to model how well-motivated citizens would converge on a particular set of principles are committed to thinking that conflicts among values can be resolved either by "dissolving heterogeneous moral considerations into a common quantifiable metric (as most utilitarians do), or by arguing that values don't conflict when properly understood (as Ronald Dworkin does), or by claiming that key values can be lexically ordered." Galston claims that all of these views are incompatible with the insights at the heart of value pluralism: value pluralists "cannot say that justice (or anything else, for that matter) is the first virtue of social institutions, full stop; in some circumstances, other considerations may take priority. And within a broad range, they cannot say that one resolution of value conflicts is preferable to another, regardless of circumstances."[20] In this sense, attempts to show how ultimate values can be seamlessly integrated, or command the assent of reasonable citizens (usually because one is preoccupied with the Kantian aspiration to explain how a political order could attain the rational consent of all of those whom it coerces),[21] are incompatible with acknowledging the plural nature of value.

Galston also insists that the experience of making normative decisions in situations of pervasive value conflict reveals that we do not need to make recourse to systematic normative theories to choose well. Thus, he recounts how when he served in the White House as an official responsible for domestic policy, he repeatedly had the same experience:

> I would be chairing an interagency task force designed to reach a unified administration position on some legislative or regulatory proposal. As the representatives of the departments argued for their various views, I found it impossible to dismiss any one of them as irrelevant to the decision, or as wholly lacking in weight.... I found it remarkable how often we could reach deliberative closure.... Many practitioners (and not a few philosophers) shy away from value pluralism out of fear that it leads to deliberative anarchy. Experience suggests that this is not necessarily so. There can be right answers, widely recognized as such, even in the absence of general rules for ordering or aggregating diverse goods.[22]

These appeals to the phenomenology of making decisions when values conflict lead value pluralists to insist that "the concrete situation is almost everything" (CTH, 18–19). On this view, no general or systematic normative theory is capable of making sense of the unique situations we face.

With this in mind, Galston claims that Berlin's work tends in the direction of a moral particularism that holds that we are able to make reasoned choices between disparate goods, values, and principles in concrete situations. Indeed, Galston claims that much of the time "reasonable observers open to fact and argument will be able to agree that one option sacrifices too much along one dimension of value compared to what is gained along another and that the alternative course of action represents a better balance among competing but worthy claims."[23] There is an interesting conjunction of attitudes at work here. On the one hand, this understanding of value pluralism evinces a basic pessimism about the ability of philosophy to deliver a theory adequate to guide our moral and political judgments. On the other hand, it also holds that well-informed, experienced agents can make good decisions when values conflict. It also implies that the correctness of such judgments will only be revealed retrospectively, further calling into question the proleptic potential of philosophical theory.

Something akin to this view is articulated by Berlin and Williams in a response they coauthored to a paper of George Crowder's.[24] Berlin and Williams took umbrage at Crowder's claim that value pluralism entails that any decision in favor of a particular course of action is, by definition, nonrational and can only be explained by that subject's particular preferences and desires. Contrariwise, they insist it is by no means clear why a particular judgment of how distinct values should be traded-off is "intrinsically less rational or reasonable than a claim to the effect that some simple priority rule should be accepted." Thus, while Berlin and Williams endorse the claim that value pluralism ensures that practical decision-making cannot be made "completely algorithmic," they deny that it entails that we cannot speak of correct or incorrect, or better or worse, decisions or judgments. Consequently, they distinguish two ways of understanding the pluralist thesis that practical decisions are underdetermined by reason, affirming the claim that "it is not a requirement of reason that there should be one value which in all cases prevails over the other" while rejecting the suggestion that pluralism is committed to the idea that "in each particular case, reason has nothing to say (i.e. there is nothing reasonable to be said) about which should prevail over the other."[25]

In light of this, the best way of rendering value pluralism's opposition to systematic, normative political theory is not by claiming that such theories are necessarily monistic, likely to generate persecution, or conceptually incoherent, even if some of them are. It is, rather, to stress that people, first, are capable of making reasoned judgments about how values should be balanced against each other and which courses of action ought to be adopted in the absence of such normative visions. Moreover, value pluralists can, second, claim that we are *more* likely to be able to make judgments that are sensitive to the inevitable value costs of our decisions if we are not in thrall to an antecedent normative theory. Accordingly, good political judgment is a matter of being guided by "awareness of the immediate, particular experiences of actual individuals," not of working out how a prior normative standard or theory can be applied or realized.[26]

Certainly, the two lines of argument I have canvassed in this section—that certain theoretical approaches are inconsistent with value pluralism and that the lack of such a theory does not inevitably ensure that we are incapable of making reasoned decisions about what should be done—do not refute the attempt to construct a systematic normative theory. This is precisely because these pluralist arguments do not depart from a set of premises about the nature or role of moral and political philosophy that pluralists of Berlin's ilk share with ideal theorists. However, they illustrate that the common refrain that we *need* regulative ideals or ideal theory to guide our political judgments and motivate political action is more controversial than many contemporary political philosophers acknowledge, who assert that without such theories our political actions lack an objective or aim.[27]

This sense of the limitations of theoretical argument in ethics and politics motivates Berlin's work on political and historical judgment. In both domains, he insists there is "no substitute for a sense of reality" (SR, 35). This sense of reality largely consists of sensitivity to the distinctive features of concrete situations. Individuals who possess a well-attuned sense of reality perceive the "unique flavours of each situation as it is, in its specific differences—of that wherein it differs from all other situations, that is, those aspects of it which make it insusceptible to scientific treatment, because it is that element in it which no generalisation, because it is generalisation, can cover" (*SR*, 24). The sense of reality, in other words, is a "capacity" or kind of "imaginative insight" (*SR*, 25). Berlin claims it enables some statesmen to understand "what fits with what: what can be done in given circumstances and what cannot, what means will work in what situations and how far, without necessarily being able to explain how they know this or even what they know" (*SR*, 32). When we attempt to describe this ability or skill, we can only revert to metaphors: we talk of people possessing antennae or a good political eye (*SR*, 45). Those in possession of this ability are able to integrate "constantly changing, multi-coloured, evanescent, perpetually overlapping data," so that effective, pragmatic decisions can be reached (*SR*, 46; see also *POI*, 139; *UD*, 188). In many ways, as commentators have noted, Berlin's account of the sense of reality is evocative of Aristotle's account of phronesis.[28] Significantly, the ability to make these kinds of judgments necessitates a certain kind of realism: "the correct perception of the characteristics of events or facts or persons without distortions produced by feelings like hope or fear or love or hate, or by a disposition to idealise or depreciate or anything else that interferes with accurate observation" (*SR*, 134).

This suggestive, but clearly underdeveloped, account of political judgment is somewhat buttressed by Berlin's portraits of various political figures that interested him. He distinguishes between two types of statesmen—a distinction similar to the one he draws between hedgehogs and foxes. "The first kind is that amalgam of simplicity of vision with intense, sometimes fanatical, idealism which is to be found in men compounded of fewer attributes than the normal human complement, but those larger than life." Berlin claims, at their best, "such men rise to the noble grandeur of the great and simple heroes of classical antiquity" (*POI*, 186). These statesmen characteristically think in binary, almost monistic terms, by unifying "the manifold particulars of any situation under a single commanding vision."[29] Along with Churchill, in this group Berlin includes Garibaldi, de Gaulle, Jabotinsky, Tito, and Trotsky. For Berlin, such statesmen typically "attract their followers by the intensity and purity of their mind, by their fearless and unbending character, by the simplicity and nobility of the central principle to which they dedicate all that they have, by the very fact that they impose some pattern so clear, so uncomplicated, upon the manifold diversity of life" (*POI*, 186). As Berlin notes, this kind of forcefulness can be used for good or ill.

On the contrary, the second type "are acutely aware of the smallest oscillations, the infinite variety of the social and political elements in which they live." Berlin claims that these statesmen "record half-consciously a vast variety of experience . . . their genius consists precisely in the fact that they are able to integrate it—not by any conscious process, but in some semi-instinctive fashion—into a single coherent picture; and then to act in accordance with this picture in a sure-footed, morally confident, firm and supremely effective fashion, responsive to the sharpest needs of their time in an infinity of sympathetic ways" (*POI*, 187–88). Among this group Berlin includes Lincoln, Weizmann, and Franklin Roosevelt. They are "naturally political" beings (*PI*, 27).[30]

As noted in the introduction, Berlin's dichotomies should not be pushed too far, and this one is no exception. It is also somewhat ironic that Berlin's discussion of the first kind of statesman reveals that monistic commitment can be a begetter of political success because this implies that a philosophical appreciation of the plural nature of value may often be in tension with admirable statesmanship. However, Berlin's discussion of these figures, alongside his remarks on political judgment, sketchy as they are, give color to his view that no set of theoretical claims can capture what it means to act well, and responsibly, in politics. To be sure, as I will argue in the next section, Berlin's account of political judgment contains some damaging omissions, such as his disinclination to think about political conduct in terms of winning and exercising authority or ensuring the compliance of subjects. Yet this aspect of his thought expresses the view that although we can only decide how we can balance the competing claims of different values in concrete circumstances, an attractive integration of distinct values can sometimes take place, but that this is something that is necessarily revealed in practice, not delivered by theory.[31]

Politics in a Pluralist Key

So far in this chapter, I have argued that Berlin's work is at odds with some aspects of moralist political philosophy, given the impure approach he favors and his skepticism about overly theoretical approaches. In this section, I argue that his value pluralism slants more directly in the direction of various considerations at the heart of recent realist thinking.[32]

Berlin is clear that if we take value conflict seriously, this proscribes some ways of thinking about the *tasks* of politics. In particular, he claims that monists typically see politics in instrumental terms: as an activity concerned with putting the antecedently discovered answer to the question of how we should live into practice. In this regard, they hold that politics raises no interesting philosophical or ethical questions of its own: the monist claims to be in possession of knowledge of the ends we should pursue and, as a result, thinks that "the only unsolved problems will be more or less technical: how to obtain the means for securing these ends, and how to distribute what the technical means provide in the socially and psychologically best manner" (*CC*, 153).[33] On this view, politics is simply a matter of working out how the antecedently established answer to the question of how we should live is to be realized, and how other people can be converted to it (*AC*, 78; see also *KM*, 30; *CC*, 153). The only conflicts that can exist in society are, therefore, conflicts of interest.

It should be clear why value pluralists cannot think about politics in this way. For them, value conflict is not merely the rationalization of conflicts of interest. Thus, the pursuit of a particular set of political goals entails the marginalization of other values and ends. At points in his later work, Berlin, somewhat pessimistically, suggests that the best that we may be able to hope for is a kind of unstable equilibrium "between the different aspirations of differing groups of human beings" that stops such groups "at the very least from attempting to exterminate each other, and, so far as possible, to prevent them from hurting each other—and to promote the maximum practicable degree of sympathy and understanding, never likely to be complete, between them" (*CTH*, 49–50). According to this vision, a commitment to liberalism amounts to the hope that a set of political institutions may succeed in preventing "people from doing each other too much harm, giving each human group sufficient room to realise its own idiosyncratic, unique, particular ends without too much interference with the ends of others" (*CTH*, 50).

Berlin recognizes that this view can seem uninspiring (*CTH*, 18–19). But, as we have seen, one of the central implications of his value pluralism is that many more ambitious understandings of political society are often conceptually confused, and sometimes potentially dangerous. We simply have to recognize that "social or political collisions will take place; the mere conflict of positive values alone makes this unavoidable" (*CTH*, 20). However, this does not necessitate conservatism and political inaction. Political collisions can be minimized and, to some degree, ameliorated. In particular, we can seek compromises between distinct goods and values. In our personal lives, we tend to realize that our life plans do not involve the pursuit of a single good to the neglect of all others and, accordingly, make trade-offs between values. Similarly, every outlook that attempts to marry more than one value represents some kind of "uneasy compromise between principles which in their extreme form cannot coexist" (*CC*, 102). Thus, Berlin intimates that reflective individuals should recognize that political life requires us to "adjust claims, compromise, establish priorities, engage in all those practical operations that social and even individual life has, in fact, always required" (*L*, 53). These compromises are, of necessity, "logically untidy," "flexible," and even "ambiguous" and involve making ad hoc, context-specific decisions, rather than applying general principles (*L*, 92; see also *L*, 173; *CTH*, 18). Indeed, in many situations, we have to think in consequentialist terms and realize the best we can do "is to maintain a precarious equilibrium that will prevent the occurrence of desperate situations, of intolerable choices" (*CTH*, 18).

Some critics have complained that Berlin is unable to articulate any criteria to help us choose between the feasible, Pareto-superior compromises that are open.[34] This observation is accurate but somewhat beside the point because it rests on what Berlin would regard as a serious overestimation of philosophy's power to resolve these kinds of normative questions, precisely because, per the argument of the last section, deciding which compromises we ought to adopt must be a matter of contextual *judgment*. The most that philosophy can do in these cases is to elucidate the nature of the values that will be traded-off against each other and explain some of the merits and demerits, or costs, of proposed courses of action.[35] While it is true that the claim that we have good reasons to seek prudent compromises between values is not especially striking,[36] the correct response to this goading is to reiterate that novel theoretical recommendations are only rarely a mark of insight or good political judgment.[37]

There are two more worrying omissions or shortcomings of Berlin's remarks on political compromises worth highlighting. First, as Berlin notes in his essay on Machiavelli, some values and goods are necessarily attenuated when pursued in this kind of "moderate" manner. Berlin notes that Machiavelli maligns those who "cannot bring themselves to resolutely follow" their goals because their lives often end in "weakness and failure" and "bungling" and "ruin" (*AC*, 47, 64). In this spirit, Berlin remarks that Machiavelli advises people to "learn to choose between" competing moral outlooks "and having chosen, not look back" (*AC*, 59). This suggests that the attempt to defend political compromises from value pluralist premises is more complicated and problematic than it is often taken to be. Second, Berlin never fully grapples with the interpersonal aspects of political compromises. He often talks as if political compromises are simply an extension of the kind of reasoning that individual agents engage in when deciding how to act. In both, we ask how to trade values off against each other so as to secure an ordering of values that we can affirm. But this fails to grasp what it means to compromise with other people who value differing goods. Neither does it tell us why or how far we should make these compromises.

In his understandably sketchy "Notes on Prejudice," Berlin remarks on the merits of the British skepticism toward political fanaticism and monomania, asserting that "compromising with people with whom you don't sympathise or altogether understand is indispensable to any decent society . . . [as] nothing is more destructive than a happy sense of one's own—or one's nations—infallibility."[38] He also intimates that such fanaticism can be arrested by the kind of understanding value pluralism exemplifies: "The only cure is *understanding* how other societies—in space or time, live: and that it is *possible* to lead lives different from one's own, and yet be fully human, worthy of love, respect or at least *curiosity*" (L, 346).[39]

There is little reason to disagree with any of this, but more can be said to offer some sense of the ethical presuppositions that undergird this way of engaging with one's fellow citizens. As we will see in chapter 4, Stuart Hampshire's more thoughtful (although by no means fully satisfactory) meditation on political compromises departs from some ethical starting points that are close to Berlin's but ends up offering more concrete institutional and political recommendations about how such compromises can be fostered.

It is also extraordinary that Berlin does not reflect more deeply on questions of legitimacy and authority. As I have illustrated, value pluralism suggests that people are not likely to converge on a set of moral principles, and any political settlement is, by definition, going to involve some values and ends being promoted at the cost of others. While both of these claims may seem rather innocuous, we can reach some important theoretical conclusions about politics with the addition of two further riders that Berlin never fully articulates but which are consonant with the spirit of his thought.

The first rider is that coercion is a constitutive feature of politics. Mark Philp notes, "that we have politics is symptomatic of the need to establish, identify, and enforce rules to govern people's behaviour in the absence of rational consensus on principles."[40] This suggests that *all* forms of politics are likely to involve some domination because any political settlement is inevitably going to involve the pursuit of an ordering of ends and values that not all members of a society will rationally assent to. The second rider is the plausible psychological claim, pithily expressed by Bernard Williams and consistent with Berlin's own understanding of liberty, that the "restriction of our activities by the intentional activities of others . . . can give rise to a specific reaction, resentment" (*IBWD*, 82). As Williams notes, if this resentment "is not to express itself in more conflict, non-cooperation, and the dissolution of social relations, an authoritative determination is needed of whose activities should have priority" (*IBWD*, 82). Putting these claims together delivers the conclusion that *any* political settlement is highly likely to be resented by at least some of those people it coerces as it will pursue an ordering of goods the value of which they may not accept.

These considerations problematize Berlin's claim, noted in the introduction, that political philosophy is fundamentally a matter of focusing of moral ends and values; that it is, as he puts it, but ethics applied to society (*CTH*, 1–2). The view of politics that I have offered above—brief, sketchy, and incomplete as it certainly is—suggests that focusing solely on these ends and values ignores the fact that some of the most important theoretical questions about politics we need to ask concern who has the authority to insist on an ordering, and to employ coercion to secure it, when people's interests diverge or they disagree about questions of value. To put it another way, if one endorses Berlin's value pluralism, there are very good reasons for thinking that politics is, in some central sense, an exercise in trying to resolve the problems that exist when there is an absence of agreement on value. While any particular view of the various ends that we ought to pursue may be very important, it is hard to see why articulating a set of preferred political outcomes or ends exhausts political theory. In fact, the line of thought I have outlined above suggests that questions of legitimacy and the grounds of authority are, in some fundamental sense, prior.

Some theorists and philosophers are likely to claim that this way of thinking about the fundamental tasks of politics—and, by implication, political theory—exaggerates the depth of conflict in contemporary (liberal) states. For such thinkers, enough citizens agree on some central values (equality, justice, liberty, the importance of political toleration, and so on) to get a moralized consensus on constitutional essentials off the ground, even if a wider-ranging consensus on more comprehensive visions of the good life is impossible. For example, Rawls implies that some kind of nascent consensus on fundamental liberal political values either exists or can be forged and that political philosophy can proceed on the basis of assuming that "reasonable" citizens, of whom there are presumably a sizable number, recognize the authority of a shared fund of basic ideas and principles that are implicit in the public political cultures of democratic societies. By taking such ideas as "provisional fixed points,"[41] we can, therefore, work toward a conception of political justice that all reasonable citizens reflectively endorse.[42] Thus, Rawlsian approaches effectively hold that the political conflicts that exist as a result of the burdens of judgment can be overcome if we collectively recognize the demands of political reasonableness. In this sense, Rawls endorses what we might refer to as a doctrine of *resolvable pluralism*.

For those attracted to Berlin's account of value pluralism, there are several basic problems with this Rawlsian doctrine. For one thing, value pluralists are likely to stress that the pluralism in our societies is deeper and more antagonistic than Rawls suggests. For example, George Klosko claims that in the United States religious belief has become more comprehensive, less reasonable, and far more politically significant than Rawls supposed, as between sixty and one hundred million American citizens hold religious views that Rawls would consider unreasonable.[43] Similarly, value pluralists might argue, following Fabian Freyenhagen, that Rawls presumes that citizens will agree on the significance of the kind of political values he focuses on and accept that they cannot, except in extremis, be overridden and that this assertion of Rawls's is very questionable.[44] Third, one might remark that in the kinds of states that Rawls is concerned with, serious political disagreement exists not only between those who accept the importance of values like freedom, equality, and justice and those who do not but also between groups who interpret these values in sharply divergent ways, as the competing political traditions that are operative in such societies make sense of these ideas in conflicting ways (*IBWD*, 77). On this basis, Bernard Williams objects to the view—which he takes to be implicit in the work of Rawls and explicit in the work of Dworkin—that we can model "conflictual political thought in society in terms of rival elaborations of a moral text" the authority of which we all acknowledge (*IBWD*, 12).

These claims about the reality and intractability of political conflict problematize the Rawlsian view that some kind of shared fund of moral principles exists that we, as theorists, only need to work out how to apply. It also, as Galston surmises, suggests that there exists a "deep compatibility" between value pluralism and "an account of politics that looks to institutions that resolve value-based conflicts through negotiation and bargaining, appealing to mutual accommodation and modus vivendi rather than principles that yield premises of action binding on all."[45] Berlin does not spend much time reflecting on institutions in this way, and this is something for which, as noted in the introduction, Jeremy Waldron reproaches him.[46] Indeed, Waldron tacitly suggests a genealogy in which Berlin should take partial responsibility for the current situation where many political theorists and philosophers exclusively focus on ends and values at the expense of more properly political questions.[47]

While I am sympathetic to aspects of Waldron's complaints with such conceptions of political philosophy, a less damning evaluation of the significance of Berlin's thought is possible. Berlin's work vividly suggests that some moralist ways of thinking about politics must be relinquished and also implies that questions of legitimacy and authority must be considered central in political theory. Even though Berlin did not directly address these latter issues himself in any real depth, as I illustrate in the remainder of this book, his account of value pluralism is a vital influence on later thinkers like Hampshire and Williams, who do think in appropriately "political" terms about these issues.

Before I turn to Hampshire and Williams, though, I conclude this chapter by examining how thinking about politics in the terms I outlined in this section can illuminate how a value pluralist might commit to a substantive political position, like liberalism. My argument is consistent with some of the notoriously contradictory things that Berlin said regarding the relationship between pluralism and liberalism. However, I make no bones about whether I articulate the definitive interpretation of Berlin's considered opinion on this question. (In fact, I am doubtful that any such interpretation is possible.) Instead, it should be seen as a preliminary discussion, to be developed later in the book, about how the endorsement of a substantive set of political convictions is possible while affirming the central tenets of the views of moral philosophy's limits with which I am concerned.

Pluralism and Liberalism

As noted earlier, at certain points, most notably the final section of "Two Concepts," Berlin intimates that there is a necessary connection between value pluralism and negative freedom, famously asserting that pluralism entails a measure of negative liberty. He claims that a liberal conception of politics that prioritizes negative liberty is a "truer and more humane ideal" than the political orders typically associated with positive conceptions of liberty because it recognizes "the fact that human goals are many, not all of them commensurable, and in perpetual rivalry with one another" (L, 216). Berlin also often makes strikingly moralized claims about the importance of negative freedom, at one point remarking that "the glory and dignity of man consist in the fact that it is he who chooses, and is not chosen for, that he can be his own master" (CTH, 214). On this view, we can move from the metaethical claim about value conflict and incommensurability to the conclusion that we ought to endorse a politics that promotes people's ability to make such choices between values and to follow them through.

That things are far more complicated than these proclamations suggest is now widely acknowledged. Many commentators have observed that value pluralists cannot insist that a value or end, such as the negative conception of liberty, must always be prioritized over competing values or ends without violating their own claims about the nature of incommensurability and the limits of rational choice.[48] This idea is given its most powerful expression by John Gray, who contends that there is no necessary connection between value pluralism and liberalism: "Negative freedom is a universal human good. . . . But human beings have weighty interests apart from that in making their own choices. . . . If universal values conflict with one another in ways that have no one right solution, it cannot also be true that negative liberty must have priority over other universal values."[49] The attempt to seamlessly move from recognition of the truth of value pluralism to a determinate set of moral or political commitments is, therefore, futile.[50] Accordingly, Berlin's defense of political orders that prioritize wide-ranging negative liberty cannot be entailed by his value pluralism. It is, rather, better regarded as an expression of his valuation of the goods that he associates with such a politics.[51]

As I noted in the last chapter, one might hold that if value pluralism is as prescriptively barren as this suggests, it must render any commitment to a moral or political view unstable. Therefore, individuals who endorse the pluralist account of value would have to admit that any moral or political convictions they endorse are no more capable of vindication than a host of other outlooks. This can, understandably, be taken to suggest that any commitment to a network of values is capricious. However, at certain points Berlin rejects the account of moral psychology that tacitly underlies these concerns about the destabilizing effects of value pluralism.[52] This is, perhaps, most evident in two letters he wrote to the philosopher Jonathan Dancy in 1995. In response to Dancy's discussion of the possibility of value pluralists choosing to adopt certain values or disvalues, Berlin retorts, "this is not a realistic piece of moral psychology." He states that he does not

> believe that we "adopt" values, as if a variety of them were offered to us in some ethical shop window, and we decide on reflection that we propose to try and realise no. 3 or no. 7. We are born with certain values as a result of all the forces that create us—tradition, education, the views of the people we live among, the books we read, our own thoughts, etc. Of course we can reject any of them, and of course we can imagine different ones [but] . . . [we] begin with some kind of constellation of values and disvalues, some kind of outlook, and can alter it as the result of thought or imagination, or some shock of recognition or crisis in our or other people's lives. This is not selection or adoption: we live our lives in the light of a constellation of values, perhaps uncritically accepted (but not "adopted"), or perhaps critically—emerging as a result of reflection or self-criticism or the like. You speak as if we simply decide to choose this or that value out of those available to us, and this is surely psychologically not true. (A, 504–5)

This implies that it is an error to think of individuals uncovering the metaethical truth of value pluralism and then deciding, from some kind of disinterested standpoint, which values they should adopt.

Something close to this thought is also present in Berlin's response to the claim that his value pluralism ensures that there are no rational grounds for preferring one value over another. Berlin retorts that one can give "excellent *reasons*" in support of one's value choices but that "what rationality means here is that my choices are not arbitrary, incapable of rational defence, but can be explained in terms of my scale of values—my plan of life, an entire outlook which cannot but be to a high degree connected with that of others who form the society, nation, party, Church, class, species to which I belong" (*CTH*, 308–9). For Berlin, this is not a celebration of irrationalism but a realistic assessment of the limits of rational argument.[53]

Significantly, this suggests that so long as our outlook is not worryingly monistic, or constructed on the kind of metaphysically suspect foundations that value pluralism calls into question, it may continue to make reflective sense to us. Yet approaching things in this way radically alters our sense of the aims of philosophical reflection and argument. Rather than hoping that philosophy might conclusively answer the question of how we should live, we must instead decide if our commitments are consistent with or repudiated by what we come to learn about value in light of the truth of value pluralism. In this sense, reflection in the light of value pluralism is inherently self-reflexive: it examines whether our convictions can be stable without the metaphysical support that more traditional metaethical approaches promise.

Value pluralists typically think that our convictions can be stable without such foundational support because they do not think that absolute justification of the sort that many philosophers pursue is a prerequisite of commitment. Stuart Hampshire expresses one of the underlying assumptions of this way of thinking about ethics and politics especially clearly when he writes, "We have no pressing need for satisfactory total explanations of our conduct and our way of life. Our need is rather to construct and maintain a way of life of which we are not ashamed and which we shall not, on reflection, regret or despise, and which we respect. Our thinking generally is, and always ought to be, directed to this end, being practical and imaginative rather than an expression of theoretical curiosity" (*MC*, 168). Seen in this light, the recognition that value pluralism cannot be logically connected to a particular political position immediately seems less unsettling. Consider Gray's claim that once we acknowledge the impossibility of proving, in a priori terms, that pluralism has any particular political implications, we must proceed by illustrating why in particular historical circumstances there may be good reasons for favoring either "one value, or constellation of values, over others" or "one regime over another."[54] Berlin's work suggests that it may be possible to give a defense of liberalism on these grounds in at least three distinct ways.

First, we might hold that though there are no strict logical relations between pluralism and liberalism, there are certain psychological affinities that reveal the ways in which pluralism is amenable to liberalism, particularly because pluralists are likely to be especially prone to recognize the value of toleration. Thus, Berlin claims that if I understand the values realized in distinct ways of life, I will be inclined "neither to ignore nor to suppress" distinct ways of life, nor to "behave as if they didn't exist and mine was the only culture—the best, which can afford to ignore or despise the others" (*UD*, 87). In this sense, because pluralists recognize the "validity of a variety of forms of human life," their view encourages toleration, even if it does not logically compel it.[55]

Second, one strand of Berlin's thought continually expresses the belief that there is "nothing more destructive of human lives than fanatical conviction about the perfect life, allied to political or military power." In this respect, he claims that the search for a "minimally decent society" is the sine qua non of politics (*CIB*, 47) and that "the first public obligation is to avoid extremes of suffering" (*CTH*, 18). This suggests a politics that takes seriously the attempt to protect and promote the minimum content of natural law. But Berlin also recognizes that we should, if doing so does not sacrifice something of comparable importance, permit different people to pursue distinct values and ensure that distinct networks of value can exist side by side, "so that, so far as possible, there arises no situation which makes men do something which is contrary to their deepest moral convictions" (*CIB*, 143). It is possible to see how these considerations might enable one to make a case for liberalism. To wit, we might hold that regimes that practice toleration and promote a good degree of negative liberty have, in fact, done better at respecting the minimum content of natural law, securing tolerable coexistence among their citizens, and promoting a number of distinct goods and values than their ideological competitors in the present and recent past.[56]

Third, drawing on my earlier arguments, one might simply point out that, as a matter of fact, in social circumstances in which a wide array of different—and potentially antagonistic—values and outlooks are endorsed, there is a good reason to believe that political settlements that grant subjects a wide degree of negative freedom are likely to be considered more legitimate than those that do not. This is because it is highly likely that people will only continue to acquiesce to political orders if they do not systematically frustrate their attempts to live the kinds of lives that they pursue.[57] William Galston explicitly suggests a link between value pluralism and liberalism in these terms. As Galston sees it, pluralists hold that

Because there is no single uniquely rational ordering or combination of such values, no one can provide a generally valid reason, binding on all individuals, for a particular ranking or combination. There is, therefore, no rational basis for restrictive policies whose justification includes the assertion that there is a unique rational ordering of value.... This argument draws its force from the underlying assumption that coercion always stands exposed to a potential demand for justification. Individuals and groups whose desires and values are thwarted by existing arrangements have an incentive to question those arrangements, and they are entitled to a reply.[58]

As I will illustrate in chapter 6, Bernard Williams's political thought essentially proceeds to develop points two and three by explaining how a metaphysically and ethically parsimonious conception of liberalism—Judith Shklar's liberalism of fear—can be defended without relying on the more ambitious conceptions of morality that he, Berlin, and Hampshire call into question. The account that Williams offers represents, in my judgment, a plausible route for those who are sympathetic to Berlin's account of value pluralism to adopt in response to the question of how value pluralists can affirm liberalism. Of course, some moralist political philosophers will object that this approach rests on a very de facto understanding of politics. This is basically correct, at least to the extent that it sees legitimacy as resting in the recognition of the governed, rather than some antecedent principles that allegedly determine when and how political power can be rightly exercised. But given the pictures of ethics that Berlin, Hampshire, and Williams endorse, this is surely an advantage and not a shortcoming.

So rather than committing to the delusive aspiration that every member of the polity will consent to the authority of the liberal state, value pluralists who affirm liberalism are better advised to stress that "most human beings bridle at repressive policies and resist them when they can."[59] Moreover, such value pluralists should remind themselves that human beings are predisposed to acquiesce to institutions that, in actual fact, have a track record of enabling people to pursue their interests by securing the preconditions of commodious social coexistence, most chiefly peace and order.[60] If value pluralists think that actually existing liberal states do better than their rivals in these respects, there is no reason why they should immediately renounce their political convictions. This political judgment is not seamlessly derived from the value pluralist claim about the pluralistic and incommensurable nature of values. It is possible that a socialist, for example, might hold that the actions of actually existing liberal states need to be seen in a much less sanguine light. Consequentially, they would disagree with the opinion that actually existing liberal states adequately respect the minimum content of natural law, avoid repressing their citizens, and do in fact tend to secure the recognition of the governed, identifying this as a particularly specious kind of wishful thinking that some people fall victim to because they are passionately committed to the status quo.[61]

To the extent that liberalism's critics can provide convincing arguments to this effect, the way of defending liberal politics that I have gestured to here will obviously be undermined. This is as it should be; if our interpretation of the political world changes, our political allegiances should too. The aspiration for a more bulletproof justification of liberalism—or any other set of substantive political views—is not in keeping with the view of the limits of philosophy that is integral to Berlin's understanding of ethics.

Conclusion

In this chapter, I have argued that despite his avowedly moralistic understanding of political theory, Berlin's work gives credence to a number of ideas at the heart of the recent calls for realist approaches. Berlin's account of the impurity of political theory and view of the limited authority of normative theory suggest that political judgments cannot be seamlessly derived from moral philosophy. Moreover, as value pluralism claims that it is futile to expect that conflicts among values can be resolved in a reasonable manner accepted by all citizens, I have argued that Berlin's work should encourage us to see questions of authority and legitimacy as of first importance in politics. For these reasons, I have claimed that Berlin's work inadvertently pushes in the directions that contemporary realists have advocated. I have also argued that elements of Berlin's work can be employed to generate an account of how we might vindicate a set of moral and political convictions without violating the spirit of his value pluralism.

It is certainly true that Berlin does not examine how we might think about politics in the kind of realist terms that I have argued his work inspires. In the remainder of this book, I turn to two thinkers who were greatly influenced by Berlin and whose political thought begins from the view that political philosophy is not simply a matter of articulating the moral ends and values that we would like politics to realize. In similar but distinct ways, Hampshire and Williams both recognize that political philosophy cannot merely be regarded as a branch or subset of moral philosophy and, as a result, seek to articulate fundamental normative standards that are compatible with the basic circumstances of politics.

PART TWO

Stuart Hampshire

3

The Vitality of Conflict

In this chapter, I examine Stuart Hampshire's claims that morality and conflict are inseparable and that the search for harmony and consensus in morality and politics is, therefore, delusive. This touches on something of direct importance to the realist turn in contemporary political theory. As noted in the introduction, political realists stress that we must not shy away from the agonistic elements of politics. However, many realists simply see conflict as an empirical fact of moral and political life that we must accept, the basis of which they often do not explain. Others take a different tack and argue that some kinds of conflict and disagreement ought to be celebrated, which can seem puzzling. One of the reasons that Hampshire's work merits attention is that it suggests that there are good arguments for adopting such an attitude toward conflict. Indeed, for Hampshire, moral and political conflict is not a brute fact that must chasten or constrain the normative aims of any self-styled, realistic moral or political theory. Rather, he insists that within certain bounds, conflict is a sign of the healthy operation of human thought and the moral imagination. So according to his view, understanding the sources and nature of conflict plays a constructive role in helping us think realistically about morality and the ethical demands of politics.

Hampshire claims that adequately making sense of conflict necessitates a "moral conversion" on our part (*JC*, 34). In this regard, one of the central purposes of his work is to repudiate the prevailing picture of morality and reason—one that sees conflict as an aberration to be overcome, rather than as a mark of the proper functioning of human beings' distinctive capabilities and capacities—that many philosophers assume and that, he thinks, continues to distort moral and political philosophy. This chapter therefore examines the ways in which Hampshire's work gives voice to a set of underlying philosophical commitments that might ground a realist endorsement of an agonistic vision of ethics and politics.[1]

I begin by exploring Hampshire's engagement with Aristotle's work and his criticisms of Kantianism and utilitarianism. I then turn to his distinction between the "two faces of morality" (the convergent and the divergent), detailing the depth and character of his value pluralism and exploring where it overlaps with and departs from Berlin's. In the final section, I explore the significance of Hampshire's claim that "all determination is negation" and his account of the vitality of conflict.

Human Nature, Pluralism, and the Imagination

The idea that we should not only anticipate but also celebrate the wide-ranging diversity witnessed in the moral prescriptions that human beings endorse, and in the types of conduct and lives that they esteem, lies at the heart of Hampshire's moral philosophy. One of the best entry points into his thought is his engagement with Aristotle. Hampshire admires Aristotle's work because it does not appeal to any standards independent of human nature and our moral experience when examining how we should live. Instead, it is concerned with systematizing our moral intuitions and explaining how they can be seen as specifications of more general principles. On this view of ethical reflection, which Hampshire endorses, "the superiority of one moral theory to another is established by showing that it gives a more simple and more comprehensive, and a less exception-ridden, account of the whole range of one's moral beliefs" (*MC*, 27).

For Hampshire, one of the central advantages of the Aristotelian approach is that it reveals, contrary to the claims of some philosophers, how "unexceptional" moral judgments are (*MC*, 30). In particular, Hampshire lauds the fact that Aristotle adopts a thoroughly naturalistic and unproblematic account of how the word "good" functions in ordinary language (*FOM*, 64–86). As Aristotle sees it, moral philosophy is an exercise in practical rather than theoretical reason as moral decision-making is a matter of "choosing between lines of conduct" rather than "arriving at true statements and beliefs" (*MC*, 101). Accordingly, when we call something "good," we do not have to suppose a special domain of moral considerations that stand apart from the rest of nature. There is nothing peculiar in talking about good novels, good friends, or good chairs. When we think in these terms, we simply ask what it is for something to function well. Aristotle thinks that we do the same thing when we inquire into the good life, relying on our intuitive judgments about what makes lives go well in order to elicit more general principles and to describe various virtues that admirable human beings display.

Yet Aristotle holds that we cannot merely list the various human virtues that we intuitively esteem but must also explain why such virtues enable us to class someone as a good human being. This requires us to formulate an order of priority among the virtues and to give an account of the rationale behind such an ordering by invoking an idea of the highest good. Thus, if someone decides to devote themselves to a particular pursuit, like politics or pottery, they will refer to the ideal politician or potter to guide their conduct, "but these ideals must find their place within the ideal of the complete human being. They are subordinate ideals, to be explained by the contributions . . . [they] make to the exemplary human being." In this sense, Hampshire claims that Aristotle holds that "a person will have a satisfying life if and only if he realises in his activities all the essential potentialities of human beings at their best, with nothing wasted, no loss in a complete life" (*IE*, 27).

Hampshire rejects the claim that moral philosophy must proceed in this way. Aristotle holds that, in principle, it is possible to give an account of an exemplary human life in which all the virtues are displayed. This in turn commits him to thinking that an exemplary person might be able to balance the virtues in a maximally inspiring way. Hampshire, on the other hand, is adamant that there is no reason to endorse such a perfectibilist view of human potentialities (*FOM*, 78). While Aristotle assumes that there must be such an ideal because practical reasoning could not be conclusive without it, Hampshire contends that even if this is the case it would not prove that such a form of life was identifiable; it might just tell us something significant about the limits of practical reasoning. Moreover, Hampshire flatly denies that there is much reason to expect the human virtues to be subsumable under any general criterion. Like Berlin, he claims that our moral intuitions "are not instances of one, or instances of very few, much more general prohibitions or injunctions" but are "irreducibly plural" precisely because "human beings are not so constructed that they have just one overriding concern or end." In this sense, we constantly find ourselves "trying to reconcile, and assign different priorities to, widely different and diverging and changing concerns and interests" (*MC*, 20). He also follows Berlin in insisting that historical reflection reveals that multiple styles of life are admirable and worthy of our esteem, even if the virtues and values they realize diverge, sometimes sharply.

In this sense, "good" human lives do not obviously point toward a determinate ideal or give much credence to the idea that flourishing human beings find a way to unify disparate commitments or balance the virtues in a uniform way. Furthermore, realistic social and historical understanding reveals that certain virtues "can only be attained at the cost of certain others, and that the virtues typical of several different ways of life cannot be freely combined" (*MC*, 91).[2] Accordingly, there is little reason to hope that we could live a life that realized all the virtues or forms of flourishing that we revere. Any life can only ever be "a balance between, and combination of, disparate elements" (*MC*, 20).

These claims are at one with Hampshire's belief that we frequently find ourselves in situations in which contrary moral requirements press upon us. We intuitively accept a diverse range of moral prohibitions because we consider various acts "morally repugnant, shocking, indefensible, inhuman, vicious, disgraceful," even though we cannot find a "simple connection between them" (*MC*, 20). We also often experience situations of deep moral conflict where any choice will leave a moral stain (*MC*, 34, 115). Hampshire frequently employs an example from his own life to illustrate this point. Toward the end of the war, he was tasked with interrogating a traitor to the French resistance who refused to cooperate unless he was allowed to live. Hampshire knew that the man was condemned to die but promised him a reprieve to elicit the information he required.[3] For Hampshire, this was a clear example of a situation in which an abstract moral theory is incapable of grasping the nuances of the situation or explaining the pull of the different options and the evident regret that *any* decision would generate. Some moral theories try to explain away such conflicts by appealing to an overriding principle, like the principle of utility. But Hampshire is adamant that if we are uncorrupted by misleading theory, we will naturally think of "a multiplicity of moral claims, which sometimes come into conflict with each other, just as we think of a multiplicity of human virtues, which sometimes come into conflict with each other." This just is "the stuff of morality as we ordinarily experience it" (*MC*, 116).

In light of these considerations, Hampshire insists that we should follow Aristotle in beginning our ethical inquiries with reference to our moral intuitions and an understanding of human nature but stresses that even though the "good" person will exhibit some distinctive human characteristics to an exceptional degree, it is a mistake to think that any one person could exhibit them all or find a uniquely rational way of "balancing" them. It does not follow that anything can be classed as a human virtue or that any kind of life represents an ideal to be aspired toward. Human beings "need to be free of a minimal set of gross defences if they are to be praised," but excellence comes in many forms above this minimum (*IE*, 28–29). In particular, there is no reason to agree with Aristotle that good lives are "rounded and balanced, necessarily not eccentric and lopsided" (*IE*, 28). We often deeply admire men and women who single-mindedly pursue a solitary aim and disregard many commonly shared human interests and who, as such, do not display some of the characteristic virtues others exhibit but who excel nonetheless (*IE*, 29).

Thus, like Berlin, Hampshire insists that multiple "ways of life" realize distinctive forms of human flourishing and disparate sets of virtues. Consequently, though focusing on human nature can persuade us that certain ways of life are not admirable expressions of human potential, this focus cannot deliver a conclusive, determinate judgment about how human beings should live. Hampshire therefore holds that admirable human beings often exhibit a wide range of virtues and that these are derived from the distinct "ways of life" they endorse.[4] On this basis, in a number of the papers in *Morality and Conflict*, he endorses a "three-tiered conception of morality" (*MC*, 124). On this view, a morality involves (1) the endorsement of a set of injunctions and prohibitions that are (2) explained by the valuation of a set of virtues that are (3) derived from a commitment to a distinct way of life (*MC*, 91).

Ironically, Hampshire claims that if we focus on human nature, we must pay attention to two distinctive domains of thought: reason and imagination. He claims the kind of thought that has usually been regarded as reason directs forms of inquiry that are not "confined by the notations employed in them to any specific culture, nor tied to any particular language." This form of thought is "designed to be universal in the sense of ecumenical." For example, theorems in mathematics are "immediately accessible to everyone everywhere, whatever language they speak, sometimes with a relatively trivial call for translation" (*IE*, 42). Another kind of thought that human beings engage in—imaginative invention—contrasts with reason by generating diversity and "a process of seclusion" (*IE*, 43). The example of imaginative thought that Hampshire most often draws on is learning to speak one's own language. He notes that learning a language "is precisely and conspicuously to acquire a power that separates one's own people from the great mass of mankind" (*IE*, 42). In this sense, natural languages set up "frontiers" between people and serve to divide humanity (*IE*, 43). This style of thought is essentially divergent and idiosyncratic: our imaginative capacity is the source of linguistic, cultural, and moral diversity (*IE*, 30).

Hampshire claims that both forms of thought have a role in morality. As we will see shortly, some elements of morality are universal, but others are the result of "particular and distinguishing memories and of particular and distinguishing local passions" (*MC*, 135). Human nature cannot disclose a particular way of life that is best for all; it is natural for human beings to develop, imitate, and affirm distinctive ways of life that are underdetermined by reason (*IE*, 118). Thus, though Hampshire endorses Aristotle's claim that the virtuous man immediately acts in accordance with internalized moral dispositions, similar to the way in which language users communicate effortlessly without fretting about their language's underlying grammar (*MC*, 103–4), he insists that ways of life and languages are always "overlaid" by specific requirements that cannot be understood by focusing on universal considerations (*MC*, 142). Just as "linguistic conventions of grammar and idiom change with changing circumstances, so also the moral conventions that support a particular way of life change" (*MC*, 159–60). It is natural for imaginative thought to affect morality in this way.

In this sense, Hampshire claims that defending the particular virtues and prohibitions that form part of our way of life is not a matter of articulating universal principles but of pointing out "the distinctive and peculiar virtues of one way of life" and the ways that these are mutually dependent (*MC*, 136). It is part of the very purpose of languages and moral outlooks "to mark off a group of men and women, uniting the group and dividing humanity" (*MC*, 141–42). And just as there is no reason to regard natural languages as an approximation of an ultimate or perfect language, we should not "think of past and present ways of life, with their supporting and dominant virtues, as phases in the development towards the one perfect way of life" (*MC*, 160).

Putting the imagination at the center of our understanding of human nature has significant ramifications for our understanding of ethics. Truthfulness to history, and to our own moral experience, generates the skeptical realization that no moral judgment can plausibly claim to grasp all of the morally relevant features of a situation on which other human beings might focus (*MC*, 24–25). The result is a kind of unending openness to competing sets of moral distinctions and alternative ideals.[5]

Moreover, any particular life an individual pursues, either through conscious choice or as a result of their upbringing, precludes the achievement of other ways of life and their concomitant virtues. When we are in situations of moral conflict, choosing between two courses of action can have wide-ranging consequences for the kind of person we will become. Reflecting on Sartre's example of a young man who has to choose between being a resistance fighter or fulfilling familial obligations, Hampshire writes,

> The first commitment will demand the virtues of courage above all, of dedication, selflessness, also of loyalty; it will also call for violence, skill in deceit, readiness to kill, and probably also false friendship and occasional injustice. The second will demand the virtues of friendship and affection, gentleness, justice, loyalty, and honesty; it will also call for acquiescence in public injustice, some passivity in the face of the suffering of others, some lowering of generous enterprise and energy because of political repression. These are two

different ways of life, because they demand different dispositions and habits of mind, different social settings, and different ends of action. The young man has to choose between two possible types of person, each with his own set of virtues and defects, now incompatible sets. (*MC*, 33)

Likewise, enculturation in any way of life involves the acquisition of specific habits, dispositions, and methods of evaluating the world that ensure that one type of human being among others is formed. In this sense, enculturation entails that some potentialities of a person's nature will not be realized. Reflective individuals, therefore, realize that alternative ways of life were open or reasonable possibilities for them, but that they, and the very people they may have become, have been suppressed. Hampshire claims that this idea is one of the central ethical resonances of the logical principle "all determination is negation" (*MC*, 146).

These considerations underwrite Hampshire's rejection of Kantian and utilitarian ethics. By presenting themselves as articulating nonnegotiable moral injunctions that capture the truth about how we must act, both approaches fail to recognize that

> A man may be dissatisfied with his own conduct and with his own intentions, not because he has failed to do that which he knew to be right, but because he suspects that he is enclosed within a system of habit that does not present the varied possibilities of action open to him. His regret and uneasiness do not arise because he thinks that he makes the wrong response to the clearly identified problem. Rather he thinks that he overlooks many of the problems and that he fails sometimes to notice the features of a situation, and fails to make discriminations in conduct, which would be evident to him, if he had been trained in different habits and conventions. It is not that he recognises his rational and superior will is sometimes overcome by desire and that he fails from weakness of will; rather that he has too narrow and too crude a conception of the possibilities of behaviour and expression. He is aware, perhaps for the first time, that there are ways of discriminating and noticing differences in situations confronting him, and in manners of performance, that have never hitherto entered into his thought and intentions. He is waiting rather for a further enlightenment of his perceptions and of his intelligence, and not for admonition, addressed to his will, telling him to behave as he already knows, in his clearer and more rational moments, that he ought to behave. (*TA*, 209)[6]

For Hampshire, then, every way of making moral distinctions reflects a particular moral standpoint and will, inevitably, fail to capture something that other people could reasonably judge as having moral relevance. As a result, we are likely to wish to widen our frame of thought and judgment and to ensure that we are open to new ways of reflecting on the situations we find ourselves in. Yet we must also recognize that even a more enlightened standpoint could never capture everything that could reasonably be considered morally salient by another rational person. Taking the imagination seriously, therefore, requires us to give up on not only the hope of articulating an account of the ideal life but also the search for a moral standpoint that captures all the morally relevant features of any situation.

In a related way, Hampshire claims that thinking in terms of general principles often requires one to exclude aspects of particular situations that do not fit the abstract criteria that are employed. In so doing, "much that is puzzling, exceptional and difficult about those practical questions which are called moral issues has been cleared away" (*MC*, 113). We have no trouble thinking of situations in which "the particular circumstances of the case modified what would have been the expected and principled decisions, and for reasons which do not themselves enter into any recognized principle" (*MC*, 114). Hampshire remarks on the tendency to circumscribe "a lived-through situation" into a "clearly stated problem." Yet he insists that this often fails to do justice to the particular problem one faces at a particular point in time. When musing on his wartime experience of interrogating a captured spy that I touched on earlier, he remarks that "on different occasions, and without any clear intention, I tended to stress different features of the situation as relevant to the problem, and that I did not always even include the same elements of the situation as belonging to the story." In this regard, even speaking of a particular moral problem as being clearly defined is often "to oversimplify by a false individuation" (*MC*, 114).

These criticisms of utilitarianism and Kantianism are not conclusive, but rather than attempting to prove that such views are logically incoherent, Hampshire stresses that we can merely highlight "the actual variety of conflicting ends which we know that intelligent men have had in view at different times and in different places." While this does not refute utilitarianism or Kantianism, it urges defenders of such "single-criterion" theories to reflect on whether they may have "overlooked or failed to understand" the nature of ethics (*MC*, 22).[7]

If we take the imagination seriously, we must conclude that it is impossible to make a priori moral judgments about which forms of ethical life are superficial and which are profound and genuinely valuable (*IE*, 133).[8] On this basis, there is an important strand of self-reflexivity underpinning Hampshire's work. If we take seriously the failure of perfectibilist conceptions of human nature and the inadequacy of single-criterion theories, we should realize that our particular moral beliefs "are only one set among many" (*IE*, 135). Hampshire notes that some people manage to "recognize and accept the pathos of their situation, the narrow limits of their experience, of their range of feelings, of their knowledge of the world, but others do not" (*JC*, 70–71). His moral and political thought is an exercise in examining how we must proceed if we are to refrain from thinking in such hubristic terms. Accordingly, Hampshire is adamant that there is something deeply inhuman about the aspiration to present ourselves as delivering such moral pronouncements from a vantage point "beyond the rim of the world, observing it from the outside" (*MC*, 9). Our moral and political judgments express a particular point of view, one of many such points of view that reasonable human beings have either endorsed in the past, currently take up, or are likely to express in the future.

Convergence and Divergence

Once we center both reason and imagination in our understanding of human nature, we must make the distinction between two kinds of moral claims essential to our understanding of morality: the universal and convergent and the distinctive and divergent.[9] According to Hampshire, aspirational accounts of human excellence and social life "are infinitely various and divisive, rooted in the imagination and in the memories of individuals and in the preserved histories of cities and states" (*JC*, xi). Yet there exists another class of norms that relate to observable facts about human life and respond to some basic universal needs and interests we share. With regard to this minimal set, there is a degree of convergence. Hampshire refers to this as the *natural* element of morality.

> The idea that moral distinctions are found in the nature of things implies there is an underlying structure of moral distinctions, partly concealed by the variety of actual moral beliefs, a structure that is defensible by rational argument and by common observation of human desires and sentiments, when a covering of local prejudices and superstitions has been removed. If the underlying structure of moral distinctions has no supernatural source, it must be recognized by rational inquiry as having its origin in nature and, specifically, in human nature: that is, in constant human needs and interests, and in canons of rational calculation. (*MC*, 128)

This leads Hampshire to hold that there is a common core of morality, universal in reach, that relates to an invariant set of shared human needs and interests. These are "comparable to biological needs" as they constitute "the minimum common basis for tolerable human life." Respecting these needs stops human life from becoming "nasty and brutish, less than human" (*IE*,

33). On this basis, there exist some universal prohibitions that are rationally defensible concerning what kinds of conduct, and what kinds of social arrangements, are minimally acceptable.

As these needs are so widely shared, Hampshire insists that the central evils of human life are not culturally relative: throughout history people have bemoaned the horrors of "murder and the destruction of life, imprisonment, enslavement, starvation, poverty, physical pain and torture, homelessness, friendlessness" (*IE*, 90). These evils are independent of divergent conceptions of the good, and the assertion that they must be avoided is not "a matter of divided opinion, requiring argumentative support" (*IE*, 99). The similarities with Berlin's understanding of the empirical content of natural law, which I examined in chapter 1, should be immediately clear.

Moreover, Hampshire insists that despite a marked diversity among different historically conditioned moralities, each celebrates a set of essential virtues, including "courage, justice, friendship, the power of thought and the exercise of intelligence, [and] self-control," even though the particular forms these virtues will take vary greatly in different cultural and social settings (*MC*, 37). Indeed, we can only recognize different moral systems as being instances of the more general phenomena of morality with reference to this common core. This is markedly similar to the basic idea at work in Berlin's account of the human horizon.

Hampshire is more forthright than Berlin in explicitly stating that averting the evils he speaks of is the central presupposition of morality.[10] He writes,

> That destruction of human life, suffering, and imprisonment are, taken by themselves, great evils, and that they are evil without qualification, if nothing can be said about consequences which might palliate the evil; that it is better that persons should be free rather than starving in prisons or concentration camps—these are some of the constancies of human experience and feeling presupposed as the background to moral judgements and arguments. They correspond, as the constant evils presupposed, to such regularities as the effects of gravity, or the alternation of night and day, presupposed in everyday natural explanation. All ways of life require protection against the great evils, even though different conceptions of the good may rank their prevention in very different orders of priority. (*IE*, 90–91)

Hampshire claims that these great evils are directly *felt* as such, and that the word "feeling" is of great significance because it enables the immediate labeling of those horrors as great evils "by any normally responsive person, unless she has perhaps been distracted from natural feeling by some theory that explains them away: for example, as necessary parts of God's design" (*JC*, xii).

The named great evils do not seamlessly lead to a set of human rights, as is indicated by Hampshire's inclusion of the misery of friendlessness. Although we would expect a person to find a life of friendlessness miserable, it is problematic to think that others might have an obligation to befriend them (and not only because genuine friendships do not tend come about with a cloud of guilt or responsibility hovering over them). In addition, Hampshire does not think that only the great, universal evils can be genuinely classed as evil. His point is, rather, that judgments about evils that are not immediately felt as such by "normally responsive people" necessarily take place from within a particularizing frame of reference and must, therefore, be "revealed and certified by argument as evil before they can be felt as evil" (*JC*, xii). Among this class of evils, we consequently ought to expect a plurality of competing judgments to obtain at different times and in different places.

Hampshire's belief in a "natural" element of morality leads him to insist that the central question of morality and politics is how "a standard of bare decency in social arrangements is to be maintained; for this standard is always under threat" (*MC*, 168). This aspect of Hampshire's thought is motivated by his work as an intelligence officer in World War II, an experience that fundamentally changed his philosophical and political beliefs by revealing just "how easy it had been to organise the vast enterprises of torture and murder, and to enrol willing workers in this field, once all moral barriers had been removed." A disquieting realization followed: that "unmitigated evil and nastiness are as natural . . . in educated human beings as generosity and sympathy" (*IE*, 8). This leads Hampshire to stress that any viable postwar moral and political philosophy has to recognize that humanity is not on an inexorable path of moral improvement. Hampshire claims that a refusal to acknowledge the importance of some sense of moral restraint lies at the heart of evil (*MC*, 156). From a philosophical perspective, he argues that the most striking feature of Nazism was its goal to establish a society that attempted to discard moral barriers. By seeking to create a politics in which notions of justice and fairness had no place, the Nazis envisioned a society based on force, subjection, and domination.

Evil ideologies, like Nazism, aim to thoroughly subvert all of the values that the concept of justice highlights: "argument on two sides, respected procedures of gathering evidence, impartial adjudication, the avoidance of violence, distribution of rewards and penalties in accordance with rationally defensible and well-established criteria" (*IE*, 69). In this sense, Hampshire believes that by understanding the nature of evil we gain a better appreciation of the fundamental nature and point of justice as a negative virtue: a bulwark or barrier that stands against the ruinous results of force and domination. As we will see in the next chapter, Hampshire sketches an account of how we should conceive of justice by focusing on what it "prevents rather than what it engenders" (*IE*, 68).

Even though these arguments somewhat chasten Hampshire's pluralism, the common core of morality radically underdetermines how we should live. Thus, much of the time moral reflection requires us to engage in forms of understanding that are more characteristic of historical, humanistic analysis than that of the natural sciences (*MC*, 3). This has ramifications for our understanding of rational justification in ethics and politics. We are embedded in a particular way of life that is not fully subservient to a set of general moral principles or prohibitions and that cannot be fully understood in light of them. It is natural for us to internalize the particular customs and ideals that we endorse from within our way of life and to act in accordance with them. (Following David Hume, Hampshire argues that many moral commitments are expressions of human beings' "second nature.") Hence with some moral concerns, "the complex description of a whole way of life, and of its history, does fill the place occupied in other moral contexts by general principles" because "justification stops when the interconnections of practices and sentiments within a complete way of life are described" (*MC*, 5). Hampshire refers to this kind of justification as holistic because we appeal to our ways of life taken as a whole to explain our allegiance to particular customs, practices, or ideals, which are themselves mutually dependent on one another and intermeshed in ways we cannot always fully grasp. In consequence, highly abstract styles of philosophical reflection can preclude us from understanding the virtues and vices that distinct ways of life exhibit.

Hampshire is aware that many philosophers consider this a willful exercise in irrationalism but stresses that his point is not that rational argument has no place in ethics. He accepts that much of the time "rational considerations of human welfare and justice override, and ought to override, all more intuitive perceptions of the value of particular relationships and practices and sentiments." But he denies that such considerations exhaust morality. As a result, the attempt to think about ethics solely in terms of abstract, general principles must be relinquished. As moral agents, we never find ourselves "unclothed in the sole light of reason, computing what is best for mankind as a whole . . . and guided by no considerations of another less rational kind" (*MC*, 161). Rather, our moral decisions and evaluative attitudes are often explained by the feelings and perceptions our distinctive ways of life generate by means that defy transparent rational reconstruction: "An action or policy may be felt to be, or perceived to be, squalid, or mean, or disloyal, or dishonourable, even though the agent can give no very precise and explicit account of why on this particular occasion he perceives the situation in this light . . . reasonably trusting his reflective feelings about it, which may have arisen because he has noticed features of the situation that he does not know that he has noticed and that he cannot spell out and analyse" (*MC*, 157). Significantly, Hampshire insists that it is not irrational to reflectively endorse our intuitions and particular judgments if they take this form because "strict reasoning" cannot legislate for all areas of moral concern.

In this sense, Hampshire claims that ethics is resolutely resistant to reductive theorization. We are born into a society that is constituted by a particular set of moral conventions, and we learn to live morally by imitating these. There comes an inevitable point at which we must accept that we cannot rationalize our particular practices any further. It does not follow that we should disown them. Although there is no overriding rational obligation to support any particular ethical practices (beyond the core minimum of morality), Hampshire insists that we can derive a prima facie duty that is conditional upon two things: first, a respect for "possibly overriding considerations of justice or utility," and second, "an evaluation of the way of life in question, taken as a whole, as comparatively respect-worthy and as not morally repellent and destructive" (*MC*, 7). Provided these conditions are met, there is a sense in which we should respect "some set of not unreasonable moral claims of a conventional kind, because some moral prescriptions are necessary" and we are "reasonably inclined to respect those prescriptions which have in fact survived" (*MC*, 137). The aspiration to reorder the world in the light of a fully determinate rational vision of how we should live is hopeless and can only lead to self-deception.

This account of the two faces of morality disrupts some standard philosophical dichotomies. It is a gross error to think that the universal/particularizing distinction neatly maps onto the old philosophical distinction between reason and sentiment. It is also a mistake to align the superficial with the variable or transient and to contrast it with the deep and constant. In fact, many things with regard to which different moral outlooks issue divergent prescriptions—familial relations, sexual etiquette, or friendships, for example—have profound importance for us, and some of the time our recognition of their particularity contributes to our sense of their significance (*MC*, 153-54). Moreover, it is a mistake to paint our particular sentiments and concerns as "blind excitements." Precisely because we take these aspects of our lives with the utmost seriousness, we often discuss their reasonableness, or lack thereof, in great detail. In this regard, Hampshire does not deny that "moral sentiments can be adopted, endorsed and repudiated as a consequence of reflection" (*MC*, 9). While we cannot uncover a systematic account of how we should live that is grounded in an incontrovertible vision of the best life for humanity, Hampshire insists that it is a superstition to think that we need such a vision. Our need is rather to "construct and maintain a way of life of which we are not ashamed and which we shall not, on reflection, regret or despise, and which we respect" (*MC*, 168).

All Determination Is Negation

Hampshire's celebration of moral and political conflict is one of the most striking features of his thought. In an interview published in *Philosophy Now*, he states that his thinking was influenced by what he considered to be the "big gaps in the thinking of Bernard Williams and Isaiah Berlin, who appear to adopt a kind of pluralist view without giving any non-Nietzschean grounds for it."[11] He offers three different lines of argument that, he claims, explain why his account of pluralism moves beyond Berlin's and Williams's.

First, as we have seen, Hampshire argues that any way of life requires us to develop a certain set of capabilities or powers that are realized at the cost of other capabilities and powers, and their associated virtues (*MC*, 146). In this sense, pursuing a particular way of life requires exclusionary specialization and negates the possibility of living one of the many other kinds of valuable lives open to human beings. Hampshire's position has much in common with Berlin's in this regard. Yet Hampshire insists that, according to Berlin, it is possible to draw up "a definite list of essential virtues, deducible from human nature alone . . . even if there will always be conflicts between them" (*MC*, 159). This possibility is something Hampshire denies. As one of the two faces of morality is irreducibly grounded in convention and our imaginative capacities, the particular ways of life that human beings aspire toward inevitably evolve and change throughout history in ways we could never hope to grasp in advance. Hampshire insists that this problematizes any account of value pluralism that stresses the inevitability of conflict between timelessly valid moral values and commitments (*MC*, 159–60).[12]

Second, Hampshire holds that conflict often plays a role in generating values that we come to endorse. Part of what we admire, what we value, and who we take ourselves to be is determined by what we reject and regard as worthless, inferior, shameful, or reprehensible. In this sense, Hampshire repeatedly states that "self-determination by moral opposition is the moral equivalent of the old logical principle '*Omnis determinate est negatio*' [all determination is negation]" (*JC*, 26). It is not merely the case that the imagination leads human beings to pursue multiple, conflicting ways of life and their virtues. Our deepest hopes and aspirations are also sometimes generated by our opposition to, and rejection of, alternative ways of life that we think lack value. Accordingly, hostile judgments play a role in determining what we pursue and esteem. This is why Hampshire claims that his account of ethics rests on a strong and distinctive thesis about "the superior power of the negative" (*JC*, 34). Conflict is, in a sense, a begetter of moral commitment. Thus, he insists that "most influential conceptions of the good have defined themselves as rejections of their rivals: some of the ideals of monasticism were a rejection of the splendors and hierarchies of the Church, and this rejection was part of the original sense and purpose of a monastic ideal. Some forms of fundamentalism, both Christian and others, define themselves as a principled rejection of secular, liberal, and permissive moralities" (*JC*, 34–35).

This understanding of the place of conflict and negation in moral lives is highly distinctive. Hampshire is not suggesting, as Berlin does, that conflict is inevitable because a plurality of valuable ways of life exist. Rather, he intimates that conflict plays a constructive role in establishing new values and commitments because we have a tendency to define ourselves in light of what we reject. This gives Hampshire's view a distinctively realist shape as he begins with a view about the centrality of social and political conflict in our lives, from which he goes on to defend a set of claims about the plural nature of value, rather than proceeding in the converse direction.[13]

Third, Hampshire claims that Spinoza's metaphysical speculation that human life is in part constituted by "unavoidable conflicts of interest in the pursuit of survival" also applies to "conflicts between conceptions of the good to which people are passionately identified" (*JC*, 39). So there is a sense in which "the individuality of any active thing depends on its power to resist invasion and the dominance of the active things around it." On this view, "Men and women are naturally driven to resist any external force that tends to repress their typical activities or to limit their freedom. This is true of individuals, families, social classes, religious groups, ethnic groups, nations. They are all, these different units, struggling, wittingly or unwittingly, to preserve their individual character and their distinctive qualities against encroachment and absorption of other self-assertive things in their environment" (*JC*, 38–39). In light of this, conflict is an expression of our natures and something to be celebrated, not merely tolerated, because it is the inevitable result of the exercise of the imagination, which is itself the precondition of our choice and pursuit of moral ends (*IE*, 139).[14] Diversity, and the deep and pervasive conflict between antagonistic conceptions of the good that accompanies it, is therefore an inevitable and predictable result of the ordinary, healthy functioning of human thought.

Thus, it is foolish not only to think that we might have stumbled upon a theoretical understanding of how we should live that will perpetuate itself over time by gaining the assent of all rational beings. Even if this were possible, it would herald a distinctive kind of loss by representing the end of the collective exercise of the human imagination and mark a stunting of our natural potential. A stable moral consensus would negate the possibility of a future in which there are "leaps of the imagination, [and] moments of insight . . . which will lead to transformations of experience and to new moral ambitions and to new enjoyments of living" (*MC*, 125). This is why Hampshire insists that "there is every reason to hope that history will continue to show moral and aesthetic diversity and competition, as humanity develops new sciences, new styles of expression, new conceptions of the good, new ways of life" (*IE*, 141). We endorse competing moral ideals and aspirations and antagonistic visions of how we should live because it is our nature to do so. As a result, we should neither expect conflict to vanish nor want it to: "The diversity and divisiveness of languages and of cultures and of local loyalties is not a superficial but an essential and deep feature of human nature—both unavoidable and desirable" (*JC*, 37).

This account of the vitality of conflict has far-reaching implications for political thought that are misunderstood by those who insist on seeing claims about the inevitability of conflict as the expression of resigned acquiescence to the brute fact of political disharmony. If we refuse to see moral conflict and moral disagreement as an irrational aberration, or as evidence of the malfunctioning of human nature, there is little reason to endorse moral and political theories that regard conflict as something to be overcome. According to Hampshire, such theories are not only phenomenologically inadequate; they are also unattractive and unconvincing because they fail to understand human nature. This requires us to reject a picture of morality deeply "entrenched both in philosophical ethics and in ordinary language" (*IE*, 38). Hampshire claims that much of the Western tradition of philosophy, following Plato, views the undivided soul, ordered by reason, as the sine qua non of human flourishing. Yet Hampshire dismisses Plato's image of a well-ordered soul, where reason disciplines the other lower elements, as "a philosophical invention," developed for the purposes of defending a particular political ideology (*IE*, 34). In contrast, he favors the Heraclitean vision, according to which "every soul is always the scene of conflicting tendencies and of divided aims and ambivalences." On this view, "our political enmities in the city or state will never come to an end while we have diverse life stories and diverse imaginations" (*JC*, 5).

Thus, we must see the internal conflicts we experience between competing ways of life in our souls, as well as the conflict between competing conceptions of the good that we encounter in the city, as a sign of the healthy operation of human thought, rather than the malignant victory of unreason. Once this is accomplished, we have achieved the kind of "moral conversion" that Hampshire claims is needed if we are to better understand ourselves and the vagaries of politics (*JC*, 33–34). Hampshire thinks that ignoring the "reality of conflict" is lamentable because it is an "aversion from reality" (*MC*, 155). But taking conflict seriously is important not merely because it expresses a kind of realism and truthfulness, helping to guard against endorsing a set of "unrealistic" or "utopian" moral aspirations, which is how most people interpret the realist commitment to taking "real politics" seriously. For example, according to Lorna Finlayson, political realists move from claiming that some phenomena are important to claiming that they are constraints on what is politically possible, in order to argue that some forms of political thinking are "too ambitious" as they fail to "pay due heed to the limits of feasible political change."[15] Thus, Finlayson claims that self-styled realists hold that "being realistic means looking (an unappealing reality in the face); looking at reality in the face results in pessimism; pessimism brings us to curb our political hopes and ambitions."[16] On this reading, realism is a form of defeatism.

This may be a fair characterization of some understandings of political realism, but as this chapter illustrates, it is not the kind of argument that Hampshire makes.[17] Hampshire does not think that conflict is merely a brute fact to which any self-styled realistic conception of politics has to resign itself. Rather than holding that reflection on a recalcitrant reality should lead us to abandon a set of ideal moral or political principles and lower our normative vision, Hampshire encourages us to understand the sources, and necessity, of conflict because this will allow us to achieve a deeper understanding of ourselves, our ethical commitments, and the best possibilities of moral and political life. Foregrounding our moral and political theorizing in an understanding of the vitality of conflict is, therefore, not a matter of chastening our expectations by noting how reality will inevitably fall short of what is often taken to be the "ideal" by contemporary political philosophers—a society that exhibits a moralized consensus on substantive principles of political morality. Rather, appreciating the nature and sources of conflict is a precondition for thinking more clearly about what is "ideal" and what is worth hoping for in the first place.

To be sure, if one presupposes that moral conflict and disagreement are aberrations to be overcome, one will be inclined to interpret Hampshire's remarks about the inevitability of conflict in pessimistic terms. Hampshire is very explicit that "we ought not to plan for a final reconciliation of conflicting moralities in a perfect social order; we ought not even to expect that conflicts between moralities, which prescribe different priorities, will gradually disappear, as rational methods in the sciences and law are diffused" (*MC*, 160). This leads him to reject the suggestion that it can make sense to conceive of an ideal political society as one that is marked by the absence of fundamental moral and political disagreement in the way that many ideal theorists do. But this is not a heavyhearted expression of despair or some kind of mournful resignation. It is simply wrong to read Hampshire as endorsing the kind of position that holds that moralized consensus on substantive political values is not "intrinsically unattractive, but . . . [merely] incompatible with moral pluralism."[18] The point is not merely that that we should not seek such a consensus because it is unattainable; even if it were attainable, it would represent a stunting of the exercise of the imagination and our freedom.

Taking this idea seriously requires us to think differently about the ethical possibilities of politics and should alter our sense of an ideal political society in a very fundamental way. If one follows Hampshire in thinking that "the glory of humanity is in the diversity and originality of its positive aspirations and different ways of life," one should also recognize that we ought not to hope for a moralized consensus on substantive principles of justice and political morality. That desire is the political analogue of the delusive hope that "mutually hostile conceptions of the good should be melted down to form a single agreed conception of the human good" (*IE*, 107–8, 109). Hampshire's point, therefore, is manifestly not that moral and political theorists ought to accept that conflict is something that must constrain their normative visions or moral and political prescriptions. Rather, it is that understanding the vitality of conflict can help us to think constructively about the nature of moral and political values. As we will see in the next chapter, Hampshire offers such a constructive account by attempting to persuade his readers to disavow the idea that the aim of political thought is to uncover substantive political ends that should command the assent of any rational person and to instead see justice as a purely procedural virtue that enables us to manage political conflicts fairly.

Hampshire claims that the arguments of political philosophers who seek to defend more substantive ends and goals always seem "to be trapped in circularity" because "the conclusions derived from their own arguments supplied the only criterion of rationality and acceptability that they were prepared to accept" (*JC*, x). To this end, he insists that a lot of political philosophy amounts to little more than the search for "adequate premises from which to infer conclusions already and independently accepted because of one's feelings and sympathies" (*JC*, xiii). In this sense, Hampshire would be sympathetic to Gerald Gaus's assertion that political philosophy should not be "merely an intellectual game in which you defend what you want to believe."[19]

For Hampshire, political philosophy must not lose sight of the fact that the first job of political institutions is to protect us from the perennial evils that blight human lives—"physical suffering, the destructions and mutilations of war, poverty and starvation, enslavement and humiliation" (*JC*, xi)— and to facilitate "untidy and temporary compromises between incompatible visions of a better way of life" (*IE*, 109). His view is not that in an ideal world politics would be an instrument for achieving a harmony between substantive moral ends but that reality reveals this is unfeasible. More fundamentally, Hampshire expresses the view that politics both is and should be a domain of controlled hostility, conflict, and disagreement.

Conclusion

In this chapter, I have illustrated why Hampshire holds that hoping for consensus and agreement on the positive aspects of morality is both impossible *and* undesirable. His account of human nature stresses that human beings will inevitably endorse diverse and often antagonistic moral ideals. This has important implications for our understanding of politics. At its best, Hampshire claims that politics is a continuous exercise in forging compromises that people are prepared to accept by creating and maintaining political institutions that secure people's allegiance. As we will see in the next chapter, he accordingly claims that basic procedural justice is a good that people, if they are thinking honestly, will recognize and appreciate as it stands against the ruinous horrors of force and domination.

Although we can aspire to achieve more positive goods than basic procedural justice in politics, these aspirations will inevitably be divisive and reflect a particular conception of the good. The central purpose of politics is, therefore, to help us to live together, given our conflicts and disagreements about the positive requirements of morality. The yearning for a consensus on substantive principles of justice or a conception of the good is deeply rooted in philosophical ethics and political philosophy, but it is a misconception we must relinquish. In the next chapter, I ask if Hampshire's account of justice as a negative virtue offers an attractive vision of how we should think about the ethics of politics in light of his claims about the conflictual nature of morality.

4

From Conflict to Compromise

In the last chapter, I illustrated why Hampshire holds that there is no sense in hoping for harmony and consensus in our moral and political lives. But if conflict is both a fact of morality and politics and (at least in some forms) healthy, how can we hope to generate acceptable political settlements that preserve the civil goods of political order and earn the acquiescence of subjects? Hampshire attempts to answer this question by articulating an account of basic procedural justice. He claims that conflicts that arise in the city should be mediated and can be restrained by respecting the institutions that foster just forms of adversarial reasoning. In this chapter, I scrutinize this account of procedural justice.

I begin by setting out the central elements of Hampshire's account of procedural justice, paying particular attention to the account of rational decision-making that undergirds his position. I then draw out some of the underlying complexities and subtleties of Hampshire's understanding of how issues of procedure and substance intertwine. Following this, I probe two ways of interpreting Hampshire's claims about the requirements of procedural justice. First, I examine what I term the *thin* reading, raising some concerns about its undemanding nature. I then distinguish between two thicker readings and argue that one of these is plausible, although it exposes some salient lacunae in Hampshire's thinking. Despite these concerns, I conclude by arguing that Hampshire's work in moral and political philosophy has various salutary features. It powerfully suggests that we must renounce mainstream views that hold that well-ordered politics must be grounded in a moralized consensus of some kind, urging us to accept that the central task of political institutions is to secure the acquiescence of different groups by generating acceptable settlements between conflicting claims. In so doing, his work upsets views of morality and politics that encourage us to see compromise, bargaining, and negotiation on matters of principle with disdain and suspicion. These are important insights for future realist political theory to take up.

Basic Procedural Justice

As he insists that we inhabit a moral universe containing diverse and antagonistic conceptions of the good, Hampshire attempts to articulate a "rock-bottom" minimum concept of justice that tells us how to respond to existing conflicts in society, one which is independent of specific and divisive conceptions of the good (*IE*, 72, 78). Hampshire proceeds by trying to outline inherent procedural standards of conflict management observable in a diverse range of societies (*IE*, 14, 182, 188).[1] At its most rudimentary, Hampshire's aim is to persuade his audience to accept a negative conception of justice as a form of fairness in negotiations when conflicts occur. As such, he posits a basic distinction between justice and fairness in matters of substance, such as in "the distribution of goods or the payments of penalties in a crime," and justice and fairness in matters of procedure, which simply tell us how to manage conflicts that exist in the city in order to avoid "brute force and domination and tyranny" (*JC*, 4–5).

It is easy to see why this route might appeal to value pluralists who deny that it is reasonable to expect a concurrence on substantive moral principles among a citizenry of any great size. If moral reasoning does not converge on substantive moral principles that all reasonable people can be expected to affirm, then perhaps the best we can hope for is a more limited agreement on how to mediate the inevitable conflicts that arise in society. Although the attempt to secure a rational consensus on issues of substance is illusive, Hampshire believes that some universal standards of procedural rationality do exist and that these should command the assent of all members of the polity when they find themselves in conflict with adversaries.

Hampshire begins by observing that disputes and disagreements are pervasive in every society and that issues of policy are debated in an assembly of some kind or other, be it "democratically or aristocratically chosen . . . or an assembly chosen simply by a monarch or tyrant." In this regard, he claims that "the institution of articulating and reviewing contrary opinions on policy is of necessity species-wide" (*IE*, 51–52; *JC*, 7–8). Importantly, Hampshire claims that all procedures of conflict resolution have a philosophically significant prescription at their heart: a minimal conception of fairness that holds that the justice of public procedures depends on hearing different sides of a dispute in order to genuinely weigh and balance contrary arguments. It is this idea—captured by the legal prescription "audi alteram partem" (hear the other side)—that Hampshire terms the *principle of adversary argument* (*JC*, 8–9). This principle is realized when procedures of hearing the other side are embodied in institutions of conflict management respected by the denizens of a society (*JC*, 54). Hampshire claims that hearing the other side in this way is "acknowledged as a value in most cultures, places, and times" (*JC*, 4–5). It gives ethical expression to the very basic, rational requirement that evidence should be assessed and evaluated before one comes to a decision (*IE*, 94). If contrary claims are not heard, a process cannot be regarded to be just and fair, even if it delivers "the judgement that probably would have been reached if there had been full and fair argument" (*IE*, 53). Thus, Hampshire's account of procedural justice simply tells us how to engage with opponents and adversaries without prescribing how to resolve our political conflicts.

Hampshire claims that our inner processes of dealing with conflict shadow the way adversarial situations are resolved in the city (*IE*, 52; *JC*, 9). Accordingly, he insists that interpersonal and intrapersonal practical reasoning have the same character and that his account of procedural justice is "founded upon the antecedent claim of rationality to universal respect; and this claim, in turn, is founded on, and is supported by, a universal feature of human behaviour" (*JC*, 53). This is why Hampshire sometimes refers to his as a transcendental argument. As he sees it, everyone unavoidably engages in the "balancing of pros and cons" in the pursuit of their own good, "as well as in common prudence, in pursuit of his own interests" (*JC*, 42). Even those who seemingly disavow any respect for procedural rationality in public life balance pros and cons when faced with inner conflicts. Accordingly, Hampshire claims they should recognize that reason requires them to consider both sides in political conflicts too (*JC*, 65).[2]

In contrast to the substantive theories of justice defended by many contemporary political philosophers, Hampshire's position is strikingly minimalist. He refuses to draw any substantive conclusions about how such conflicts should be resolved. The outcome of such processes of adversarial reason-giving might be considered substantively unjust, yet Hampshire claims that his account delivers a clear-eyed understanding of the core of injustice: "the recourse to attempted conquest and domination when conceptions of the good come into conflict, even though fair and equal negotiation is still possible" (*IE*, 154).

The account of rational decision-making that drives Hampshire's argument has been criticized, however. John Horton claims that Hampshire fundamentally misunderstands the nature of rationality:

> Not only do we not in fact typically put to ourselves all of what could, in some sense, be thought of as relevant considerations when faced by a conflict about

how to act, it is far from clear that we think we should. Some reasons or options we might not consider because for us they are "unthinkable," in the sense that we should not even consider them. . . . So, for example, faced with a conflict about what I should do, I do not, say, consider as one of the options that I might steal from my mother. And what is important is that *I do not consider it*, not that I think about it, but after careful deliberation decide that it would be the wrong choice to make. . . . In such cases, not only do we not consider both sides of the argument, we believe it a good thing—perhaps a mark of a virtuous character—that we do not do so.[3]

As a political analogue, Horton argues that if I am "set against racism," it makes little sense to say that reason demands that I hear the other side of the case. This suggests that, just as some actions would not arise as possibilities to be considered by the perfectly just person, some courses of action would not be countenanced in a just state.

There is no reason to dispute Horton's claim that virtuous agents are unlikely to consider certain (immoral) courses of action. As Bernard Williams helpfully puts it, "if an agent has a particular virtue, then certain ranges of fact become ethical considerations for that agent because he or she has that virtue" (*ELP*, 10). For this reason, as Williams sardonically notes, "one does not feel easy with the man who in the course of a discussion of how to deal with political or business rivals says, 'Of course, we could have them killed, but we should lay that aside right from the beginning.' It should never have come into his hands to be laid aside" (*ELP*, 185). However, it is not clear that this undermines Hampshire's view of procedural justice. Hampshire does not suggest that rational decision-making requires that we weigh *every* possible course of action, and at one point in *Innocence and Experience*, he asserts that "from the moral point of view," that a certain possibility may not occur to someone is "a significant fact" (*IE*, 101). Hampshire is simply not interested in offering a substantive account of the considerations that would (or would not) present themselves to the just individual, or in the perfectly just city. His is a procedural point, that rational individuals weigh the arguments that *do* present themselves to them. While we may agree that a perfectly just person would not countenance various racist attitudes, if they are rational in the sense Hampshire is alluding to, they do weigh the alternative courses that appear to them before deciding how to behave, and this is all that is required for Hampshire's analogy to function because it reveals that a certain method of weighing pros and cons prevails in both the city and soul. Hampshire's point is that substantive positions, such as racist political proposals, must fairly be weighed *if* they are raised, in much the same way that they would be weighed if they presented themselves to the agent who rationally decided how to act.

The principle of adversary argument is realized in institutions and practices that manage adversarial conflicts. Beyond the injunction that each side to a conflict may put its case, Hampshire insists there is "no rational necessity about the more specific rules and conventions determining the criteria for success in argument in any particular institution" (*JC*, 17–18). In certain historical periods, dueling was regarded as such a procedure while mere fighting was not (*JC*, 18). Locally existing institutions—parliaments, law courts, councils, and so on—specify the requisite forms of fairness in light of their peculiar histories (*JC*, 54). Accordingly, the concrete requirements of procedural justice can differ enormously, even though the basic rational requirement they serve is universal.

The institutional aspect of Hampshire's argument has two central implications. First, it suggests that "bringing into existence institutions and recognized procedures should have priority over declarations of universal principles." Second, it holds that so long as an institution for adversarial argument has a record of resolving societal conflicts in an acceptable manner over a period of time, it satisfies the requirements of basic procedural justice, even though the specific ways that it resolves disputes are rationally underdetermined (*JC*, 40). In this sense, Hampshire seemingly envisions some kind of sufficiency threshold. Even if the procedures employed may not be as "ideally fair" as we could imagine them being, we may conclude that they are fair enough to warrant our respect (*JC*, 56). This is why he claims that a respect for procedural justice and a respect for history come together: "Arguments in negotiation turn on precedents and the comparison of cases in their historical setting" (*IE*, 138).

Significantly, Hampshire insists that "domination, the suppression of conflicts by force or by the threat of force is a great political evil that any citizen may be expected to feel as evil. . . . Even those men of religion who are disgusted by the easygoing tolerance of secular liberals will have a rational ground for respecting the institutions that enable such liberal attitudes and practices to survive alongside their own. The rational ground of respect is rationality itself, the habit of balancing pros and cons in argument, a norm that they cannot without disaster discard in their own thinking" (*JC*, 79–80; see also *IE*, 119). On this view, human beings are naturally predisposed to esteem basic procedural justice in much the same way that Hampshire claims that normally responsive human beings directly feel the universal evils to be evil.

By thus linking justice and fairness with this account of practical reasoning, Hampshire expresses his thoroughgoing naturalism. Representing justice in these terms enables us to give a realistic account of how such a norm can develop from the natural features of human life (*JC*, 13–14). At its most basic,

Hampshire's claim is that human beings need to live in societies of some kind and that when they do, they will live among other people who endorse divergent conceptions of the good. Accordingly, they need to develop a principled way of managing their conflicts, the authority of which they can all recognize so that their conflicts can be contained.

Yet Hampshire is careful to insist that he does not think that the principle of adversary argument must always override countervailing considerations (*IE*, 140). When he refers to the duty to support procedural justice as absolute, he does not mean that it necessarily trumps all other considerations. Rather, it is "a duty for everyone, whatever ends he or she may be pursuing" (*IE*, 140). This idea is most fully developed in his essay "Public and Private Morality," when he claims that "a moral claim . . . is absolute when it is not conditional upon, or subordinate to, any further moral claim or purpose. . . . The prohibition contains its own sense, and explains itself" (*MC*, 115). On this view, it is possible that absolute moral claims can conflict with one another, and when this occurs, "one of them is in the final decision overridden, even though it has not lapsed" (*MC*, 116). A similar circumstance transpires if you refuse to abide by the norms of procedural justice in order to resist evil or if your adversaries demand you "sacrifice a number of the more essential features of the best way of life" (*IE*, 142, 154). In such cases, one may reasonably decide that "the cost of peaceful co-existence on an agreed and fair basis is unacceptably high," but so long as this has not occurred, it is "contrary to reason to refuse to abandon some less essential features of your preferred way of life in a reasonable exchange of concessions with your adversary" (*IE*, 154). We shall return to this last significant point.

The institutions of conflict management do not transcend political conflict. We routinely disagree about how political conflict should be managed and whether existing procedures are as ideally fair as they should be (*JC*, 26). This is why procedural justice "tends of its nature to be imperfect and not ideal, being the untidy outcome of past political compromises" (*JC*, 32). Yet one ought to abide by the understandings of fair discussion and negotiation that prevail unless "one has reasonably rejected those procedures as being themselves unjust and unfair" (*IE*, 140). To illustrate this point, Hampshire claims that if the basic decencies of procedural justice are denied to some people, as they were in Apartheid South Africa, the subjugated have no reason to abide by the verdict of the extant institutions. In this regard, we judge the basic unfairness of the extant institutions of conflict management with the same rough tests that we employ to question the fairness of particular procedural outcomes. Thus, we ask, "Are the moral claims fully presented? Do the interested parties have reasonable access? Is there genuine argument and counter-argument? Are precedents, if any, respected? Are the rules of procedure reasonably consistent and known? Is the procedure free from threats of physical force?" (*IE*, 141). If the existing institutions fail to meet these conditions, we will regard them as instruments of injustice and domination.

This is a self-consciously untidy picture that disavows precise institutional prescription in favor of historical, political, and psychological realism. Yet even if we recognize that procedural justice will not always trump all other moral considerations, this does not mean that it is practically inert. There is a particular kind of chastened confidence in Hampshire's thought; he believes a thin conception of procedural justice can secure our allegiance if we bring our understanding of justice in line with a realistic grasp of the nature, and sources, of conflict.

Hampshire's critique of Rawls illustrates how his minimal account differs from the more moralized conceptions prevalent in contemporary political philosophy.[4] Hampshire rejects Rawls's picture of justice on two grounds. First, he accuses Rawls's political liberalism of not being "narrowly procedural enough" (*IE*, 187). That is, Hampshire complains that Rawls determines what is reasonable "by the traditional standards of liberalism" and argus that, for this reason, it is "hard to see how political liberalism avoids becoming merely another competing comprehensive moral doctrine."[5] He also claims that as a result of this, Rawls has little to say about how liberals should interact with nonliberals, beyond pointing out that nonliberal conceptions of the good are incompatible with substantive liberal commitments. To this end, Rawls "bypasses the outstanding political problem of our time" (*JC*, 23–24).

Second, Hampshire claims that Rawls's view that an overlapping consensus on liberal principles of justice is a realistically utopian ideal rests on an overestimation of the ability of rational argument to channel us toward a moral consensus. Hampshire flatly rejects Rawls's supposition that a political society will not be stable "unless an implicit consensus is first discovered and then is made explicit and reinforced" (*IE*, 189). Living together in political society requires acquiescence to institutions that have emerged to manage adversarial conflicts, rather than a consensus on substantive principles of justice (regardless of how "freestanding" they are claimed to be). This is why Hampshire argues that it is misleading to suggest that one of political philosophy's tasks is to settle various fundamental political questions "once and for all" by ensuring that some issues are not "suitable topics for ongoing public debate."[6] Just as the "life of the soul is a series of compromise formations, which are evidently unstable and transient," Hampshire claims "every successive state of society is evidently unstable and transient" (*IE*, 189). Our task is to explain the value of seeing politics as a domain of compromise and conciliation and to consider how we might think about justice as a negative virtue, one that enables us to live alongside our adversaries without descending into conditions of violence and disorder.

The Vicissitudes of Convention

As I have illustrated, Hampshire holds that people are generally predisposed to recognize the appropriateness of adversarial reasoning in the city. This supposition is, however, in tension with the fact that we know of societies in which certain groups clearly feel no compulsion to hear the complaints of those they dominate. It is easy to point to a litany of cases in the recent past when this has occurred, most obviously in situations of pervasive ethnic conflict.[7] But there are other less extreme examples lacking the kind of widespread social breakdown and killing that often accompanies explosions of ethnic hatred, where the denizens of such societies subjugate others without appearing to have any sense of the injustice of their behavior. These cases are more illustrative of this tension because they can be presented as situations of "ordinary politics."

For example, in his discussion of Greek slavery, Williams claims that most Greeks were not deceived about what slavery involved; some even regarded being enslaved as a "paradigm of bad luck." However, questions about the practice of Greek slavery were not raised because most people took slavery to be a necessary presupposition of their political, social, and cultural life: "life proceeded on the basis of slavery and left no space, effectively, for the question of its justice to be raised" (*SN*, 124). Cases like this reveal that it is not uncommon for some members of society to deny that all human beings' claims need to be heard in the way that Hampshire's principle of adversary argument suggests they must. It seems that human beings often feel nothing wrong in refusing to hear the other side, and this has the potential to discredit Hampshire's account, given that it starts from the claim that human beings are predisposed to recognize the value of basic procedural justice.

However, Hampshire is sensitive to these kinds of concerns. He insists such a situation can arise when members of a society are unable to "abstract themselves sufficiently from their own way of life" (*IE*, 59). In these cases, due to our enculturation, we believe that certain practices are, in some sense, unavoidable. As a result, alternatives to these practices and institutions are not "envisaged as real possibilities." Yet questions about the justice of treating people in certain ways "will be effectively raised only when and if an organised social group is strongly pressing its own claims in the name of elementary justice" as this kind of mobilization makes changing the practice at hand "a real possibility to be debated" (*IE*, 59). Thus, "practical possibilities have to be vividly imagined and actively explored," and groups who are treated unjustly (enslaved peoples, conquered populations, minorities denied the same rights as majorities, the severely economically vulnerable, and so on) "must organise themselves as strongly as they can in order to present an effective demand for justice." If this has occurred and the arguments of marginalized or oppressed groups are still not fairly weighed, Hampshire asserts that they may justifiably fight and agitate "until their substantial claims are fairly considered" (*IE*, 185).

On this basis, we might interpret Hampshire as holding that once demands become *politically audible*, the principle of adversary argument comes into play.[8] Even though many of the people who inhabited or inhabit certain political societies did or do not feel compelled to "hear" the complaints of those they dominated or dominate, Hampshire insists this does not undermine the claim that we are predisposed to recognize the value of hearing the other side. In such situations, a confluence of factors warp people's natural moral sentiments, resulting in some people's claims being politically inaudible.[9]

Such situations will only be ameliorated when procedural and substantive conceptions come into tension with each other. Reflecting on such cases, Hampshire posits that the following process occurs: "First come the precursors, the 'premature' advocates of a just cause which will finally seem to most people obviously just, but which at first seems a denial of the natural and divine order of things, not open to practical reasoning; then comes the formation of pressure groups which represent some powerful interests in society, usually, but not always, material interests; third, within the institutions of the state, democratic or otherwise, arguments for and against . . . have to be weighed and adjudicated within prevailing, but also changing, conceptions of justice" (*IE*, 56; see also *JC*, 31). In such societies, a belief in the inevitability of various features of social life makes sense because social myths make social arrangements appear fixed. Societies that endorse such myths subscribe to what Hampshire calls the *fallacy of false fixity*.[10] This has the effect of placing such considerations "outside the sphere of practical reasoning" (*IE*, 56). Yet once we critically scrutinize these practices, the rationale of various social conventions is debated, and in many cases the justifications are revealed to be baseless. So Hampshire claims that although there would have been long periods in history when people would not have thought that "absolute monarchy leads to injustices; that it is unfair and exploitative to exact a day of ten hours' labour in filthy conditions from factory workers; that slavery is a grossly unjust institution; that it is unfair that women should not receive equal pay for equal work," we can conclude that people who believed these things were blind to the injustices of such practices, and "we are right to think this" (*IE*, 57–58). But, in order for members of society to start deliberating about such institutions, "a large shift in the non-rational, or imaginative, presuppositions of a culture or community has to occur" (*IE*, 60).

In addition, Hampshire claims that in adversarial debate, parties "are supplied with the raw material for argument by the practices, the moral principles, and the precedents that prevail in a particular culture or community." In this regard, "there is no way in which entirely abstract arguments from the bare concept of justice can by themselves produce a determinate conclusion about the justice of a particular social practice" (*IE*, 61).

Thus, conventional attitudes and opinions intertwine with the basic concept of procedural justice in complex ways. First, our enculturation often constrains the political audibility of complaints about practices (such as not paying women equally at work) or existing institutions (such as slavery). Second, the arguments that are made in adversarial debate also appeal to practices, principles, and precedents that prevail in a particular polity. Therefore, even though Hampshire insists that the disposition to esteem adversarial reasoning is a universal feature of human nature, the political audibility of various claims is often constrained by features of our social lives that we are unable to distance ourselves from sufficiently in order to scrutinize them. (Indeed, we are unlikely to be able to make ourselves aware of the myriad ways this occurs.) Moreover, there is no reason to think that there is natural progress in recognizing instances of injustice (*IE*, 65). As such, there is an ineliminable pessimism in Hampshire's account.

This aspect of Hampshire's thought implies that one of political theory's most important roles is to examine the social myths of our own time and place, to ask if our conventional views may commit the fallacy of false fixity, and to vividly imagine and explore alternatives to our existing political and economic systems. Reflecting in these terms can raise "our consciousness of political possibilities" and help us stop seeing some issues as "natural misfortunes" and instead regard them as "political failures" (*JC*, 43–44).[11] This manner of political thought does not, however, require us to systematize our moral intuitions in order to generate general principles of substantive justice; nor is it a matter of stating and defending a set of substantive moral propositions. Rather, it requires us to consider how we might eliminate the "particular evils found in particular societies at particular times," an activity which is not dependent on a "generalizable account of a future society or of essential human virtues" (*JC*, x). This mode of political theorizing therefore enjoins us to think practically about how we might raise people's consciousness of the possibilities that are alive in their time and place.

Hampshire also offers valuable glimpses of how we should defend our political convictions in a way that is sensitive to the reality of conflict. In the preface to *Justice Is Conflict*, he remarks that the political events of the twentieth century lead him to realize that while his socialist commitments—emanating as they did from his view that poverty was a persisting evil of human life—were not unreasonable, they could not claim any kind of absolute authority (*JC*, ix–x). Yet he argues that, as a socialist, he was never deluded about the essentially conflictual nature of politics. When socialists wage political battles against poverty and deprivation in their many forms, Hampshire claims they are cognizant of the fact that by bringing these issues into the political domain, they have to generate an aggressive political consciousness and develop institutions (like trade unions) that can direct this consciousness in pursuit of its political ends. For Hampshire, the central aim of socialism is to extend the field of "political agency far beyond the domain recognized in earlier centuries" by bringing the sources of "human suffering and frustration into the political domain" (*JC*, 83). Thus, socialists of Hampshire's ilk never considered the task to be that of "solving social problems objectively defined" but that of "creating for workingmen the best attainable conditions of life and work through consolidating their mastery of the political processes" (*JC*, 89).

Significantly, when socialists and capitalists engage in political conflict, they both appeal to substantive principles of fairness to support their claims: capitalists "point to the unfairness of inadequate compensation for financial risk, and the workers will point to the unfairness of inadequate compensation for the hardship and the monotony of the work" (*JC*, 91). But the truly dangerous illusion, Hampshire claims, is that we might come to hold that a set of substantive moral and political principles can be invoked to finally resolve these disputes and disagreements, one which all parties will finally come to acknowledge as authoritative (*JC*, 89). This is a delusion that Hampshire claims certain forms of liberalism are especially prone to as they pursue a moral consensus. But the search for such a consensus is both philosophically false and politically debilitating: "false, because no universally acceptable premises exist from which the alleged principles can be deduced; debilitating, because such a hope will undermine the need for aggressive political organization in readiness for conflict when consensus has predictably proved unattainable" (*JC*, 89–90).

The Thin Reading

There is an ineliminably conservative slant to Hampshire's thought. Following Burke and Hume, he insists that if the prevailing conventional procedures of negotiation and adjudication in society are "successful and well established in the resolution of moral and political conflicts according to particular local and national conventions," we should abide by their dictates (*JC*, 26; *IE*, 138). With such passages in mind, some commentators have raised concerns about the status quo–affirming nature of Hampshire's account of basic procedural justice. They worry that Hampshire's position suggests that subjects should submit to whichever institutions of conflict management happen to obtain because we must prioritize peace and stability over and above all other political values.[12]

These worries are unjustified on three grounds. First, Hampshire's account of the universal core of morality and his remarks on the fallacy of false fixity articulate standards that we might employ to criticize and object to various procedures of conflict management. Second, as I have shown, he does not hold that we have an overriding duty to acquiesce to the existing institutions of conflict management at all times. Third, he does not claim that such institutions stand above political conflict; he explicitly states that it is permissible to make second-order and procedural questions "the subject of political conflict and negotiation" (*JC*, 29). For these reasons, it is incorrect to insist that Hampshire argues that respecting the known methods of adjudication requires us to abide by the decisions they reach in all cases. Nor does he believe that we must refrain from criticizing established social procedures and institutions of adversarial argument.

Nonetheless, Hampshire does claim that we can only judge extant procedures and institutions of adversary reasoning in local terms, asking whether instances of conflict management accorded with the prevailing norms and expectations about equal hearing in a particular society at that point in time. One might then extrapolate from this claim that Hampshire's account of procedural justice does not have any further implications—of either a concrete institutional or more attitudinal kind—for our view of how conflicts in the city should be resolved. Hereafter, I refer to this as the *thin* reading of his theory of procedural justice.

There are powerful reasons to doubt the overall adequacy of adopting such an austere view of the fundamental features of procedural justice. Most centrally, if we interpret the claims that Hampshire makes about the necessity of fair and equal access in this way, we must grant that what is meant by *fair* and *equal* access is fully determined in light of local understandings. This has serious costs because we have no trouble judging that many such local conventions do not actually accord equal hearing to all members of a polity in any plausible sense. As David Archard has remarked, "all political procedures known to humanity may have given some voice to each party to a disagreement; few of these can claim to have given every party an *equal* voice or opportunity to speak."[13] Moreover, it hardly needs to be said that one of the chief functions of the institutions, procedures, and conventions that mediate conflicts in the city is to legitimate the prevailing (often deeply inequitable) distributions of the benefits and burdens of political coexistence.

On occasion, Hampshire consciously presents his account of procedural justice in such severe terms, occasionally even dropping his common reference to equal hearing, as when he insists that "only the most general feature of the process of decision is preserved as the necessary condition that qualifies a process, whatever it happens to be, to be accounted as an essentially just and fair one: that contrary claims *are heard*" (JC, 16–17; italics added). But if procedural justice merely requires that adversary institutions give conflicting views *some* hearing, it becomes very hard to see how one might claim that a set of institutions and customs fails to reach a basic threshold of procedural justice per se (with the exception of a minority of regimes, like Nazi Germany, which Hampshire claims invert "all the values contained in the concept of justice" by attempting to ensure that power requires "no justification" and admits "no restraint" [IE, 69]). Thinking about procedural justice in this (thin) way therefore merely enables us to claim that in particular instances, the local customs and dominant conventions that determine how conflicts should be resolved either have or have not been respected. In this sense, the thin reading unfortunately ensures that Hampshire's account has much less critical bite than one might have expected a theory of procedural justice to deliver. Of course, pointing this out does not refute Hampshire, but it does demand us to concede that his account of procedural justice does surprisingly little to help us discriminate between the vast majority of the diverse procedures and institutions of conflict management that we could plausibly implement here and now. If one adopts this reading, one might therefore say that though the principle of adversary argument may not leave everything as it is, it is not a robust standard of political evaluation.

The Thick Reading

At other points, however, Hampshire delivers a more normative vision of politics as a domain of compromise and conciliation. According to this (thicker) view, basic procedural justice does not merely necessitate that we acquiesce to local standards of hearing the other side but also requires us to adopt a particular attitude or stance toward our political adversaries when we find ourselves in conflict with them. It is possible to detect two distinct ways of thinking about politics in these terms in Hampshire's late work, which I refer to as *prescriptive considerations* and *affective considerations* (though these labels are far from ideal).

On the one hand, Hampshire at times appears to suggest that in many cases of political conflict and disagreement, we have direct normative reasons—duties of justice and fairness—to pursue fair and equal political compromises with our adversaries. At other points, however, his work suggests a more indirect defense of compromise by explaining why one might come to see the value in institutions that foster compromising and mutual concession-making, even when this has costs for one's own moral and political aspirations. One might say that this latter approach supports a vision of the good of compromise that has more in the way of sentimental implications than concrete, action-guiding prescriptions.

I now consider each of these approaches in turn, arguing that the former prescriptive approach is inconsistent with Hampshire's wider account of morality and conflict and that while the latter affective route is not, thinking in this way uncovers some salient shortcomings of Hampshire's thought.

PRESCRIPTIVE CONSIDERATIONS

Intermittently in *Innocence and Experience*, Hampshire suggests that our evaluation of the rightness or wrongness of a debate on policy's conclusion is determined by whether it accords with further conditions than those outlined by the thin reading. To wit, he claims that the "moral quality" of such decisions "in part depends on the acceptability of the reasons: are they a sufficient justification of the action?" In this respect, he claims that "practical reasoning requires explicit formulation of reasons as a defence of the policy adopted" (*IE*, 52–53). This suggests two distinct requirements. First, that both parties explicitly formulate their reasons for favoring certain courses of action, and second, that if a course of action is adopted, it must be sufficiently justified by these reasons. In this sense, the principle of adversary argument seems to have some direct declarative implications.

Hampshire also claims that the principle of adversary argument does not merely require that contrary claims are heard but also that there is "equal opportunity" for both sides (*JC*, 18, 71). Thus, contrary views must be offered "equal hearing" and "equal access" so that no one view is imposed by "domination and by the threat of force" (*JC*, 41). This suggests that if procedural justice is to be achieved, adversarial reasoning must be guided by a set of roughly egalitarian norms.

In addition, Hampshire argues that the negative virtue of justice supports "swapping concessions" and "fair exchange" (*IE*, 74) as this is a feature of the kind of "common decency" that fanatics deplore. In this sense, he sometimes states that the weighing of alternatives is a matter of "judgement and compromise" (*IE*, 119). The underlying idea here is most fully expressed in a section of *Innocence and Experience* entitled "Conflicts about Duty," where Hampshire claims that if two opposing groups assert an "argued basis" for their substantive views, each should realize that "it is unjust and wrong to refuse to enter into an ordered negotiation about how you might live together with the minimum of harm, on each side, to the way of life you consider the best." It is, he insists, straightforwardly "unfair to insist on having your own way" (*IE*, 154). On this basis, Hampshire declares that it would be "contrary to reason to refuse to abandon some less essential features of your preferred way of life in a reasonable exchange of concessions with your adversary" (*IE*, 154). Developing this thought, he asserts that procedural justice requires one to "enter into negotiation on fair and equal terms in order to establish institutions and customs which distribute the frustrations of moral interests among the participants fairly and justly" (*IE*, 155). Thus, even if both parties find some elements of the settlements that their shared institutions generate "morally repugnant," he claims that they have reason to abide by them because other features of their favored way of life may have been left open "in a fair exchange of concessions." It is unfair to insist that one's particular substantive commitments be "enthroned in the institutions of society" (*IE*, 155–56).

These passages suggest that negotiating, compromising, and making mutual concessions are direct subsidiary requirements of procedural justice, even though our sense of the concrete forms they should take will be determined by "a heritage of customs" (*IE*, 74). In this sense, we might say that Hampshire encourages us to recognize that fairness itself demands that we pursue broadly egalitarian compromises with our adversaries.

Is this way of thinking about the demands of procedural justice compatible with Hampshire's wider view of morality and conflict? I doubt it. To see this, it is worth asking *why* one might think that it is unfair or unjust to insist on having your own way when ordered negotiation and mutual concession are possible. The answer cannot be that refusing to do so is contrary to rational decision-making—the equivalent of refusing to hear the other side—for the obvious reason that one can hear the other side without agreeing to acquiesce to their demands. (In much the same way, I can rationally deliberate about whether I want to keeping working in the library this afternoon or go home early and take my daughter to her soccer practice, without having to do a bit of both on pain of irrationality). As Hampshire himself recognizes in his discussion of Aristotle, it is not the case that when confronted with conflicting demands, reason demands that we *must* settle on some balance between the alternatives. As I showed in chapter 3, Hampshire explicitly repudiates the suggestion that the good person is necessarily balanced and not lopsided, acknowledging that we can admire people who dedicate their lives to a single aim or end at the cost of other forgone reasonable aims and ends.

If we accept that this is not irrational, we must acknowledge that adversary reasoning does not necessarily require us to pursue fair compromises in situations of conflict. That genuine ethical commitment often requires agents to single-mindedly pursue some goods at the costs of others, and to see their choices through despite the value costs that are involved in so doing, is a staple of value pluralist understandings of ethics. This represents a problem for a defense of a politics of compromise on grounds of practical reasoning alone. The political analogue to this is not a commitment to perpetual political compromise and negotiation but a form of political decisionism where some substantive ends and values are pursued at the costs of others.

Nor can the refusal to compromise in such situations be presented as irrational because it threatens "peaceful coexistence." We know of regimes that are peaceful and that secure important civil goods in which politics is not best understood as a matter of bargaining, compromising, and the balancing of interests. Simply put, there is a philosophically and politically salient distinction between recognizing the importance of accepting local institutions and precedents for conflict resolution because they secure peace and providing a positive argument for compromising as the most just or fair way of securing peaceful coexistence.

As these two routes fail, it seems that we ought to take Hampshire at his word when he claims that we should come to see that, in such situations, refusing to compromise is unjust and unfair. But we still need to ask *why*. The recent contributions to the literature on compromise in political theory attempt to do something akin to this. They hold that disagreement and conflict generate moral reasons to accept political positions that we regard to be "morally inferior" to the ones we would pursue were it not for the existence of political opposition.[14] Such views hold that moral considerations apply at two levels. On the first level, we endorse divergent and conflicting conceptions of the good and substantive principles of justice. On the second level, we recognize that if people disagree with us at the first level, we have principled reasons to seek compromises with them.[15]

So far, so good. However, theorists who have recently contributed to this body of literature in political theory recognize that such compromises must be grounded in a substantive, second-order value, the most prominent candidates being reciprocity,[16] mutual respect,[17] or the value of public justification.[18] Obviously, Hampshire cannot invoke such grounds because these are, more or less, liberal values and, as we have seen, he insists that we cannot base the requirements of basic procedural justice on claims derived from substantive political positions.

So it seems that, for his direct defense of compromise to function, Hampshire must have some purely proceduralist conception of fairness or justice in mind—one that is, as it were, independent of divisive conceptions of the good—that generates direct normative reasons for us to foster compromises with our opponents. But per my argument above, this cannot be the idea of hearing the other side, for that rational requirement does not have this implication.

Of course, one might argue that Hampshire's ethical skepticism undermines whatever putative justification one might have for imposing one's view and ends on others when compromise and reasoned negotiation is possible. However, arguments that say it is impermissible to impose a set of first-order views for this reason typically bottom out in a substantive set of claims of their own, usually holding that "people are owed equal respect, and that fact, when taken together with the fact that reason is indeterminate, delivers the conclusion that we ought not to impose a conception of the good on those that do not hold it."[19] For the reasons stated above, it is hard to see how Hampshire could employ something like a principle of equal respect at this juncture.

Finally, one might point to Hampshire's declaration that his account of basic procedural justice, unlike approaches that derive substantive principles of justice from divisive conceptions of the good, refrains from solving conflicts by engaging in "moral conquest" (*IE*, 135). By merely requiring that conflicting parties abide by the requirements of basic procedural justice, Hampshire claims, his view avoids the kind of moral harassment that substantive approaches favor (*IE*, 139).

The idea that a political society ought to be a domain of compromise in order to resist becoming a system of moral conquest is less troublingly related to many of Hampshire's ethical starting positions than the other approaches that we have canvassed. This is because it delivers a negative, and instrumental, argument for compromise that highlights the harms and evils that compromises avoid, rather than claiming that compromises realize or express a particular value or principle. However, if moral conquest is as harmful as Hampshire suggests in these passages, one might ask why he doesn't draw more radical conclusions about how our political societies should be organized. To wit, if being asked to give up the essential features of one's way of life is something we all have reasons to avoid, the most effective remedy is likely not simply abiding by the minimal requirements of the principle of adversary argument but a radically different account of the way that distinct groups should coexist. That is, rather than merely counseling us to fairly deliberate with our adversaries, acquiesce to the local institutions that manage our political conflicts, and engage in compromise and negotiation, it would make more sense to hold that, so far as it is possible while preserving peace and avoiding disorder, we ought to actually avoid compelling "people to live by standards they cannot accept."[20] If so, we might favor a politics in which distinct groups inhabit different jurisdictions that allow them to live according to the demands of their way of life, so long as a degree of peace and order is maintained in society as a whole. On such a view, we should pursue a politics that realizes a system of maximal toleration, rather than resting content with creating institutions that realize the principle of adversary argument. Consequently, I do not think that this negative approach can explain why we should compromise with our adversaries in the way that Hampshire alludes to.

It is therefore very hard to vindicate the claim that we have direct normative reasons to forge compromises when we find ourselves in situations of political conflict while staying true to the underlying view of morality and conflict on which Hampshire's account of procedural justice is built. It is hard to see why a respect for procedural justice and fairness might mandate compromise and mutual concession-making without tying procedural justice and fairness to reciprocity, mutual respect, public justification, or some other substantive value. However, doing so is inconsistent with the central motivations behind Hampshire's turn to minimalist proceduralism.[21]

AFFECTIVE CONSIDERATIONS

In other places in Hampshire's work, a more indirect way of making sense of the value of compromise can be found. Instead of attempting to isolate some first- or second-order values that ground a principled commitment to compromise, one might say that Hampshire at times attempts to provide a revaluation of compromise, one which promises to affect our sentiments and emotional responses. In other words, by stressing that conflict is perpetual, Hampshire tries to generate a vivid appreciation of the necessity and good of compromise.

The most evocative expression of this approach to thinking about compromise occurs in *Justice Is Conflict* when Hampshire writes:

> For the individual also, as for society, compromise . . . is certainly the normal, and often the most desirable, condition of the soul for a creature whose desires and emotions are usually ambivalent and always in conflict with each other. A smart compromise is one where the tension between contrary forces and impulses, pulling against each other, is perceptible and vivid, and both forces and impulses have been kept at full strength: with the tension of the Heraclitean bow. An example would be a singer's effort to hold together in her

singing complete technical control with complete spontaneity of expression. This unresolved tension of opposites is felt in excellent musical performances and in great works of art and literature. We do not normally live like this, with sustained and undiminished tension, whether as individuals or as communities. We are not masterpieces in our own lives, and the lives of communities are not master classes. We look for some relaxation of tension, but, until death, we do not expect the neat disappearance of conflict and of tension, whether in the soul or in society. As individuals, our lives will turn out in retrospect to be a rough and running compromise between contrary ambitions, and the institutions that survive in the state have usually been cobbled together in the settlement of some long past conflicts, probably now forgotten with the moral indignation of time. (JC, 32–33)

Derek Edyvane interprets this in the following way: "For those who have accepted the normality of conflict, it is possible to take pleasure . . . in the symmetry and tension of a fair compromise. Hence, while the achievement of procedural justice is always marked by prohibition and conflict, it can also, simultaneously, represent an object of pleasure and robust enthusiasm."[22] Read in this way, Hampshire does not attempt a philosophical justification of political and moral compromise akin to the egalitarian accounts that one finds in the literature in contemporary political theory. Instead, he seeks to explain why one might come to see the value in resigning one's moral commitments in the name of procedural justice.

The influence of Spinoza on Hampshire's thought is evident here. According to Hampshire, Spinoza holds that the basic purpose of philosophical reflection is to "put in place in a person's mind the objective view of a situation, and the objective view discounts the bias due to the standpoint of the individual subject. The correction after reflection of our perceptions, emotions, desires and beliefs is always a movement towards objectivity and a movement away from immediate subjective impressions" (SS, xxiii). So we shift our perspective from that of an agent to that of an observer, and "a single process is constantly presenting two different aspects of things" (SS, xxi). For Hampshire, the search for this kind of intellectual enlightenment is one of the most distinctive and interesting aspects of Spinoza's work. In his essay, "Two Theories of Morality," Hampshire writes that Spinoza's *Ethics* suggests that rather than being content with a self-centered standpoint, the purpose of philosophical reflection is to understand "our own beliefs, sentiments, and attitudes from a more objective, less confused, point of view—ideally from the standpoint of impersonal reason" (MC, 50).

Although Hampshire notes that as his work developed, he came to "disbelieve that the claims of morality can be understood in these terms" (MC, 1), in his late work he still envisages human beings as occupying multiple standpoints or perspectives that enable them to see themselves, and their activity, under different aspects. For example, the kind of robust enthusiasm that Edyvane speaks of requires parties to avoid merely viewing political conflict from the particular, committed standpoints they have as partisans of a particular conception of the good or a set of substantive ends. To feel this kind of enthusiasm for the unresolved tension of opposites, they must adopt a second perspective, that of a member of polity marked by various kinds of conflict, which enables them to appreciate the value in well-crafted, smart compromises that preserve the civil goods of political order. Hampshire does not suggest that this is a Spinozist position of impersonal reason. For example, one might commit to a political conflict as a devoted socialist while, at the same time, viewing the activity from the perspective of the citizen of a democratic regime and appreciating, from that perspective, the achievement of a well-designed compromise.[23]

Underpinning this enthusiasm is a basic, natural reverence that Hampshire claims we have for argument, advocacy, negotiation, and mutual concession-making. He holds that people often "delight in the exercise of political skills in negotiation, and in the calculation of probable outcomes," and that this enthusiasm "often outweighs or at least greatly complicates, an interest in the ultimate ends to be achieved" (*IE*, 176). In this regard, a feeling for procedural justice is "grounded human nature" (*JC*, 72). Procedural justice is, therefore, shored up by a natural impulse to revere persuasion and debate.

That this reverence can conflict with our partisan ends and commitments is evident, but Hampshire holds that acknowledging the existence of both perspectives and refusing to subsume one to the other is vital if we are to properly understand ourselves and, therefore, morality and politics. Because "every soul is always the scene of conflicting tendencies and of divided aims and ambivalences" (*JC*, 5), he insists philosophy has to reject a "too streamlined model of the human mind and of its inbuilt contrarieties of feeling" (*JC*, 46). The lesson is clear: it is futile to try to overcome inner conflict between the different perspectives one might adopt on one's actions. In actual fact, we *need* to be double-minded if we are to maintain a hold on ourselves, given the rival impulses that drive us and the conflicting ideas we affirm.

In many respects this is compelling, but there are two main concerns that arise when one considers this affective route. First, even if we accept the deep-rooted value pluralist idea that contrary to the claims of monist moral and political philosophy, people can and do adopt a variety of different perspectives and see their actions and commitments under different aspects, this generates a number of questions about moral psychology on which Hampshire is disappointingly silent. The issue of how we can sustain people's ability to shift between these perspectives—on the one hand, as advocates of divisive conceptions of the good and, on the other, as political citizens who respect the processes and institutions that manage conflicts in their city—matters deeply if one thinks about politics in the terms that Hampshire encourages. It seems highly likely that certain social and political institutions and/or distinctive cultural attitudes help facilitate the shift between these perspectives, and manage the strains and pressures that they generate, by sustaining the "institutional loyalties" and "deep seated habits of living together and arguing with each other" (JC, 94) that underpin a commitment to institutions of adversary reasoning, while different institutions and/or cultural formations will exacerbate these tensions in various problematic ways. Thus, even if one is inclined to agree with Hampshire's disparagement of the Rawlsian search for stability for the right reasons, it is hard to shake the thought that those attracted to this way of thinking about politics need to address these issues of moral and political psychology in far more detail. Moreover, it is possible, perhaps altogether likely, that were one to think in this way, Hampshire's insistence that his theory of procedural justice is entirely general across different regime types would be undermined (JC, 46). For example, if we have good reasons to believe that regime-type x is more likely to foster relevant attitudes and dispositions than regime-type y, it appears that valuing procedural justice would give us reason to favor x over y. In other words, if some regime types facilitate the underlying attitudes that are required to sustain a commitment to basic procedural justice while others undermine them, this would surely give us reason to endorse some substantive political views or positions over others, suggesting that the principle of adversary argument may have direct bearing on the question of which substantial political commitments we ought to endorse in a way that Hampshire fails to consider.

Second, the considerations I have examined in this section suggest that though Hampshire claims that his "rock-bottom" concept of procedural justice is independent of specific and divisive conceptions of the good, it is not independent of a controversial account of human nature. Pointing this out does not necessarily reveal a fatal inconsistency on Hampshire's part—an account of human nature is not analogous to a divisive conception of the good or a distinctive way of life. However, if we are driven to thinking about purely procedural standards of justice because substantive principles of justice are too divisive to constrain moral and political conflict, it is hard to see how an account of procedural justice that depends on a controversial account of human nature is not vulnerable on the same grounds.

At one point, Hampshire insists that Rawls's political liberalism is implicitly committed to a more comprehensive set of claims than Rawls acknowledges and should be rejected for this reason (*IE*, 187–88). However, given the role that a controversial view of human nature plays in his own thought, there is a sense in which Hampshire's attempt to offer a "nondivisive" theory of procedural justice must be called into question on similar grounds (*IE*, 78). This is an important lesson. That any position in moral and political philosophy is, in the end, likely to be dependent on a controversial, substantive view of one kind or another (be it a conception of the good, an account of the nature of value, a vision of human nature, or a portrayal of the character of political rule) is something that realists need to be realistic, and upfront, about.

Conclusion

In this chapter, I have raised some critical questions and concerns about Hampshire's account of procedural justice. But despite these, I believe his thought has some important, salutary features that are worth highlighting in this conclusion. First, by stressing the inevitability and normality of conflict, Hampshire urges us to repudiate pictures of reason, morality, and politics that see conflict as a "sign of vice, or a defect, or a malfunctioning" (*JC*, 33). This is also a conclusion that Berlin's thought delivers, but Hampshire displays a better sense of the political implications of value pluralism than Berlin. Rather than suggesting that the key political question is how we might design policies that help us realize a wide array of goods, he rightly recognizes that the central issue is how we can live with other people who value competing goods without our conflicts descending into violence and disorder.

Second, Hampshire's work takes important steps in upsetting the moralist idea that we must treat political compromises on matters of principle with suspicion and scorn.[24] According to such views, there is something inherently dishonorable about compromising on matters of principle because if we are genuinely justified in endorsing *p*, there cannot be good, normative reasons for compromising on *p*, even if there are pragmatic reasons to do.[25]

Alin Fumurescu eloquently expresses some of the anxieties at the heart of such views when he notes: "in moral terms compromise is bound to remain for most people at least a suspicious concept, insofar as it appears to endanger something precious in the self . . . the positive occurrences point mostly towards some external, objective compromise ('the matter was settled by compromise,' 'they have reached a compromise,' etc.), while the negative ones predominantly relate to the personal sphere ('he compromised himself,'

'I will not compromise my reputation,' etc.)."[26] Hampshire's account of the normality of conflict enables us to see why such anxieties might be misplaced. His work suggests that those who think about compromise in these terms set up a false and misleading contrast between a stable internal domain of principled moral endorsement and integrity and a chaotic public domain of unprincipled, pragmatic negotiation. If we reject this and hold that our plight in the soul is to engage in compromises between competing goods and ideals to which we may reasonably aspire but which cannot be simultaneously achieved, as the self is never settled but is constantly developing and shifting as a result of the compromises that individuals choose to make, compromise will not be regarded as something that we only engage in externally when we try to enact our political commitments; it will also be seen as a necessary precondition of choosing to live a specific ethical life that attempts to marry conflicting values and ideals.

By suggesting that compromising between conflicting values and claims is something that comes naturally to human beings, Hampshire's work can also play a valuable role in undermining the views of morality that give impetus to moralist political philosophy's skepticism about principled compromise. I have expressed some doubts that it delivers the conclusions that we have reasons to forge fair compromises with our political opponents at the bar of justice or that if one is in a situation of principled political conflict with a reasonable adversary, it is simply "unfair to insist on having your own way" (*IE*, 154). Still, Hampshire importantly suggests that compromising on matters of principle need not be considered as troubling as much recent moral and political philosophy supposes.

Third, once we accept that moral and political conflict is perpetual, it becomes apparent that one of the primary tasks of political theory is to provide an account of how conflict can be managed and contained, rather than overcome, as in so much moralist political theory. In this sense, Hampshire's work powerfully suggests that any appropriately realistic political theory should not seek a moralized consensus on substantive principles as the sine qua non of a well-ordered politics. In turn, it forcefully reminds us that there are very good reasons to value institutions that secure temporary compromises between conflicting claims by earning the acquiescence of subjects. Swaths of moralist political philosophy, which model a consensus on a substantive set of principles, do not counsel us to see the good of politics in these terms. Such views tacitly, and sometimes explicitly, imply that we ought to look upon the bargaining, negotiation, and compromising that compose much "real politics" with a kind of despondency and dejection. One of the most provocative and appealing aspects of Hampshire's thought is his insistence that such views rest on a deep-rooted misconception about the nature of morality and reasoning. His work reminds us that another vision of morality, one which stresses the inseparability of morality and conflict and the array of "polymorphous ideals and diverse conceptions of the good" that reasonable human beings have pursued (*JC*, 52), submits that it is a mistake to rail against these aspects of real politics. Given the types of beings we are, these features of politics should be regarded for what they are: indispensable. The real question is not whether political compromise, bargaining, and negotiation are necessarily unprincipled—it is how they can be done well.

Finally, though I have criticized elements of Hampshire's thought, the claim that the central question of politics is what kind of political institutions are capable of generating settlements that the members of a polity can come to affirm and acquiesce to is important. It is also significant that answers to this question are not derivable from a (supposedly) more fundamental and substantial theory that tells us how the benefits and burdens of political society must be distributed to satisfy a set of substantive moral principles that politics must, supposedly, either enact or be constrained by.

Hampshire is probably right that there is not a great deal that we can say about what kinds of institutions will successfully generate such settlements, and reliably secure the acquiescence of their subjects in specific historical and political circumstances, at the philosophical level. But though the idea that proceduralist considerations will play a central role in any view that recognizes that moral philosophy cannot tell us how to resolve our conflicts is close to irresistible, I am skeptical that this way of thinking about politics requires us to uncover a set of procedural norms that are fully independent of divisive, substantive views of various kinds. I have shown that Hampshire's account of procedural justice is itself dependent on a contentious view of human nature. In addition, his view of the absolute but overridable nature of the obligation to act in line with the dictates of procedural justice suggests that people will only regard their political institutions in these terms if they are widely judged to be both procedurally fair *and* actually avoidant of frustrating many people's most important substantive goals and beliefs.

The inevitable rejoinder to the claim that politics can only ever be the kind of settlement that Hampshire expounds—that this is an overly despondent or pessimistic view—itself relies on a picture of ethics that Hampshire insists we must disavow. If we see our lives as irredeemably shot through with conflicts and compromises between competing values and claims and refrain from supposing that we have somehow managed to transcend "the narrow limits" of our experience "with some vision of a knowledge of perfect justice" (*JC*, 71), we shall not be disposed to think that justice must consist of some kind of unattainable harmony and consensus. We might, instead, be more comfortable with the idea that justice is a virtue of procedures and institutions that settle conflicts in ways that are considered by many subjects to be good enough, even though the settlements they produce fall short of many people's view of which states of affairs would be morally ideal.

PART THREE

Bernard Williams

5

Standing Up to Reflection

Bernard Williams's work in moral philosophy is peppered with a number of startling assertions that have a tendency to stop readers in their tracks. Perhaps chief among these is his insistence that "ethical thought has no chance of being everything that it seems" (*ELP*, 135), a statement both alluring and bewildering, which turns out to be central to making sense of his later political thought. The arresting quality of Williams's work is one of many reasons why he is often not especially easy to read.[1] Nor, for that matter, is he especially easy to write about. His work in moral philosophy contains groundbreaking discussions of utilitarianism as well as accounts of the sources of belief and reasons for acting, the relations between luck and moral assessment, and the prospects of possessing moral knowledge. It is not always simple to see how these reflections all fit together, let alone how they relate to the political ideas he developed most fully late in his life. This is not because Williams was unconcerned with whether his thought was grossly contradictory. He acknowledges that "it is a reasonable demand that what one believes in one area of philosophy should make sense in terms of what one believes elsewhere" and holds that "one's philosophical beliefs, or approaches, or arguments should hang together (like conspirators, perhaps)." However, he insists that "this demand falls a long way short of the unity promised by a philosophical system."[2] All of this in turn risks frustrating the reader.

The deliberately unsystematic manner Williams adopts ensures that any attempt to encompass every facet of his moral philosophical work in a final unified system is an unpromising approach to his corpus. Rather than attempting to do so, in this chapter I focus on those elements of Williams's work in moral philosophy that are most central for understanding his political thought. In particular, I examine how he thought we could go on, avoiding moral and political paralysis, even when we accept that we cannot ground our moral and political commitments by appealing to some external, objective standard. This question is central to the recent debates about realism and moralism in political theory. Many moralists suggest that the realist critique of moralist theory in effect generates outright skepticism about our capacity to reach any claims about what individuals or polities ought to do. In this chapter, I illustrate how Williams's work in moral philosophy sketches a way in which this conclusion can be resisted.

By proceeding in this way, I foreground various aspects of Williams's ethical philosophy at the expense of others. I begin by discussing Williams's skepticism about finding an objective grounding for ethics and explore the implications that this skepticism has for his understanding of the purpose of philosophical reflection. I then examine Williams's claim that we must conceive of ethical and political ideals in a way that is compatible with a "reflective and non-mythical understanding of our ethical practices" (*ELP*, 194). Then in conclusion, I examine how Williams's late work proposes that some of our convictions might be supported by various forms of genealogical and social critique.

Nonobjectivism

Williams's rejection of the idea that there is any sense in which we might be able to truthfully conclude that a particular ethical outlook has an objective foundation is central to his skepticism about philosophy's ability to tell us, conclusively and unaided, how we should live. In *Ethics and the Limits of Philosophy*, he considers two distinct routes that one might adopt to ground the claim that a set of ethical beliefs is objective. The first attempts to find some kind of vantage point external to an agent's current set of ethical dispositions and commitments that can validate them and show why any rational agent ought to act as they prescribe. Williams refers to such a justifying ground as an *Archimedean point*: "something to which even the amoralist or skeptic is committed but which, properly thought through, will show us that he is irrational, or unreasonable, or at any rate mistaken" (*ELP*, 29). If such an Archimedean point can be found, ethical thought can be said to have an objective foundation. Williams holds that the two most famous arguments of this sort are Aristotle's attempt to show that we are committed to acting ethically if we want to lead a "satisfying human life" and Kant's attempt to show that "the most minimal and abstract possible conception of rational agency" has determinate ethical implications (*ELP*, 29).

For Williams, Aristotle's argument that the ethical life is rational because it maximizes human well-being "represents the only intelligible form of ethical objectivity at the reflective level" (*ELP*, 153).³ However, Williams contends that if we dispense with the metaphysically suspect teleological elements of Aristotle's account, there is little reason to think that a determinate set of "internalized dispositions of action, desire, and feeling" is uniquely conducive to human flourishing (*ELP*, 35). Although he expresses sympathy with Aristotle's view that when we reflect ethically, we reflect from a point of view deeply colored by the substantive ethical dispositions that result from our upbringing and enculturation, Williams claims that this has more skeptical implications for us than it did for Aristotle. Williams posits a contrast between thinking about ethics in Aristotelian terms from *inside* and *outside* perspectives. From the internal perspective, it is clear that according to Aristotle, agents will insist that various things—such as the needs of others and requirements of justice and courage—have independent ethical value. Yet from the outside perspective, Williams claims that we may ask, "What has to exist in the world for that ethical point of view to exist?" The answer given by advocates of Aristotelian approaches can only be people's dispositions. In this sense, Williams claims that Aristotle's focus on well-being, character, and the virtues shows that dispositions are "the ultimate supports of ethical value" (*ELP*, 51).⁴

Williams claims that this is not a problem so long as no conflict arises between the inside and outside perspectives. That is, if our internalized dispositions of action, desire, and feeling can be presented as "a correct or full development of human potentiality," then the recognition that dispositions are the ultimate supports of ethical value need not be discomfiting. However, Williams claims that it is now simply dishonest to believe that an account of human nature will privilege a particular form of ethical life over other alternatives in the way required. Like Berlin and Hampshire, he is adamant that we now have sufficient grounds for holding that any particular form of ethical life "is only one of many that are equally compatible with human nature" (*ELP*, 52). Strikingly diverse forms of ethical life are compatible with, and expressive of, human potentialities. Williams claims this fatally repudiates the teleology underpinning any view that hopes to uncover an Archimedean point in considerations of well-being.⁵

For Williams, the most that a philosophical inquiry into the universal determinants of human well-being might be able to offer are various *negative* claims about which constraints may be considered ethically objective. Thus, it may well reveal that "any ethical life is going to contain restraints on such things as killing, injury, and lying" (*ELP*, 153). However, any adequate, historically informed approach disabuses us of the idea that inquiring into human nature might have any more positive implications. Certainly, it will not determine the superiority of a particular form of ethical life.

Williams argues that the Kantian attempt to delineate a morality of rights, duties, and obligations by focusing on the idea of rational agency fares no better. His discussion of Kantian approaches is rather impatient. He has little truck with certain elements of Kant's own position and instead questions whether a Kantian line, which avoids certain controversial aspects of Kant's metaphysics, can work. Williams denies that Kantian appeals to the form of practical reason are able to provide an objective grounding external to ethics from which one can evaluate an ethical outlook because he rejects the claim that the bare idea of practical reasoning involves a kind of impartiality. As Williams parses it, such views hold that if an agent acts on reasons, "he must not only be an agent but reflect on himself as an agent, and this involves seeing himself as one agent among others. So he stands back from his own desires and interests, and sees them from a standpoint that is not *of* his desires and interests. Nor is it the standpoint of anyone else's desires or interests. That is the standpoint of impartiality. So it is appropriate for the rational agent, with his aspiration to be genuinely free and rational, to see himself as making rules that will harmonize the interests of all rational agents" (*ELP*, 65–66). This is why Williams thinks Kantians insist that every rational agent is committed to a moral system of rights and duties. On this view, one is a defective practical reasoner when one's reasoning is conditioned by something given to it, rather than that which it gives itself. But while Williams admits that factual deliberation requires us to reason in this manner—because it is an exercise in truth-seeking that requires us to be committed to forming a consistent set of general beliefs—he denies that practical reason requires us to adopt such an impersonal perspective. Indeed, he insists that practical deliberation is "radically first-personal," in the sense that it "involves an *I* that must be more intimately the *I* of my desires than this account allows" (*ELP*, 67). This is a complex point, but, to put it baldly, Williams insists that unless one's view of practical reasoning is already implicitly colored by a quasi-Kantian set of ethical commitments, it is hard to see why we should be disposed to think that when *I* am reflecting on how *I* should act, there is any inconsistency in acting in a way that furthers *my* interests, desires, or projects. Of course, we can stand back from our desires and interrogate them, but this does not reveal that we are committed to the attempt to achieve some kind of "harmony of everyone's deliberations" or to making rule-bound claims from "the standpoint of equality" (*ELP*, 69). Accordingly, there is no reason to think we can find a foundation for adopting an impartial moral standpoint purely from a set of structural considerations regarding the nature of rational agency.

Williams's responses to Aristotle and Kant are of a kind. In both cases, once we reject either a suspect teleology or problematic metaphysics, the purported foundation invoked—human nature or the bare conditions of practical reasoning—is shown to be too minimal to provide a foundation for ethical life.

Williams's critique of Kant's attempt to defend a morality of impartiality by focusing on our rational agency expresses his deeper view that ethical theories that suggest we must be guided by impartial and impersonal considerations are likely to alienate us from some of our deepest ethical commitments and personal relationships. Williams famously repudiated some such ethical theories for offering "one thought too many" to agents who find themselves in ethical dilemmas. When discussing the example of a man who must choose between saving two people, one of whom is his wife, Williams notes how the utilitarian may invoke the maximizing consequences of a preference for spouses and the Kantian would ask which action passes the categorical imperative. Yet Williams insists that this takes reflection too far: "it might have been hoped by some (for instance, by his wife) that his motivating thought, fully spelled out, would be the thought that it was his wife, not that it was his wife and that in situations of this kind it is permissible to save one's wife" (ML, 18).

Similarly, Williams argues that utilitarianism is incapable of recognizing the value of integrity because it directs us to abstract from agents' identities to such an extent that they become nothing more than "a locus of causal intervention in the world" (U, 96). Yet, if we are solely concerned with maximizing consequences, we effectively encourage someone to see themselves as nothing more than "a channel between the input of everyone's projects, including his own, and an output of optimific decision; but this is to neglect the extent to which *his* projects and *his* decisions have to be seen as the actions and decisions which flow from the projects and attitudes with which he is most closely identified. It is thus, in the most literal sense, an attack on his integrity" (U, 116–17). Williams illustrates this point most clearly in his discussion of a hypothetical George who is offered a job in a laboratory that researches chemical and biological warfare. George initially decides he cannot accept the job, given his long-held opposition to such weapons, but he is asked to reconsider when it is pointed out that he needs the money to support his family and that if he declines, the job will go to a contemporary of his uninhibited by his scruples. Williams claims that by encouraging George to drop his principled opposition to chemical warfare, utilitarianism reveals that it considers any personal projects and commitments dispensable. However, he insists that such projects confer meaning on our lives and are, to a certain degree, the conditions of our interest in continuing to live. As he puts it, "unless I am propelled forward by the conatus of desire, project, and interest, it is unclear why I should go on at all" (*ML*, 12). So by impelling us to abandon such projects if they are not consequentially optimal, utilitarian approaches are incapable of grasping what it is to be a person with a specific character—a fatal defect for an ethical theory that purports to tell us how we should live.

The second way of thinking about ethical objectivity that Williams scrutinizes is not concerned with the attempt to uncover an Archimedean point. Rather, it holds that ethical beliefs are propositions that can be true or false in much the same way as other kinds of knowledge claims. Once again though, Williams denies that thinking about the objectivity of ethics in such terms is promising. This is because he insists there is little reason to think that there might be any kind of "convergence on a body of ethical truths which is brought about and explained by the fact that they are truths" in the way that there is in other kinds of inquiry, most principally scientific inquiry (*ELP*, 151–52). The difference between science and ethics in this regard relates to the question of *how* a convergence of opinion can be explained. Williams claims that in a scientific inquiry, it is possible that the "best explanation of the convergence involves the idea that the answer represents how things are." In ethics, on the other hand, this is not a coherent aspiration. The distinction does not turn on whether a convergence may occur. Rather, "the point of the contrast is that, even if this happens, it will not be correct to think it has come about because convergence has been guided by how things actually are, whereas convergence in the sciences might be explained in that way if it does happen" (*ELP*, 136).

This requires unpacking.[6] Williams insists that there can be knowledge in ethics because every form of ethical life employs what he refers to as thick concepts. These concepts—contemporary examples include "crony," "slut," and "bullshitter"—have both factual and evaluative components, which is why Williams refers to them as being world-guided and action-guiding (*ELP*, 129). For example, if I accuse you of being a bullshitter, I am making a factual claim about your lack of concern for speaking the truth while simultaneously condemning your character. Williams claims that thin concepts, such as "good," "right," and "wrong," must be understood differently. They are not world-guided in the way that thick concepts are, and they are so thin that they are inadequate to provide substance to personal ethical lives (*IBWD*, 49). Significantly, Williams holds that the claims we make that employ thick concepts can be straightforwardly true or false. He posits a thought experiment of a "hypertraditional" society where people have mastered the use of their thick ethical concepts and understand the actions and decisions in which the concepts are implicated. In such a situation, the judgments made by the denizens of society employing their thick concepts can be true or false. In this respect, Williams famously holds that "the question whether there can be ethical knowledge is not the same as the question whether ethical outlooks can be objective" (*MSH*, 203). To put it crudely, we may know that Donald Trump is a "bullshitter" and that Roman Abramovich is a "crony" of Vladimir Putin's. However, this kind of knowledge is necessarily local and only holds because those who employ such concepts live in a particular social setting. Reflection, nevertheless, reveals that any such shared ethical life is one among many other possible forms of ethical life. Thus, as Adrian Moore stresses, Williams holds that any convincing account of why people converge in their judgments that employ thick concepts must "include a social-scientific explanation of why they embrace the concept [at all]" and that "this explanation cannot itself invoke the [thick] concept . . . because it must be from a vantage of reflection outside the social world in question." In this regard, such an account cannot take the form of saying that "people converge in their beliefs about *x* because they are suitably sensitive to truths about *x*" (*PHD*, xvii). This is not the case in scientific inquiry because scientific explanation can "show how the perceptions are related to physical reality and how they give knowledge of that reality" (*ELP*, 150). Thus, Williams holds that science can "claim to represent the world in a way to the maximum degree independent of our perspective and its peculiarities" (*ELP*, 138).[7] Knowledge claims that invoke thick concepts, on the other hand, cannot.

Williams calls the resulting picture painted by science the *absolute conception of the world*, the idea being that this conception could be arrived at by any investigators, even intelligent and inquisitive extraterrestrials, no matter how greatly they differed from us (*ELP*, 139).[8] He insists that ethical claims using thick concepts cannot meet this standard: "Unlike the inhabitants of the fictionally pre-reflective society, we do have the thought that other people have had different concepts, and that people may come to do so in the future. So we are aware, when we come to think of it, of something that less reflective people were not aware of, that these concepts are not simply given."[9] Subsequently, with regard to whether ethical knowledge can be objective, Williams is unequivocal: "science has some chance of being more or less what it seems, a systematized theoretical account of how the world really is." Ethical thought does not (*ELP*, 135).

Williams's skepticism about whether any ethical beliefs might be objective has implications for his treatment of moral relativism. Although he claims that recognizing that our ethical beliefs are not objective cannot immediately unseat our commitment to them, it ought to affect our sense of how we apply them. While it is possible for us to go on "simply saying that we are right and everyone else is wrong," Williams insists that "if we have arrived at this stage of reflection, it seems a remarkably inadequate response" (*ELP*, 159–60). Yet this does not lead Williams to embrace relativism in any straightforward sense.

Williams differentiates nonobjectivism, a position about the metaphysical status of moral claims, from relativism, which he sees as a position that expresses the attitude we should have toward moral conflict. As noted in chapter 1, he claims that "standard relativism" is absurd because it generates a claim about which actions are right in our dealings with other people and societies—being "equally well disposed to everyone else's ethical beliefs" (*ELP*, 159)—from the premise that right is relative to a given society, a proposition that disallows its seemingly tolerant conclusion. Moreover, declaring that *x* is right for one group of people but wrong for another is useless because as soon as one group is confronted with another, neither group can continue to "think of itself as 'we' and the other as 'they.'" Rather, when this occurs, there is simply "a new 'we' to be negotiated" (*IBWD*, 69).

Yet Williams asks what room can be made for thinking coherently in a relativistic manner and endorses what he calls the *relativism of distance*. This claims that we should refrain from making some ethical judgments by distinguishing between *real* and *notional* confrontations. Real confrontations occur when a group is presented with a real option of acting differently. A real option is a largely social notion. Williams claims that if a group of people can "go over" to another way of life and "live inside it in their actual historical circumstances and maintain their hold on reality, [and] not engage in extensive self-deception," it counts as a real option for them (*ELP*, 160). The life of a Bronze Age chief or a medieval samurai are, therefore, not real options for inhabitants of Sheffield in 2020 and would instead fall into the notional category (*ELP*, 161). In these notional confrontations, Williams insists that "for a reflective person the question of appraisal does not genuinely arise" because the normal point of moral appraisal is to guide action (*ML*, 141). Reflecting on what may be wrong with say, feudalism, can be a useful heuristic device for us. Yet Williams is adamant that there is little point imagining oneself as "Kant at the court of King Arthur," disapproving of the injustices of the past in moralistic terms, because this fails to help us make sense of our own ethical commitments (*IBWD*, 66).

The Morality System

Williams's denial of the claim that philosophical reflection can conclusively determine how we should live is further buttressed by his work on reasons.

Williams notes that sentences such as "A has reason to x" can be interpreted in two ways. According to the first *internal* reading, "A has some motive which will be served or furthered by his x-ing," so that if this turns out not to be so, the sentence is false. According to the *external* reading, however, "there is no such condition, and the reason-sentence will not be falsified by the absence of appropriate motive" (*ML*, 101). Williams posits as a basic thesis that it only makes sense to say A has reason to x if A could conclude to x by deliberating from the motivations they already have. In other words, there are only internal reasons.

This has significant implications for philosophical views that hold that all agents have *reasons* to act in a particular way. Most centrally, Williams rules out labeling people unreasonable for failing to acknowledge a set of requirements that a moralist may claim are binding. While there are still many things we can say about people who lack appropriate items in their subjective motivational set—such as calling a man who really does not care about his wife "ungrateful, inconsiderate, hard, sexist, nasty, selfish, brutal" (*MSH*, 39)—we cannot say that he has a *reason* to be nicer. This has direct implications for the phenomenon of blame. As John Skorupski notes, one of the desires of the external reasons theorist is to pull all people into the domain of morality so that morality is universally binding.[10] In contrast, Williams, in effect, argues that some people may not have reasons to be moral. His critique of externalist conceptions of practical reason is consequently expressive of his more general belief that ethics must work within the bounds of the contingently variable particulars of moral psychology and practical reason, rather than creating distinctive models of them that further antecedent moral aspirations.[11]

This has a consequent impact on his sense of the basic aims of moral philosophy. For Williams, the value of ethical reflection must lie in its ability "to sharpen perception, to make one more acutely and honestly aware of what one is saying, thinking and feeling" (*M*, xv). Ethical reflection, in this sense, is a way in which we might increase our self-understanding. Thus, like Berlin and Hampshire, Williams considers the main task of moral philosophy to be that of making sense of moral phenomena as they occur in lived ethical experience, rather than prescribing how human beings must live from some external vantage point.

Like Berlin and Hampshire, he also stresses that we often experience situations in which we are confronted by multiple sources of value and conflicting favorable courses of action.[12] In his paper "Conflicts of Values," written for Berlin's Festschrift, Williams asserts that the claim that values are incommensurable can be read as making four important points (*ML*, 77):

1. There is no one currency in terms of which each conflict of values can be resolved.
2. It is not true that for each conflict of values, there is some value, independent of any of the conflicting values, which can be appealed to in order to resolve that conflict.
3. It is not true that for each conflict of values, there is some value which can be appealed to (independent or not) in order rationally to resolve that conflict.
4. No conflict of values can ever be rationally resolved.

He insists that of these only (4) is false because, as we saw in chapter 2, rational considerations can be brought to bear on particular occasions of value conflict, even if there is no one way to resolve all conflicts of value. More generally, Williams asks why, if I am in a situation where competing values make claims on me, theoretical tidiness or simplicity are supposed to have any weight at all (*CC*, xvii). He insists that the pursuit of ethical theory is a prejudice requiring justification that "a good deal of moral philosophy engages [in] unblinkingly . . . for no obvious reason except that it has been going on for a long time" (*ELP*, 17). It is simply not clear why any theory has the right to "legislate to the moral sentiments" (*ML*, x).

In light of this, Williams distinguishes between two ways of approaching moral philosophy. The first, "a phenomenology of ethical life," reflects on "what we believe, feel, take for granted; the ways we confront obligations and recognize responsibility; the sentiments of guilt and shame." The other, ethical theory, "tends to start from just one aspect of ethical experience, beliefs," and sets out a "structure of propositions, which, like a scientific theory, in part provides a framework of our beliefs, in part criticizes or revises them" (*ELP*, 93). Precisely because we cannot uncover an absolute perspective from which to legislate our moral and political sentiments, Williams opts for the former.

This skepticism about some of the guiding aims of modern moral philosophy is practically important because Williams claims that a particular development of ethical thinking—which he terms *morality*—has come to have a "special significance in Western Culture" (*ELP*, 6). Morality praises certain forms of ethical conduct above others and is expressive of a particular set of aspirations, most centrally "the ideal that human existence can be ultimately just" (*ELP*, 195). It holds that moral reflection is ultimately a matter of working out which impartial moral obligations press upon us and how we can best discharge them. In this regard, morality paints our obligations and duties in comprehensive and authoritative terms—as applying to all domains of action and as necessarily trumping any countervailing considerations.[13] However, by thinking in such terms, Williams insists that morality rests on various presuppositions we have little reason to endorse, principally a conception of voluntariness that is "total and will cut through character and psychological and social determination, and allocate blame and responsibility on the ultimately fair basis of the agent's own contribution" (*ELP*, 194). He denies that this hope for a pure ethical system (which is in many respects analogous to religious conceptions of ethics) makes sense. Any remotely realistic understanding of our ethical lives must acknowledge that "we do not make our thoughts out of nothing; they come in part from what is around us, and we have a very poor grasp . . . of what their source may be" (*SP*, 327). To this end, Williams claims that the morality system speciously presents itself as making binding demands on our conduct that supposedly come from outside us but really come from within: demands that place categorical constraints on both our behavior and the behavior of others by employing the mechanisms of blame and guilt, which present themselves as externally binding but in truth are the products of deeply internalized psychological processes (and, in some cases, pathologies).

Rather than endorsing a picture of morality claiming that the demands of ethical life "lie beyond any empirical determination" (*ELP*, 195), Williams insists that ethics is a deeply socially embedded and practical activity, a matter of acting in accordance with a set of internalized dispositions that are the result of a "very complex historical deposit." Moreover, the fact that our ethical ideas have this form means that there is little reason to expect them to exhibit a systematic theoretical structure (*MSH*, 189). Instead of seeking to fit our ethical beliefs into such a system, we should examine our dispositions and sentiments, our characters and our deepest projects, and think creatively about, and with, the thick ethical concepts that give our lives meaning and purpose. As there is no kind of objective foundation for ethical life, we cannot avoid starting from our particular historical position, using the ethical material that has already been bequeathed to us. Philosophical inquiry must "seek for as much shared understanding as it can find on any issue, and use any ethical material that, in the context of the reflective discussion, makes some sense and commands some loyalty." Of course, this takes "things for granted, but serious reflection must know that it will do that" (*ELP*, 116–17). The task of philosophy is to scrutinize our ethical experience and ask which of our ethical commitments, aspirations, and ideals, if any, might "stand up to reflection" if we disavow thinking about morality in the ways that Williams rejects (*ELP*, 200).

By trying to rescue moral value from such contingencies, the morality system emphasizes a series of idealized contrasts we have little reason to endorse: "between force and reason, persuasion and rational convictions, shame and guilt, dislike and disapproval, mere rejection and blame" (*ELP*, 194–95). Since it is wrong to think that "morality just is the ethical in a rational form" (*MSH*, 246)—both because historically this has not always been the case *and* because the morality system rests on a series of philosophical misconceptions—Williams argues that morality is a threat to ethical life itself: it "makes people think that without its very special obligation, there is only inclination; without its utter voluntariness, there is only force; without its ultimately pure justice, there is no justice" (*ELP*, 196). This, according to Williams, is not only false but also ethically dangerous.

It is with this skepticism about morality in mind that Williams claims,

> We are in an ethical condition that lies not only beyond Christianity, but beyond its Kantian and its Hegelian legacies. We have an ambivalent sense of what human beings have achieved, and have hopes for how they might live.... We know that the world was not made for us, or we for the world, that our history tells us no purposive story, and that there is no position outside the world or outside history from which we might hope to authenticate our activities. We have to acknowledge the hideous costs of many human achievements that we value, including this reflective sense itself, and recognize that there is no redemptive Hegelian history or universal Leibnizian cost-benefit analysis to show that it will come out well enough in the end. (*SN*, 166)

This may look like a bitter truth, but although we cannot offer an external justification for ethical life, Williams is adamant that it would be a mistake to think that this inexorably leads to reflective nihilism or practical paralysis. We can and should seek "understanding of our motives, [and] psychological or social insight into our ethical practices." This is not merely an explanatory activity because it can critically reveal that "certain practices or sentiments are not what they are taken to be" (*ELP*, 112). Thus, there is the possibility of offering a critique of ethical practice. However, at least in *Ethics and the Limits of Philosophy*, Williams claims that at most we can "show how a given practice hangs together with other practices in a way that makes social and psychological sense ... we may not be able to find anything that will meet a demand for justification made by someone standing outside those practices. We may not be able, in any real sense, to justify it even to ourselves" (*ELP*, 114).

Contingency and Confidence

How, then, can our ethical and political commitments be stable despite the unsettling effects of this understanding of moral philosophy? How might they, as Williams puts it, stand up to reflection? In *Ethics and the Limits of Philosophy*, Williams argues that ethical conviction must be identified with what he refers to as confidence, rather than with knowledge or certainty. His discussion of confidence is, however, very condensed and has largely mystified commentators. Williams asserts that confidence is "both a social state and related to discussion, theorizing and reflection," and, in a certain sense, "a basically social phenomenon" because it is "a social and psychological question what kinds of institutions, upbringing and public discourse help to foster it" (*ELP*, 170–71). Williams claims that the key question we must answer "is how people, or enough people, can come to possess a practical confidence that, particularly granted both the need for reflection and its pervasive presence in our world, will come from strength and not from the weakness of self-deception and dogmatism. (Confidence is not the same as optimism; it could rest on what Nietzsche called the pessimism of strength.)" (*ELP*, 171).

Williams elaborates a little in his Festschrift, stating that we need to think about what is involved when an ethical concept survives reflection. He claims that an ethical concept can do so "in the sense that we would not have encountered any considerations that led us to give it up, lose hold on it, or simply drift away from it, as modern societies in the past two centuries or less have, for instance, done one or more of those things in relation to chastity."[14] But even if this happens, we should recognize that we nonetheless lack "any knowledge to the effect that we have a definitively desirable set of such concepts" because we are aware that "other people have had different concepts, and that people may come to do so in the future."[15] Consequently, though we can make knowledge claims that can be true or false from within our evaluative perspective, given the limits of philosophy we cannot claim any knowledge about the ultimate desirability of conceptual schemes that employ these concepts. Thus, if we are to continue to use a conceptual scheme, we need to have confidence in it.

However, little is said about how such confidence might be achieved, and in *Ethics and the Limits of Philosophy*, Williams is skeptical that philosophical reflection may help to foster it (*ELP*, 171). Nonetheless, as I seek to show in the remainder of this chapter, his later works do probe how some forms of inquiry might help us to vindicate—or achieve confidence in—certain commitments we endorse.

In his last monograph, *Truth and Truthfulness*, Williams claims that historical analysis reveals the sheer contingency of our current ethical commitments and beliefs and that this recognition can undermine the perceived authority they have over us (*TT*, 20–21). This is especially unnerving for contemporary liberal political philosophy because Williams holds that most liberal theory has "a poor account, or in many cases no account, of the cognitive status of its own history" and "no answer in its own terms to the question of why what it takes to be the true moral solution to the questions of politics, liberalism, should for the first time (roughly) become evident in European culture from the late seventeenth century onward, and why these truths have been concealed from other people." To this end, Williams alleges that much contemporary liberal political philosophy "cannot plausibly explain, adequately to its moral pretensions, why, when and by whom it has been accepted and rejected" (*IBWD*, 9). Such ethics-first approaches lack what he calls a "theory of error" (*IBWD*, 11).

This insistence that moral and political philosophy must take such historical considerations very seriously then motivates much of Williams's work from the mid-1980s to the end of his life. Williams insists that once we accept that "our moral aspirations do not, cannot, mean everything that they seem to mean," we should acknowledge that "they cannot come from where they seem to come from, and another kind of inquiry will be needed to understand their hold on us."[16] In particular, if we are to determine whether our convictions stand up to reflection, we must think in distinctly historical terms and engage in genealogical critique. Williams recognizes that some philosophers hold that such historical approaches push one worryingly close to the genetic fallacy—the mistake of thinking that the history, source, or origin of x determines the current value of x. However, in a characteristically suggestive passage, he insists that these complaints overlook

> the possibility that the value in question may understand itself and present itself and claim authority for itself in terms which the genealogical story can undermine. The "morality" that Nietzsche's genealogy damaged claimed to be the expression of a spirit that was higher, purer and more closely associated with reason, as well as transcending negative passions such as resentment, and if Nietzsche's account of it, in its functional and its historical aspects, were true, it would emerge as self-deceived in that respect. Similarly, when it is argued that the values of contemporary liberalism cannot possibly be criticised in terms of their history, this will be so only to the extent that those values can be separated from the claim—one which is often made for them—that they have emerged from the spread of reason and represent a cognitive achievement.[17]

This is the basic problem Williams has with the moral universalism of thinkers like Thomas Nagel. In response to Nagel's claim that "to reason is to think systematically in ways that anyone looking over my shoulder ought to be able to recognize as correct,"[18] Williams retorts that if this were the case, we should think that if Louis XIV were looking over our shoulders, he ought to agree that our liberal convictions are correct, which Williams finds deeply implausible (*IBWD*, 66). Yet he denies that this should necessarily cause us to lose confidence in our convictions. Instead, we must take seriously the idea that any "theory will seem to make sense, and will to some degree reorganize thought and action, only by virtue of the historical situation in which it is presented, and its relation to that historical situation cannot be fully theorized or captured in reflection" (*IBWD*, 25). In consequence, moral and political theory should confront the reality that abstract reasoning is typically a rationalization of what is already implicit in a practice, and this makes the practice explanatorily (and often chronologically) prior.

Thus, while certain ideas stand fast for us—Williams mentions the view that every citizen deserves equal consideration as an example (*PHD*, 194–95)—the attempt to offer the kind of justification the moralist pursues is doomed as our most basic commitments are not validated by any antecedent theory.[19] Yet Williams also insists that if we remain in the space of our first-order reasons, we cannot say much more about many of our most deeply held beliefs other than rehearsing our self-validating justifications of them, even though we know that many people in the past and present do not share them (*PHD*, 195). So theorizing in such terms is reflectively unsatisfying. If we are to reflect more adequately on our beliefs and commitments, we must think in historical terms. This allows us to question those practices and values we endorse that, in a Wittgensteinian sense, appear to be "simply there," an inquiry that goes beyond straightforward philosophical analysis that has to stop when the giving of grounds terminates (*PHD*, 195). In consequence, Williams argues that there is no conflict among the first-order activity of acting and arguing within the framework of our ideas, the philosophical activity of reflecting on those ideas at a more general level and trying to make better sense of them, and the historical activity of understanding where they came from (*PHD*, 193–94).

Moreover, because we do not have to make judgments from an absolute point of view in the name of ethical truth, Williams denies that such historical understanding will inevitably undermine our commitments. In fact, if such an inquiry does not reveal our endorsement of certain values to be radically self-deceived, we may be able to hold on to them regardless of the fact that they lack an objective foundation. Thus, in his essay "Why Philosophy Needs History," Williams claims that if a view or conviction of ours is "stripped of its false self-understanding, important parts of what remains may indeed have a vindicatory genealogy, in the sense that we can understand it and at the same time respect it, support it and live within it. We can also urge it against alternative creeds whose own self-understandings (as divine revelations, for instance) are themselves not going to survive a genealogical inquiry."[20] (In the next chapter, I examine why Williams thought that a commitment to liberalism might stand up to reflection in these terms.)

This differs markedly from the views espoused by some historians about the unsettling effects of historical understanding. Quentin Skinner, for instance, once remarked that "one effect of learning more about the causal story is to loosen the hold of our inherited values upon our emotional allegiances. Haunted by a sense of lost possibilities, historians are almost inevitably Laodicean in their attachment to the values of the present time."[21] This, Skinner suggests, is principally because when we reflect historically, "we become disturbingly aware of the sheer contingency of the process by which our values were formed."[22] One commentator, exaggerating only somewhat, has suggested that the unedifying implication of this is that politics should be conceived either as merely "the expression of will, and therefore free of rational discipline, or else . . . [as] subject to the contingent discipline of historically arbitrary distributions of power."[23]

This is the kind of reductive move Williams's work urges us to overcome. He consistently stresses that contingency and arbitrariness are not coextensive, claiming that the kind of historical awareness he urges "does not mean that we need to be hesitant or double-minded in using our own [ethical concepts] . . . if we are not, this just shows that we can sustain them with a certain measure of confidence."[24] To illustrate, he defends the idea of a vindicatory historical understanding akin to Hume's theory of justice, insisting that we will only be dissatisfied with such a view if we tacitly yearn for an unsustainably ambitious grounding for our convictions. According to Hume's account, we can "still give justice, its motivations and reasons for action, much the same respect as one did before one encountered the explanation—or perhaps more respect, if one had suspected that justice had to be a Platonically or other-worldly idea if it was anything" (*TT*, 36). This impulse is manifested throughout *Truth and Truthfulness* when Williams sets out to defend the virtues of truth—Accuracy (care, reliability, and so on, in discovering and coming to believe the truth) and Sincerity (saying what one believes to be true)—by positing how they "could have come about, or might be imagined to have come about." To do so, he sketches a fictional state of nature inhabited by people with some basic human needs and motivations, notably the need for cooperation, with the aim of deriving from "within the story values connected with these activities . . . by way of an abstract argument from some very general, and I take it, indisputable assumptions about human powers and limitations" (*TT*, 20). He insists that Accuracy and Sincerity (which he argues cannot have any meaning unless we adopt a view of truth) will be functionally vindicated in this light.

The argumentative intricacies of *Truth and Truthfulness* must be passed over here, but the structure of the argument has important consequences for our comprehension of Williams's political thought. Accuracy and Sincerity are something like "thin" universals, but the thicker form they take in a given period will be the result of a plethora of historically contingent factors. For instance, Williams claims that we cannot regard the idea of personal authenticity as a necessary development of the twin virtues of truth because it arose in reaction to the Enlightenment's notion of "individuality," which was alien to the historical periods that preceded it. Consequently, it "cannot be seen as a development of human needs, concerns, and interests which was inevitable, or even particularly probable" (*TT*, 172). This does not mean that we should dismiss the idea that authenticity is a value. But if we are to understand the ideal of authenticity, and think through what it means for us here and now, we have to turn to history because the content of such thick expressions of truthfulness cannot be properly understood absent a historical inquiry into how they came to be accepted.

If we return to the Skinnerian view about the Laodicean nature of the historian's attachment to certain values, we can, accordingly, uncover a space for a kind of confidence that represents an improvement on the dejected acceptance invoked by Skinner. Williams effectively suggests that we can value certain things in good faith if three provisions are met: (1) they can be understood in naturalistic terms; (2) our commitment to them is not the result of self-deception (as Nietzsche claims is the case with Christian morality); and (3) they are not relics of earlier ideas that no longer make sense, as Williams suggests is the case with autonomy-based defenses of toleration (*PHD*, 127–28).

One of the guiding thoughts of Williams's later work is, therefore, that historical reflection is essential if we are to make sense of our ethical and political ideals because there is no hope of vindicating them in some kind of ultimate metaphysical terms. Consequentially, in his later works Williams, in effect, offers a view of philosophical reflection that develops and extends the rather elliptic remarks he makes about confidence in *Ethics and the Limits of Philosophy*.

Is Confidence Enough?

Mark Jenkins remarks that "although it is not particularly hard to see what Williams wants confidence to do, namely to undergird ethical conviction in a world without ethical certainty, it is much harder to see how confidence gets going or at least stays going in contemporary life." He thus accuses Williams of trying too hard to "resolve a fundamentally irresolvable tension between ethical conviction and contingency."[25] If the thrust of this criticism is correct, the vindicatory strategy sketched earlier will not stabilize our commitments in light of skeptical reflection on the contingent reasons behind our endorsement of them.

Williams addressed this problem in "Philosophy as a Humanistic Discipline," one of his last published papers, where he denies that the discovery that our convictions have a contingent history and lack any foundational metaphysical vindication has to be regarded as disappointing. In fact, if we go *"far enough* in recognizing contingency," he claims we can see why this worry is misconceived:

> Because we are not unencumbered intelligences selecting in principle among all possible outlooks, we can accept that this outlook is ours just because history has made it ours; or, more precisely, has both made us, and made the outlook something that is ours. We are no less contingently formed than the outlook is, and the formation is significantly the same. We and our outlook are not simply in the same place at the same time. If we really understand this, deeply understand it, we can be free of another scientific illusion, that it is our job as rational agents to search for . . . a system of political and ethical ideas which would be the best from an absolute point of view. (*PHD*, 193–94)

John Cottingham claims that here Williams is merely offering "a kind of resigned acquiescence, an acceptance that we have to rest content in the prospect of a life grounded in no more than how things 'merely are.'" For Cottingham, however, there is a tension here: "the very acknowledgment implicit in that 'merely' carries with it a yearning for more."[26] Cottingham insists "there is no real harmony here, just a concatenation of contingencies," as Williams is merely telling us that "we happen to be a certain way, we happen to have certain desires, and to value things in a certain way, and that is all there is to say."[27] If this diagnosis is correct, Williams fails to move us beyond Richard Rorty's ironism. Rorty influentially distinguishes between the public and private stances one takes to one's ethical commitments. He thus paints a picture according to which reflective subjects fervently endorse liberalism as an answer to various public concerns while simultaneously recognizing, as private ironists, that they are "never quite able to take themselves seriously because [they are] always aware that the terms in which they describe themselves are subject to change, always aware of the contingency and fragility of their final vocabularies."[28] For this reason, Rorty holds that the most that we can hope to offer is a "redescription" of liberal societies, rather than a "defence of them against their enemies."[29]

There are certain similarities between Williams and Rorty. Both acknowledge the historical reasons behind our endorsement of our convictions and refuse to make any claims about them reflecting some kind of transcendent ethical truth. However, Williams thinks that the basic tenor of Rorty's ironism is problematic because the ironist embraces the psychologically untenable move of committing publicly to various things "while knowing that that is all he is doing; he believes in things while knowing, in a sense, that there is nothing to believe in."[30] Williams claims that this is confused and, somewhat ironically, that the ironist stance Rorty advocates itself only makes sense against the backdrop of the metaphysically-inflected understandings of morality that hold that only a universal justification can properly sustain conviction. In this sense, he claims that Rorty's stance is "still under the shadow of universalism" because it suggests that you cannot really believe in something "unless you hold it true in a sense which means that it applies to everyone [throughout history]" (*IBWD*, 67). In this regard, Rortian ironism is "counterfactually scientistic: rather as an atheist is really religious if he thinks that since God does not exist everything is permitted" (*PHD*, 187). This leads Williams to declare that although Rorty embarked on the "immensely important" project of giving "liberalism a better understanding of itself," his work offers "not much more than a benign celebration of this task."[31]

The basic failure arises—and this applies to Cottingham's lament as much as to Rorty's purported solution—because Williams insists that such views are "relic[s] of a world not yet thoroughly disenchanted" from the failures of metaphysical justifications in ethics (*PHD*, 137). Once we purge ourselves of this hope, Williams claims that the recognition of contingency does not have to be alienating. As Miranda Fricker notes, if "a given tradition casts the authority of ethical judgements in terms of absolute objectivity—as derived from some set of values held to be metaphysically objective, or from the law of God, or from the workings of Pure Reason—then, so long as its members are at all likely to go in for sceptical reflection about the supposed source of authority, the tradition sets them up for a fall."[32] Williams's account of confidence self-consciously avoids making that kind of claim, so it is not clear why the recognition of contingency must be unsettling.

This is not to suggest that we should simply go on advocating our commitments regardless of reflection. Indeed, Williams notes that "we are very unlikely to be able to make complete sense of our outlook. It will be in various ways incoherent" (*PHD*, 194). Yet this does not mean that we should simply abandon our convictions, especially as we cannot investigate our most basic views independently from our ways of making sense of the world, and when we do so certain commitments "stand fast" for us. The absence of an Archimedean point does not, therefore, result in either the nihilistic abandonment of our commitments or the embracement of an ironic posture. For Williams, both responses tacitly buy into the assumption that conviction can only be grounded by the kind of objective justification that he denies philosophy can secure. Our reflective task is, instead, to consider whether we can continue to endorse the commitments that stand fast for us without invoking the discredited justificatory strategies of much modern moral philosophy.

Many philosophers find this disquieting, precisely because the morality system dominates their understanding of the requirements of reflective stability, which is why so much moral and political philosophy is "unnecessarily vulnerable in the face of certain traditional sceptical goadings."[33] However, Williams's work intimates that the problem may be with our Christian tradition and the expectations it has bequeathed to us. Certainly, we should be skeptical of Cottingham's assertion that "to make our ethical home within an entirely closed and contingent cosmos, and pretend that we are wholly comfortable so doing, seems a violation of our human nature."[34] If some of our commitments stand up to reflection without us claiming a foundational or metaphysical support for them, this strongly suggests that they can be sustained despite Williams's brand of skepticism about morality. One might, therefore, say that our actions and lives reveal that Cottingham's assertion is merely a superstition. For Williams, then, the only way to answer the question of the relation between reflection and commitment is at the level of fact and practice—ethical life as it is actually lived—rather than by making theoretical assertions about the necessity of ultimate justification. What we need to do, to borrow Nietzsche's phrase, is to "educate ourselves against our age"[35] and to realize that the search for some kind of ultimate justification is a chimera. If this is truly acknowledged, then we should be less inclined to think that without such a justification, we are at a loss to explain why our convictions warrant our commitment.[36]

This is why Cottingham's complaint about the uselessness of Williamsian confidence is ultimately unimpressive. He claims that "the aspiration to confidence seems very likely to be a . . . ghostly trace of the ancient theological virtue of *hope*. That virtue makes sense, for the believer . . . but if, by contrast, all you have is that 'things merely are' . . . then confidence appears arbitrary."[37] However, as I have argued, confidence is not an attitude we decide to adopt but is rather something that reflection can sustain if we engage in the right kind of examination of our commitments. Moreover, if we take Cottingham at his word, he appears to merely be counseling us to embrace theism. For most of us, this is unhelpful not only because it is likely to be deeply inauthentic but also because it will be a barrier to serious, engaged, and truthful reflection on our predicament.

For Williams, the right kind of reflective inquiry enables us to effectively judge our ethical concepts by our best ethical standards, in the way he suggests with his talk of a left Wittgensteinianism. This form of moral and political reflection rejects foundationalism and, consequently, sees our ethical and political convictions in historical terms. For this reason, Williams claims that we can deploy some parts of our ethical thought against others "so as to give a critique of existing institutions, conceptions, prejudices, and powers." In particular, there is an open possibility of criticizing what "some of 'us' do in terms of our understanding of a wider 'we'" (*IBWD*, 37). On this view, antifoundationalism does not rule out the possibility of moral and political critique, and it is not difficult to see how we might realize that certain thick concepts (like "slut," with its core of reprehensible gendered discrimination) are not going to survive genealogical reflection while others (like "crony," with its useful political condemnation) may do so.

This requires us to think anew about the central tasks of moral and political philosophy:

> To see things in this way represents the reversal of a familiar Platonic structure. For the Platonic spirit . . . the aim is ultimate truth or rationality, and the powers that could lead us to it merely need to be protected from interference by persuasion. The present picture is rather of a world in which everything is, if you like, persuasion, and the aim is to encourage some forms of it rather than others. This is not . . . as is often suggested by those of a Platonic disposition, a picture that is a product of despair, a mere second-best for a world in which the criteria of true objectivity and ethical truth-seeking have proved hard to find. To recognise how we are placed in this respect is, if anything, an affirmation of strength. To suppose that . . . things that we prize or suppose ourselves to prize are simply revealed to us, or given to us by our nature, is not only a philosophical superstition but a kind of weakness. If that is the best we can say for them, we probably do not deserve them anyway. (*MSH*, 148)

In this sense, Williams suggests that those who claim that thinking in these terms will render our convictions unstable under reflection—those who, to put it another way, suggest that it is all pessimism and no strength—invite the threat of nihilism, precisely because the promise of firmer grounding is illusory.

Conclusion

In this chapter, I have focused on Williams's critique of the "morality system" and his account of how a set of ethical beliefs and commitments might stand up to reflection. As I have argued, Williams insists that if we are to work within the limits of philosophy, we need to think more realistically about the power of philosophy to justify our ethical and political commitments from some universally binding external perspective. However, according to Williams, we also need more hope in our ability to recognize that we can still live ethically and politically worthwhile lives without this kind of justification.

As we will see in the next chapter, Williams's political thought is deeply influenced by this assessment of the limits of philosophical ethics and premised on the idea that political philosophy cannot simply be a matter of applying "morality" to politics in part because morality cannot be all that it claims to be. This leads him to endorse a different conception of liberalism from those favored by mainstream liberal political philosophers like Rawls, Dworkin, and Nagel, a conception that he claims might stand up to reflection despite his skepticism about modern moral philosophy and indeed the morality system tout court.

6

Legitimacy and Liberalism

Having addressed Williams's work in ethics, I now turn to his political thought. One might be tempted to think that Williams's skepticism about philosophical ethics vitiates the attempt to articulate any robust standards of political evaluation, but Williams develops a realist conception of legitimacy that survives his critique of morality, which he argues enables us to distinguish between better and worse regimes on distinctively political grounds. In this chapter, I scrutinize this account of legitimacy and Williams's claim that it delivers a different, more convincing approach to liberalism than those advocated by liberal political moralists.

I begin by focusing on Williams's account of legitimacy, explaining how it calls into question the idea that political theory is a form of applied moral philosophy by suggesting that the most basic evaluative political standards arise *within* politics. I then offer a defense of Williams's nonmoralist conception of legitimacy and go on to explain how this enables Williams to support a realist version of liberalism inspired by Judith Shklar's liberalism of fear. I then focus on Williams's formulation of a critical theory test, which is intended to help us consider cases when subjects' beliefs about the legitimacy of their regimes may be problematically formed. I argue that Williams's critical theory test can help us impugn some such orders but that, ultimately, it has less critical potential than he implies. This is not necessarily a fatal shortcoming, but it reveals the limited extent to which realists can impugn political orders solely on grounds of Williams's conception of legitimacy.

The Basic Legitimation Demand

Williams's political thought is grounded in his insistence on the preeminent importance of the "first political question": the securing of "order, protection, safety, trust, and the conditions of cooperation." He states that this is the first question of politics because solving it "is the condition of solving, indeed posing, any others" (*IBWD*, 3). Williams stresses that if the central point of politics is to save people from the horrors and inconveniences that usually accompany situations of widespread disorder, we must acknowledge that some political orders either fail to resolve these issues or inflict such problems themselves. Moreover, Williams insists that solving the question of order is not sufficient to settle the question of legitimation by introducing the central component of his political thought: the *basic legitimation demand* (BLD). He claims that if the exercise of political power is to be regarded as a genuine solution to the first question of politics, those who exercise power must offer those over whom power is exercised an account of "what the difference is between the solution and the problem, and that cannot simply be an account of successful domination. It has to be a mode of justifying explanation or legitimation" (*IBWD*, 5).

The need to offer such a justification arises when "A coerces B and claims that B would be wrong to fight back: resents it, forbids it, rallies others to oppose it as wrong." By making such demands, Williams submits, A "claims that his actions transcend the conditions of warfare, and this gives rise to a demand of justification of what A does," and when "A is the state, these claims constitute its claim of authority over B" (*IBWD*, 6). To this end, he claims that the BLD "implies a sense in which the state has to offer a justification of its power to each subject" (*IBWD*, 4). (I will argue shortly that this point of Williams's is often misinterpreted and that what Williams in fact means by this is subtler than this rough characterization suggests.)

When those who exercise power claim to solve the first political question by offering a legitimation of their actions, we move beyond a situation of unmediated coercion. To illustrate, Williams utilizes the example of the Helot population of Sparta, who were often openly regarded as enemies by the Spartans. When a radically disadvantaged group such as the Helots are treated no better than a group of enemies, we do not have "per se a political situation" because "the mere circumstance of some subjects being de facto in the power of others is no legitimation of their being radically disadvantaged" as there "is nothing to be said to this group to explain why they shouldn't revolt" (*IBWD*, 5). Two key points follow. First, that the inability to protect a disadvantaged group can invalidate the claim that the rulers exercise authority and warrant obedience. Second, that we can treat as axiomatic that "might does not imply right, that . . . the power of coercion offered simply as the power of coercion cannot justify its own use" (*IBWD*, 5–6).

In this sense, Williams holds that when a group claims to exercise political authority, there are reasons inherent in this act that necessitate offering a legitimation of its authority to those who are coerced. This is why he insists that if the BLD is a moral principle, "it does not represent a morality that is prior to politics"; it is, as he puts it, "a claim that is inherent in there being such a thing as politics" (*IBWD*, 5). Therefore, by offering an account of its actions in such terms, an account that it thinks its subjects ought to accept, the state recognizes that power cannot be justified by the bare ability to coerce. Williams thus focuses on the character of political relationships and the standards that he takes to be *internal* to the exercise of political power.[1] These are not imported from an external moral standpoint but arise within politics.

On this view, a political situation obtains when a group claims authority and offers a legitimation of their actions to those who they claim to rightfully coerce. If a sufficient number of people accept the legitimation, we can conclude that the order has achieved legitimacy.[2] This successful satisfaction of the BLD then distinguishes legitimate from illegitimate solutions to the first political question. In this sense, a state successfully satisfies the BLD when it *makes sense* (MS) to its subjects as an intelligible order of political authority (*IBWD*, 10). I will discuss what this involves in more detail shortly, but the key issue is the extent to which the justification makes sense in the specific setting in which it is offered. Indeed, Williams stresses that a solution to the first question of politics is required "all the time" (*IBWD*, 3). Consequently, legitimacy is not a utopian moral ideal but a reachable threshold affected by historical circumstances and the feasible possibilities of time and place. Significantly, Williams also claims that it cannot be a necessary condition of "there being a (genuine) demand for justification that someone demands one" because people can be "drilled by coercive power into accepting its exercise." For this reason, he endorses a *critical theory principle* that holds that "the acceptance of a justification does not count if the acceptance itself is produced by the coercive power which is supposedly being justified" (*IBWD*, 6). Given the significance of this idea, I return to it below.

For Williams, then, legitimacy is not achieved when a state meets various prepolitical moral standards that determine when and how political power can be morally justified once and for all. Rather, it is conferred by subjects and ultimately rests in their recognitive judgments.[3] In this respect, his view contrasts sharply with moralist approaches. To employ a famous example, A. John Simmons argues that a legitimate state must be consented to in quasi-Lockean terms because of the "voluntarism" that derives from his rights-based view, and he consequentially infers that no existent states are legitimate.[4] From the perspective Williams advocates, this is problematic precisely because Simmons begins with an antecedent moral standard that he claims political orders must meet and proceeds to impugn politics on this basis because none ever will. More generally, Williams holds that political moralists tend to mistake judgments about what makes sense as an order or authority in a specific historical situation (and why) with the basic conditions of satisfying the BLD. This is a staple of views that closely connect judgments about political legitimacy to a particular theory of social justice. Such approaches reduce questions about the basic nature of political legitimacy to those concerning the author's judgment of the specific ends and values we should pursue in politics. That these questions are importantly distinct is the cornerstone of Williams's realist political theory.

When the legitimation story is accepted in the relevant way (I discuss what this involves shortly), rulers exercise *political* authority because they do not merely coerce or subordinate their subjects but stand with them in a political relationship in a way that, for example, a warlord does not. Legitimacy is therefore not determined by whether the state realizes or respects particular principles of justice but instead by its subjects' belief that the state acceptably solves the first political question. Moreover, for Williams, legitimacy does not require a moralized agreement or consensus on constitutional essentials. Any purported solution to the first political question will always, in some sense, be a kind of modus vivendi.[5]

These starting points do not lead Williams to deny that "there can be local applications of moral ideas in politics, and these may take, on a limited scale, an enactment or structural form" (*IBWD*, 8). When we ask what kind of legitimation story makes sense to us, we pose a normative question because "what (most) MS to us is a structure of authority which we think we should accept." So discussions about the requirements of legitimacy here and now take place in first-order terms and invoke "our political, moral, social, interpretative, and other concepts" (*IBWD*, 11). However, Williams is adamant that we must refrain from thinking that these judgments capture universal truths about the moral conditions of rightful political action. In addition, given his work in moral philosophy, he claims that there is no reason to believe that moral reasons are necessarily authoritative when we think in these terms. Claims about the justice of a political society will often be a competing factor in subjects' judgements that they ought to abide by the claims that a political authority makes on them, but there is no reason to think they will, or indeed ought, to trump all other considerations. This is one of the reasons why judgments about the acceptability of the state are manifestly not the same as pondering what a perfectly just society may look like.

This does not preclude us from claiming that certain features of existent states are objectionable, but Williams stresses that when we ponder which normative goals we should presently pursue, this is a question "that belongs to the level of fact, practice and politics, not one that lies beyond these in the very conditions of legitimacy" (*IBWD*, 17). I may think that the British economy should be reformed to ameliorate the plight of the severely economically disadvantaged or hold that certain decisions my government makes are morally indefensible, but such claims can be made without me concluding that the state lacks legitimacy.[6] Judgments about legitimacy are judgments about whether the state is a realistically acceptable order of coercion that can secure the conditions of cooperation among groups of people with disparate moral beliefs and conflicting interests. To this extent, Williams endorses the Hobbesian claim that no functioning political state could exist if claims about its legitimacy had to cohere with all citizens' judgments about the optimal set of moral principles that should govern political life.

Williams's view is also compatible with the common realist insistence that moral precepts cannot, and often do not, preempt the political project of establishing order; because solving the first political question creates the conditions in which we can have a moral and ethical life, the act of securing order may not be compatible with a strict adherence to the same standards.[7] Yet because we assess legitimation stories in light of what makes sense to us as a justifiable order of authority, Williams claims that we impose more stringent conditions of legitimacy than were operative in the past. Crucially, though, such judgments cannot be seen as the "foundation of the liberal state" because they are a "product of the same forces that lead to a situation in which the BLD is satisfied only by a liberal state" (*IBWD*, 8). Accordingly, "inasmuch as liberalism has foundations, it has foundations in its capacity to answer the 'first question' in what is now seen . . . as an acceptable way" (*IBWD*, 8). As we will see, Williams thinks that a particular conception of liberalism can indeed be vindicated in such terms, but it is a far more chastened conception than the "high liberalism" proposed by mainstream political moralists like Rawls and Dworkin.

Defending the Basic Legitimation Demand

Before I address Williams's realist liberalism, I respond to various criticisms of his account of legitimacy. I focus on four lines of attack, arguing that they all trade on various misunderstandings of the BLD and the conception of politics at its heart, which allows for multiple (but not infinite) variety about which purported solutions might make sense as answers to the first political question.

THE SCOPE OF THE BASIC LEGITIMATION DEMAND

Matt Sleat argues that Williams's insistence that the state has to offer a justification of its power to each subject "fall[s] back . . . upon some foundational moral premise that all persons matter," which disqualifies Williams from articulating a genuinely realist alternative to political moralism. For Sleat, if we are to keep "political realism and political moralism distinct it has to be the case that it is possible to fully explicate politics and the necessary conditions of legitimacy without recourse to external moral conditions."[8]

Sleat's criticism has some basis in Williams's statements,[9] but a charitable reading suggests that the scope of the legitimation story is best understood as being offered to those persons considered to be citizens or political subjects, rather than simply those who are subjected to the state's power on other grounds (like the Helots). Williams's point is that unless the state offers a justification to each person it constrains, the relationship between it and those persons is not politically authoritative in the sense Williams is concerned with. It does not follow that these regimes should thereby be classed illegitimate in a binary sense, as Sleat suggests.

Consider that Williams explicitly does not suggest that we can consider Sparta illegitimate because of its treatment of the Helots. He observes that the Helots were considered alien people and states that it is only when there "is an attempt to incorporate" the radically disadvantaged as political subjects that we can conclude that the BLD "has not been met" (*IBWD*, 5). This idea of "incorporation" and the subsequent claim to authority is significant:

> There can be a pure case of internal warfare, of the kind invoked in the case of the Helots. There is no general answer to what are the boundaries of the state, and I suppose that there can in principle be a spongiform state. While there are no doubt reasons for stopping warfare, these are not the same reasons, or related to politics in the same way, as reasons given by a claim to authority. In terms of rights the situation is this: first, anyone over whom the state claims authority has a right to treatment justified by the claim of LEG [legitimacy]; second, there is no right to be a member of a state, if one is not a member . . . ; third, there is no claim of authority over enemies, including those in the situation of the Helots. In virtue of this last point, such people do not have a right of the kind mentioned in the first point . . . the significant cases for the present problems are those in which the radically disadvantaged are said to be subjects and the state claims authority over them. (*IBWD*, 6)

Once we see the idea of "incorporation" as framing the scope of the BLD, we can distinguish between those to whom a justification of power is offered and those to whom it is not, who may instead be simply subjected to coercion.

Williams is especially clear about this in "From Freedom to Liberty: The Construction of a Political Value," when he writes that the legitimation story "is supposed to legitimate the arrangement to *each* citizen, that is to say, to each person from whom the state expects allegiance; though there may be other people within the state, slaves or captives, who are nakedly objects of coercion and for whom there is no such legitimation story" (*IBWD*, 95).

Williams's basic aim is to delimit the nature of political authority, and he recognizes that the state need not stand in political relations with all those it coerces. The state's legitimacy therefore depends on justifying itself to those who are incorporated as political citizens and thereby from whom allegiance is demanded. There is no timeless, prepolitical moral standard that determines to whom the BLD must be directed. It is possible that certain groups will be coerced for reasons that only make sense to the state's desired constituency. Williams helps us recognize that in such situations, political relations exist between rulers and the subjects to whom their legitimation story makes sense, even if there are other people who do not see their relationship to the state in such terms.

When Williams claims that "now and around here" all persons must be treated as political subjects, this is a historical development, one related to the disenchanted nature of modernity that he, following Weber, highlights when he notes that traditional hierarchical justifications of inequitable treatment no longer make sense.[10] He is not claiming that all political orders throughout history should be judged legitimate or illegitimate according to this standard.

THE CONSENSUS CRITIQUE

A number of critics, on a variety of related but distinct grounds, have alleged that Williams commits to a problematic "consensus" view of politics of the sort that realists criticize political moralists for endorsing. Jonathan Floyd insists that there is no "pre-existing arrangement to be found about which forms of political authority are acceptable"[11] and concludes that Williams's account fails because "the attempt to identify and then reconcile us to some putatively latent set of ideals in our local way of life is on a hiding to nothing on account of the very plurality of ideals which surrounds us."[12] Michael Freeden makes a similar point when he argues that Williams's claim that a state could make sense to its subjects in the way that the BLD offers is an "unfeasible return to an ideal-type expectation."[13] Likewise, Sleat contends that by "grounding his theory in the hope or actuality of agreement ... Williams's theory becomes vulnerable to exactly the same challenge that other realists have posed to liberalism as a consensus-based theory."[14]

These complaints rest on misinterpretations. Sleat insists that Williams holds that judgments about the acceptability of the state will be unanimous, claiming that, for Williams, "universal acceptance is a necessary condition of legitimacy."[15] Yet Williams states explicitly that having "something to say to each person" does not imply that "this is something that this person or group will necessarily accept" because there may be "anarchists, or utterly unreasonable people, or bandits, or merely enemies" (*IBWD*, 135–36). In consequence, satisfying the BLD "does not coincide with this insatiable ideal of many a political theoretician: universal consent" (*IBWD*, 136n8):

> *Who* has to be satisfied by the BLD is a good question, and it depends on the circumstances. Moreover, it is a political question, which depends on political circumstances. Obviously, the people to be satisfied should include a substantial number of the people: beyond that, they may include other powers, groups . . . young people who need to understand what is happening, influential critics who need to be persuaded and so forth. (If this position seems alarmingly relativist, it is important, indeed essential . . . to reflect that in the end no theorist has any way of advancing beyond it. He or she may invoke absolute or universal conditions of legitimacy, which any "reasonable" person should accept; but in doing this, he or she speaks to an audience in a given situation, who share these conceptions of reasonableness.) (*IBWD*, 136)

This is manifestly not a view that argues that legitimacy is dependent on the unanimous acceptance of the legitimation story. Rather, if the state makes sense to a sufficient number of people (we cannot be more precise than that), the situation transcends the conditions of unmediated coercion in which politics is impossible. Just as there is no timeless prepolitical, moral standard that determines to whom the state must try to legitimate itself, there is also no prepolitical, moral standard that determines how wide the acceptance of the legitimation story must be. It is possible—and altogether likely—that some subjects will insist that the legitimation does not make sense and refuse to recognize their relation to their rulers as being political in kind. Yet Williams acknowledges that it is often crude to make binary claims about legitimacy, which is why he stresses the scalar nature of legitimacy judgments. It may be impossible at times to legitimate power to all, and we may have to accept that some people are simply being subordinated (paramilitary republicans in Northern Ireland spring to mind as a recent example), but Williams demonstrates that for those to whom order can be legitimated, a political relationship with the state obtains.[16] The difference between situations where a story is offered and generally accepted and where the powerful either fail to offer any justification or offer one that fails to make sense to their subjects should in principle be clear.¹⁷ The point is not that the claim to political authority is always "settled or uncontested" but that "all parties that claim a relationship of political authority, rather than one of mere domination, must recognize the basic legitimation demand as something that needs to be addressed."¹⁸

Having disposed of this "universal-acceptance" misreading, we are in a better position to assess a more viable variant of the consensus critique. Floyd suggests that though modernity may rule out some legitimation stories, it does not help us choose which ones we ought to accept. As he puts it, even if "modern populations *do* find the notion of the divine rights of kings unacceptable [this] does nothing to guide our choices between say, social democracy or neo-liberalism, luck-egalitarians and libertarians . . . and so on and so forth."¹⁹ However, by repeating the moralistic mistake of conflating our judgments about optimal theories of justice with the idea that a state may be an acceptable solution, Floyd misses the crux of what truly concerns us when evaluating legitimacy. The appropriate criterion of making sense is not "Does this capture my favored conception of justice?" but "Do I accept this order of authority's demands on me, given that I must coexist with other citizens who have conflicting interests and commitments?"

In the next section, I will examine Williams's claim that only liberalism makes sense "now and around here" in more detail. But in response to Floyd's objection, it is worth bearing in mind two things: first, the importance of securing order and the conditions of cooperation, and second, Williams's capacious description of liberal societies as those that aim "to combine the rule of law with a liberty more extensive than in most earlier societies, a disposition to toleration, and a commitment to some kinds of equality" (*TT*, 264). With these points taken into consideration, we ought to be less disposed to object to Williams's point that some liberal orders make sense in the way he describes. For one thing, our experience of the last century has shown that, at least throughout the western world, regimes that are loosely designated by the term *liberalism* actually have by and large succeeded in making sense to their members as orders of authority. Moreover, even though some people will deny that liberalism in Williams's terms makes sense, in order for these complaints to be politically convincing, they must account for their belief that viable alternatives exist that are likewise presently able to ensure order and the conditions of cooperation. Although we cannot simply declare that this is impossible, Williams's view is buttressed by the fact that twentieth-century history confirms that recent alternative political creeds have on this score failed spectacularly.²⁰

Once we grasp the force of this point, we are in a better position to ask if social democrats, neoliberals, and luck egalitarians—or, better, the citizens who endorse the commitments these philosophical positions rationalize—actually disagree about the basic legitimacy of the liberal state simply because they disagree about its moral optimality. This is less obvious than Floyd implies. Even if some political philosophers who closely link justice and legitimacy disagree about the acceptability of actually existing liberal states in the way he has in mind, this likely tells us more about the esoteric nature of their understanding of politics than the opinion of their fellow citizens. Indeed, the acquiescence of most citizens seems to suggest that winning a democratic election, competent economic management, respecting the capacious liberal values that Williams focuses on, and not violating some basic human rights are enough to confer legitimacy.

Once we accept these points, the concern that Williams endorses the unrealistic "consensus" view immediately becomes less persuasive. Of course, certain groups may think that the liberal state "makes no legitimate demand on them" (*IBWD*, 136). However, unrealistic understandings of what forms of political society people actually do find acceptable may be avoided by moving in a quasi-Humean direction and holding that judgments about acceptability are conditioned by our psychological propensities. As such, the BLD can be satisfied if authority is exercised by rulers and acquiesced to by the population.[21] If a state fails to secure the goods involved in solving the first political question, many people will, understandably, conclude that it makes no sense to recognize its authority. In contrast to what the consensus critics suggest, there is reason to think that most subjects "now and around here" accept the thin sort of liberalism Williams has in mind. As Mark Philp notes, "while that opinion is not necessarily enthusiastic and positive, and for some groups is nothing more than a *modus vivendi*, nonetheless, the centre can and does hold in many orders, and does so with our collective concurrence (albeit motivated very differently for different groups)."[22]

THE BASIC LEGITIMATION DEMAND AND ITS NORMATIVE CONTENT

Charles Larmore contends that "it is not so much the BLD as rather the justification of state power, whatever it may be," that must "express a 'morality prior to politics': it has to embody an idea of what constitutes the just exercise of political order—specifically, an idea of what constitutes the just exercise of coercive power—and that is not only a moral conception but one whose validity must be understood as antecedent to the state's own authority by virtue of serving to ground it."[23] In his more recent reiteration of this point,

Larmore argues that any legitimation story must apply "what it takes to be a prior moral truth to the actual political situation" and that, consequently, "claims to legitimacy must always rest on assumptions expressing a morality prior to politics."[24] To support this claim, he utilizes Williams's own argument that here and now we think liberalism makes sense because we endorse "an ethically elaborated account of the person" (*IBWD*, 8).

It is true that judgments about what makes sense are normative—as noted, Williams agrees that "when we get to our own case, the notion 'MS' does become normative, because what (most) MS to us is a structure of authority which we think we should accept" (*IBWD*, 11). However, claims about the necessity of a legitimation story "embodying" an antecedent conception of the just exercise of political power or "applying" a set of prior moral truths fail to grasp what Williams is getting at. Realists like Williams insist that a legitimation story may invoke a wide array of sources—economic, ethical, social, interpretative, religious—and be deemed acceptable in the requisite sense by bundling them in a particular manner that makes sense to the state's subjects. In these terms, there is no reason to assume that moral considerations necessarily trump all others precisely because realists reject the suggestion that morality stands in a hierarchical relationship to politics. Politics cannot, therefore, simply be seen as an exercise in applying moral ideals. To this end, the BLD adheres to realist as opposed to moralist political thought by not conceiving of the "*basic* relation of morality to politics as being represented by either the enactment or structural model" (*IBWD*, 8). While Larmore is correct to observe that Williams's account references various moral/normative judgments, this does not make the BLD a species of the "applied moral philosophy" approach to political theory that Williams seeks to undermine. Ethical considerations are one among a host of resources the state may draw on to legitimate itself.

Moreover, the point Williams makes immediately after discussing liberalism's ethically elaborated account of the person, which Larmore curiously refuses to quote, is revealing. As noted, Williams insists that such moral ideals cannot be seen as the "foundation of the liberal state" because they are a "product of those same forces that lead to a situation in which the BLD is satisfied only be a liberal state" (*IBWD*, 8). In this sense, Williams urges political theorists to get past the notion that moral principles must not only underlie but also precede political practice in the way that, for example, we might consider a written constitution as settling the moral background from which politics can then occur and by which politics is (supposedly) constrained. If we take this seriously, then when we come to reflect on our moral ideals, and the way in which they impact our judgments about what kinds of political authority make sense (and why), we have to engage in the sort of genealogical inquiries I outlined in the last chapter.

On this view, it makes little sense to regard the moral ideas that may be appealed to in any act of legitimation as expressing a morality that can meaningfully be said to exist *prior* to politics. This is particularly clear in Williams's papers on toleration, where he maintains that "instead of trying to reach the politics of liberalism from a moral assumption that concerns toleration"— namely a morally elaborate view of autonomy—"we should consider first the politics of liberalism, including its practices of toleration, and then ask, what, if any, kinds of moral assumption are related to that" (*IBWD*, 135). When we do so, it is hard to "discover any one attitude that underlies liberal practice" because toleration requires "social virtues such as the desire to cooperate and to get on peaceably with one's fellow citizens and a capacity for seeing how things look to them . . . some scepticism, the lack of fanatical conviction on religious issues, and so on" (*IBWD*, 138).

Consequently, people come to accept, in a less reflective manner than Larmore seemingly acknowledges, that certain arrangements make sense to them. Much of the time, the reason that something makes sense to us has little volitional quality.[25] In this sense, Larmore fails to grasp the centrality of Williams's contention that in politics, as in much of life, we must remember that *in the beginning was the deed*.

THE ALLEGED UNREALISM OF WILLIAMSIAN POLITICS

Other critics have claimed, more damningly, that Williams idealistically misunderstands politics. Thus, according to Freeden, Williams should be maligned for retaining the unrealistic liberal view that political rule is best understood in "terms of trust and cooperation, a theme quite central to Locke's and Rawls's versions of liberalism," and for failing to recognize that "legitimacy is not necessarily an attribute of all political arrangements, even if sought after by a large number of political actors and thinkers."[26] Freeden appears to worry that Williams's contention that there is something unique about the nature of political rule, given the peculiarity of its claim to authority and the concomitant demand for justification, is baseless because countless examples exist where rulers have routinely disregarded the BLD's core axiom "might is not right" and failed to offer a justification of their power that makes sense to their subjects while remaining "political" in some sense.

This observation is true, but it does not undermine Williams's account. Mark Philp's discussion of Nazi Germany—a regime that clearly falls into the category Freeden invokes—is demonstrative in this respect. Philp claims that it is absurd to deny that the Nazi regime acted politically insofar as it "sought to adapt and extend existing forms of political authority [and] relied on an array of traditional political institutions and mechanisms to achieve [its] ends." Yet he argues that it is equally hard to insist that it exercised *political authority*. For one thing, its actions led "to an increasingly distorted set of political ambitions and an increasingly coercive political regime," and this ensured that "the order retained . . . a political form but it was less concerned with securing its authority as opposed to establishing its domination."[27] Furthermore, that the most abhorrent policies were carried out in secret suggests that "the state could not legitimate its activities and would have forfeited its claim to a right to rule had its activities been made public."[28] Philp, therefore, concludes that Nazi Germany was in effect "being run by a cabal within the state—an inner state that had no publicly legitimated . . . right to rule" and that when "things move in this direction . . . it becomes increasingly incoherent to describe the relationship between the political order and its victims as political in character."[29]

This reminder about the peculiar nature of regimes that fail to recognize something akin to the BLD's demands help demonstrate that although malevolent regimes can appear to be "political" in some sense—they use state institutions and so on—the relationship that they have to some of the people whom they coerce may not be political in kind. Once this is granted, it is hard to see why the existence of such regimes impugns Williams's attempt to delineate some central features of properly political relationships. As Philp notes, these examples can simply be seen as deficient in this respect. Hence, it is not problematic that some regimes clearly did (and do) not exercise legitimacy in Williams's sense because when they act in this manner it is difficult to describe their relationship with their subjects as being political in kind.

To this end, Williams helps us comprehend the ways in which regimes like Nazi Germany not only are morally abhorrent but can be said to pervert politics. Even though political power is coercive, not all coercion is political, in much the same way that war may be diplomacy by other means, but war is not politics by other means. Thus, the appropriate response to the reminder that some states violate the "might is not right" axiom is not to conclude that Williams's account fails but to reiterate that legitimacy is an evaluative standard that some coercive orders will, unsurprisingly, fail to meet.

Making Sense of Liberalism

Despite his rejection of political moralism, Williams does not think that we must relinquish a commitment to a version of liberalism.[30] To be sure, he disavows the "imperialistic" claim "that reason itself is liberal reason, and that an ethical practice which is other than the morality of autonomy involves the refusal to listen to reasons at all" (*IBWD*, 22–23). On related grounds, he is adamant that our historical self-consciousness vitiates the attempt to offer a "cognitive" vindication of liberalism, which sees the historical path as a matter of uncovering some timeless and universal moral truths about how human beings should do politics. Such an account would, in his view, be committed to thinking that we could apprehend the transition from nonliberal to liberal politics "in such terms that both parties (the holders of the earlier outlook, and the holders of the latter) have reason to recognize the transition as an improvement" (*PHD*, 189). However, there is little reason to think that our transition to liberalism can be understood in this manner: "The relevant ideas of freedom, reason, and so on were themselves involved in the change. If in this sense the liberals did not win an argument, then the explanations of how liberalism came to prevail—that is to say, among other things, how these came to be our ideas—are not vindicatory" (*PHD*, 190–91). So how does Williams seek to explain a commitment to liberal politics?

Williams notes that some philosophers, whom he refers to as "queasy liberals," are tempted to think that "if one does not think of one's morality as universally applicable to everyone, one cannot confidently apply it where one must indeed apply it, to the issues of one's time and place. Some people do seem to think that if liberalism is a recent idea and people in the past were not liberals, they themselves should lose confidence in liberalism" (*IBWD*, 67). As we have seen, he accepts that liberalism is a (relatively) recent idea but is adamant that if we endorse his realist view of legitimacy, we can confidently commit to liberalism for a number of reasons. Primarily, some universal constraints regarding the coercive activities of states derive from the logic of answering the first question of politics. In particular, the BLD's central "might is not right" axiom rules out "abuses of power that almost everyone everywhere has been in position to recognize as such" (*IBWD*, 26). Thus, Williams claims that the best conceptualization of human rights focuses on the problem that occurs when a purported solution to the first political question becomes part of the very problem it is meant to resolve. At the most basic level, he claims that we have a clear sense of when this transpires and, therefore, a good grasp of "what the most basic violations of human rights are," claiming that "in the traditional words of the Catholic Church, the most basic truth on this matter is *quod semper, quod ubique, quod ab omnibus creditum est*" (*IBWD*, 63). In this regard, Williams recognizes as the most blatant denials of human rights "torture, surveillance, arbitrary arrest, and murder: the world of Argentina under the junta, the story, only partly ever to be told, of those who disappeared" (*IBWD*, 26).

On his view, focusing on these core violations is both politically and philosophically prudent because we ought "to make our views about human rights, or at least the most basic human rights, depend as little as possible on disputable theses of liberalism or any other particular ideology" (*IBWD*, 74). The core violations that flow from the BLD are immune from being charged as expressions of liberal ideology because they are paradigmatic examples of "people using power to coerce other people against their will to secure what the first people want simply because they want it" (*IBWD*, 23). In this respect, Williams's account of human rights is part of his attempt to think about how our moral and political commitments might stand up to reflection if we refuse the consolations of overambitious accounts of morality. Of course, this strictly demarcated set of rights does not exhaust our sense of the conditions of legitimacy in the present. Nor does it logically compel one to endorse liberal politics. But Williams elucidates further considerations that explain why his realist approach leads him to endorse *a* version of liberal politics.

For one thing, he insists that we have very good reasons to reject solutions to the first political question that do not accord fundamental decencies to all subjects (perhaps on the on the basis of race, gender, or religious identity) because such views are incompatible with the basic precept of Weberian disenchantment: "the retreat from believing that the order of how people should treat one another is somehow inscribed either in them or in the universal realm."[31] Put another way, political arguments that invoke such discrepancies in treatment usually result in claims that we have no reason to endorse.[32] Thus, one might say that we employ what Williams refers to in his paper "The Idea of Equality" as the *reasonably weak principle*: "for every difference in the way people are treated, a reason should be given" (*IBWD*, 107). Once such reasons are given, we begin the business of assessing them.[33]

Similarly, Williams claims that we now reject the view that hierarchical structures are inevitable and hence self-legitimating: "Once the question of their legitimacy is raised, it cannot be answered simply by their existence (this is a necessary proposition, a consequence of the axiom about justification: if the supposed legitimation is seen to be baseless, the situation is one of more coercive power)" (*IBWD*, 7). He thus endorses the historical proposition that, in modernity, we receive a "constraint of roughly equal acceptability" from the BLD. This explains why liberty is such a special value for us. As we repudiate transcendental justifications of hierarchy, "in telling our legitimation story we start . . . with less. In interpreting and distributing liberty we allow each citizen a stronger presumption in favour of what he or she certainly wants, to carry out his or her own desires" (*IBWD*, 95).

Williams refers to this kind of skeptical unmasking as the *negative narrative of the Enlightenment*—the spirit of critique that led people to suspect traditional justifications of hierarchy (*SP*, 329). Although this cannot be seen as the grand unfolding of reason, when we ask what makes sense to us in the historical and sociological circumstances of modernity, we have grounds for holding that liberal regimes—with their commitment to the rule of law, wide-ranging political freedom and toleration, and some conception of political equality—represent the most appropriate answer to the first political question for us (*IBWD*, 9). Williams puts this most schematically when he writes that "LEG + Modernity = Liberalism," stating that we endorse liberal solutions, in large part, because "other supposed legitimations are now seen to be false and in particular ideological" (*IBWD*, 8).

In this light, Williams claims that a particular conception of liberalism—Judith Shklar's liberalism of fear—can be vindicated if we think in the realist terms he favors. This is because the liberalism of fear's normative impetus, like his account of the first question of politics and understanding of human rights, derives from the fact that it "takes the condition of life without terror as its first requirement" (*IBWD*, 61). Shklar contrasts the liberalism of fear with a Lockean liberalism of natural rights, "which looks to the constant fulfilment of an ideal pre-established normative order," and with a Millian liberalism of personal development, which holds that freedom is necessary for "personal as well as social progress."[34] She claims that the liberalism of fear does not consider "the basic units of political life . . . discursive and reflecting persons, nor friends and enemies, nor patriotic solider-citizens, nor energetic litigants, but the weak and the powerful," and "the freedom it wishes to secure is freedom from the abuse of power and intimidation of the defenceless."[35] Accordingly, the liberalism of fear is "entirely nonutopian"[36] and refrains from articulating a summum bonum, instead beginning "with a *summum malum*, which all of us know and would avoid if we could. That evil is cruelty and the fear it inspires, and the very fear of fear itself."[37]

Shklar recognizes various objections may be raised against the liberalism of fear. Some critics claim it is reductive, but she insists "there is nothing reductive about building a political order on the avoidance of fear and cruelty unless one begins with contempt for physical experience."[38] Others say that its fearfulness of state power lends it a logical affinity with anarchism. In response, Shklar counsels us to remember that "the actualities of countries in which law and government have broken down are not encouraging." Thus, the "original first principle of liberalism," the rule of law, differentiates the two views.[39] Finally, Shklar argues that the liberalism of fear is not simply a recasting of a rights-based liberalism because it encourages us to see rights not "as fundamental and given" but as "licenses and empowerments that citizens must have in order to preserve their freedom and to protect themselves against abuse."[40]

Some commentators claim it is unclear how Williams's political realism and the liberalism of fear link up.[41] However, this brief summary enables us to see why Williams claims an affinity between Shklar's view and his own. To be sure, thinking about the basic acceptability of political institutions with reference to the concerns about power and powerlessness at the heart of the liberalism of fear does not comprehensively justify every aspect of liberal practice that we may presently affirm. It also, clearly, underdetermines one's substantive political views. Yet Williams insists that thinking about liberalism in Shklarian terms provides the "least ambitious and most convincing justification of liberalism" (*TT*, 208).

In a sense, his argument is similar to his postmetaphysical defense of truthfulness. Just as Accuracy and Sincerity are thin universals that would be intrinsically valuable in any hypothetical state of nature, the materials of the liberalism of fear—"power, powerlessness, fear, cruelty, a universalism of negative capacities" (*IBWD*, 59)—are universal. Moreover, just as the ways in which Accuracy and Sincerity develop historically have been, and will continue to be, the result of various historical contingencies, so will the various solutions to the first political question that make sense to their subjects. And while the negative narrative of the Enlightenment may have destroyed some of the justificatory stories that (moralist) liberals like to tell themselves about liberalism's emergence, Williams claims that the resources of the liberalism of fear, "which work everywhere, may keep it afloat" because liberal societies are "more successful in the modern world than others in helping people (at least in their own territories—their influence elsewhere has been less benign) to avoid what is universally feared: torture, violence, arbitrary power, and humiliation" (*TT*, 208). In other words, while we cannot meet the demand for a cognitive genealogy of liberalism—viewed as reason uncovering the correct moral solution for politics (a historical story that views our attachment to liberalism as a discovery)—"a lot can be said in favour of liberal society" on these grounds, even though "at other times and places these things have been effectively controlled by other political means" (*TT*, 265).

This should not obscure the fact that some elements of Williams's argument are more problematic than he acknowledges. For one thing, the bold slogan—LEG + Modernity = Liberalism—is harder to square with Williams's account of legitimacy than he acknowledges, especially in light of his belief that the relativism of distance does not apply in the contemporary world. As Robert Jubb notes, "One does not have to subscribe to claims about the superiority of alleged Asian values to see that various states in East Asia seem to be accepted by most of their citizens yet are neither liberal nor under-developed compared to the North Atlantic democracies Williams presumably had in mind when equating liberalism and modernity."[42] We can best interpret Williams here as holding that there is no reason to refrain from judging the basic legitimacy of different states throughout the modern world in the terms that the BLD encourages while recognizing that this does not require us to impose our views of what "makes sense" on those regimes. This does, however, suggest that a viable view of the role relativist considerations should play in our judgment of "real" political confrontations must be more fine-grained than some of Williams's bolder statements about liberalism, modernity, and the relativism of distance imply.

In addition, the plausibility of Williams's account increases if we add two quasi-Hampshirean considerations. The first is that our acquiescence and confidence will often lie with actually existing institutions as well as with liberal principles and values. As John Gray notes, the judgments that are employed when thinking about whether political institutions do, in fact, make sense to us question our "attachment to a particular political community and its animating common culture, with the actual history and distinctive characteristics that it contingently has."[43] Second, if we accept that well-intentioned subjects will inevitably disagree on matters of the good and right and that these conflicts will, therefore, have to be settled by abiding the judgments of political institutions and procedures, our evaluations of liberal political institutions' acceptability are likely to be deeply conditioned by our view of whether they satisfy certain procedural norms that make sense to us. As we saw in chapter 4, Hampshire notes that judgments about whether such institutions meet the demands of basic procedural fairness are bound to be highly relevant in this regard. However, so are judgments about whether such institutions succeed in "respecting" different members of the polity in the requisite way, whether they actually do treat their subjects more or less equally, and so on and so forth. Unfortunately, Williams says surprisingly little about liberal democracy on these grounds, preferring to think more abstractly about the basic conditions of legitimacy and the central values of liberalism.

Despite these shortcomings, for Williams the philosophically significant point is that thinking in Shklarian terms enables us to commit to liberalism in a reflectively stable manner because we can confidently hold from a historical perspective that liberal institutions are reasonably good, though by no means perfect, at curtailing abuses of power over the powerless and at acceptably answering the first political question.[44] In this sense, Williams's defense of liberal politics avoids the question whether earlier peoples were in cognitive error about the objective truths of morality. We have to judge the legitimation stories we are offered in terms of the best judgments we can muster. This is a matter of deciding which of the stories that we tell ourselves about our values, convictions, and political institutions stand up to reflection—an activity that requires us to show fidelity to "historical and social truthfulness, rather than the phantasm of ultimate ethical truth" (*MSH*, 147).

Nonetheless, an outstanding issue affects Williams's attempt to articulate a vindication of liberalism. As noted, Williams claims that though much can be said for liberal society, from the perspective of the citizens of liberal states, with regard to the negative universals the liberalism of fear focuses on, the influence of liberal regimes on outsiders has often been far "less benign" (*TT*, 208). It clearly matters if the merits of liberal societies that Williams highlights come at the cost of human rights abuses and humiliation abroad. It is not implausible to think that recent work on the entangled history of liberalism and imperialism, in formal and informal modes, calls the defense of liberalism that I have articulated in this chapter into question.[45]

Williams accepts that liberal regimes are "high on hypocrisy" (*TT*, 265) for these and other reasons, which is undoubtedly true. Yet there are some things to be said *for* liberal regimes when these criticisms are posed by liberalism's detractors. For one thing, the fact that liberal society fosters social conditions under which people can articulate problematic questions about the bases of liberal politics is itself something to be commended, when many other forms of politics purposefully attempt to prevent subjects from asking such questions, knowing that truthful answers will discredit their legitimation stories. That we can pose these questions shows that we, unlike the Greeks in relation to slavery, recognize that questions about the justice of liberal states' actions in these respects matter.

Moreover, as I argued in chapter 1, if we reflect about ethics and politics in the kind of historically sensitive ways that Berlin, Hampshire, and Williams advocate, we should not be surprised that many of our values are connected in complex ways to lamentable acts. Williams was not naive about liberalism in this respect. He explicitly states that "the circumstances in which liberal thought is possible have been created in part by actions that violate liberal ideals and human rights, as was recognized by Hegel and Marx, and, in a less encouraging spirit, by Nietzsche" (*IBWD*, 25). However, he insists that it is a mistake to think that this should automatically lead us to reject liberal politics. Rather, we must decide how to advance in spite of the horrors that have created both our social world as well as our own thoughts about how we should act in it.

In this respect, Williams judged that it is possible to be cognizant of, and to object to, the humiliation and violence perpetrated by liberal states while still retaining a commitment to the liberalism of fear. According to Williams, this is in part because realistically available alternatives to liberalism are unlikely to fare any better relative to the universal standards the liberalism of fear highlights. Thus, he remarks that "it is not easy to imagine, let alone find, a radically different alternative [to liberalism] that would be possible in the conditions of the modern world and would do better by these universal measures" (*TT*, 265). This will not satisfy liberalism's critics, but it raises further unignorable questions. Honest observers of international politics must simply accept that all states often act indefensibly toward outsiders and that the record of powerful nonliberal regimes' relations with outsiders does not warrant much celebration. Of course, this does not excuse, and it should not lead us to forget, the atrocities that liberal states have perpetrated and continue to perpetrate. But it enjoins us to consider whether renouncing the liberalism of fear for these reasons also requires us to renounce every other known manner of doing politics.

That liberal regimes often engage in acts of cruelty that violate the rights and protections Williams and Shklar highlight does, however, show that reflective advocates of the liberalism of fear should feel deeply ambivalent when they reflect on the history of liberalism and the actions of liberal states. The most respectable intellectual stance is one that avoids the intellectual consolations of either an utter cynicism that merely highlights liberalism's manifest failures in this regard or a naive triumphalism that solely focuses on its equally real successes. As ever in politics, impurity abounds.

It is also worth highlighting that if liberal regimes show themselves to be so incapable of responding to the challenges of politics in the twenty-first century that Williams did not address—chief among them global migration and climate change—without engaging in systematic cruelty, then the claim that liberalism is concretely defensible in terms of Shklarian negative universals will become utterly preposterous. At present there may indeed be reasons for thinking that this is not especially unlikely. Still, Williams did not believe that this point had been reached in his lifetime, and this conclusion was obviously not born of complacency. Nonetheless, it is clear that whether we judge the cruelties liberal states inflict on outsiders as deviations from norms that should command our allegiance, rather than as evidence of a darker truth about the inherent features of liberal politics, depends significantly on the future actions of liberal states. The deed, after all, is primary.

The Critical Theory Principle

As noted earlier, in response to the concern that subjects' views of what makes sense may be a result of coercion by the politically powerful, Williams advocates a critical theory principle. Unfortunately, *In the Beginning Was the Deed* only contains five or six fragmentary, rather unilluminating remarks on the critical theory principle. Williams acknowledges that the challenge "lies in deciding what counts as having been 'produced by' coercive power in the relevant sense" (*IBWD*, 6), but beyond this he only offers elusive snippets about what taking these concerns seriously involves. He remarks that legitimations based on rationalizations in terms of race and gender are invalid no matter how widely they are endorsed because "the acceptance of them by the dominating party is readily explained, while their being accepted by the dominated is an easy case for the critical theory principle" (*IBWD*, 7). In addition, he holds that if a political order exists in which a group of "happy slaves" do not experience any frustration about their plight, this does not preclude us from denying the order's legitimacy. In particular, if the enslaved people's lack of frustration persists despite the fact that "they are not allowed to satisfy some desires that human beings in general might be expected to have (e.g., they cannot marry or travel or stop work)" and they "do not have certain other desires or aspirations which others have *in those historical circumstances*," we can conclude that their desires are a product of the political regime they live under and negatively impugned as such (*IBWD*, 89).[46]

Most readers will agree with Williams's judgments of these cases, but it is hard to see what broader lessons this imparts, especially as Williams notes that the "happy slaves" case is a "rather objectionable fantasy" (*IBWD*, 89). His remarks about race and gender have a more palpable basis in contemporary politics, but the fact that they are "easy cases" suggests that their significance for our grasp of the underlying theoretical issues at play may be slim.[47]

Williams's fullest discussion of these concerns occurs in *Truth and Truthfulness* when he articulates his version of a critical theory test. As a first articulation of how we might think about the critical theory test, he suggests the following: "Suppose that of two parties in the society, one is advantaged over the other, in particular with respect to power; and suppose that there is a story which is taken to legitimate this distribution, a story which is at least professed by the advantaged party and is generally accepted by the disadvantaged; and suppose that the basic cause of the fact that the disadvantaged accept the story, and hence the system, is the power of the advantaged party: then the fact that they accept the system does not actually legitimate it, and *pro tanto* the distribution is unjust" (*TT*, 221). Williams also notes that if the story is not "at least professed" by the advantaged, this can be regarded as a case of enforced false-consciousness. The more philosophically interesting and politically realistic cases are those in which both the advantaged and the disadvantaged accept the story and manipulation may not be intentional or its methods too blatant.

Drawing on Raymond Geuss's argument in *The Idea of a Critical Theory*, Williams insists that we must approach these questions contextually, rather than in the transcendental (quasi-Kantian) terms favored by theorists such as Habermas.[48] He proposes the following test for the beliefs held by disadvantaged groups: "If they were to understand properly how they came to hold this belief, would they give it up?" (*TT*, 227). This helps us avoid excessively labeling too many coercive orders illegitimate, as we do not have to include all beliefs that result from the exercise of political power (such as content children learn at school) (*IBWD*, 89n19). Yet he recognizes an ambiguity regarding the "understand properly" clause: "If we are supposing that the background is simply these people's current set of beliefs, then almost anything will pass the test . . . [while] if we suppose, on the other hand, an entirely external frame of reference, then nothing very distinctive is achieved by the test" (*TT*, 227). For this reason, he claims that we must start with people's current beliefs but can envisage a process of criticism where reflection on the formation of beliefs can lead to repudiation.

Williams thus sketches a four-step process (*TT*, 227–29). The disadvantaged initially believe

1. The distribution of powers and advantages in the system is basically just.

They then reflect and acknowledge that

2. They believe (1) only because members of the more powerful party (call them the instructors) give them appropriate training.

In making this claim, Williams says that we assume that questions concerning the justice of the social system have arisen but that, by and large, its members endorse (1). Williams claims that we can also assume that almost everyone in the society recognizes (2) in some form. With this in mind, he argues that the disadvantaged can now reflect that

3. It is only if (1) is true that the instructors are in a sound position to claim that (1) is true: the basis of their authority comes from the system itself.

Hence, the disadvantaged will recognize that "one way or another . . . the justice of the system, the authority of the instructors, and hence their own reasons for accepting the justice of the system all hang together." They can then ask "if there are any independent ways of assessing the instructors' authority" that might determine whether it is "more or less likely that they have got it right" (*TT*, 228).

This can yield the thought that

4. There are perfectly good explanations of the instructors' belief in their own authority. This means, granted (3), that there are good explanations of their teaching (1) that do not imply that (1) is true.

Thus, in contrast to the Platonic and Kantian traditions, which involve the idea that there is an external means by which we can establish "the truth about justice and other such matters," Williams argues that this process can make sense in negative terms because it uses the "weak" assumption, granted (3) and (4), that the "processes of instruction do *not* have the authority that is claimed for them" (*TT*, 229). He consequently claims that the disadvantaged may come to realize that they accept the instructors' legitimation claims only because it is in the instructors' interest that they do so. If this happens, the legitimation story will no longer make sense to the disadvantaged, who will begin to recognize their domination.

Williams's account is sketchy and difficult to evaluate for this reason.[49] However, I believe that, depending on how we interpret the four-step process, Williams's critical theory test will either impugn any society marked by significant power/advantage asymmetries, regardless of how subjects have formed beliefs about those orders' legitimacy, or merely impugn the "easy cases"—orders marked by egregious rationalizations of disadvantage that Williams claims are "false or by everyone's standards irrelevant" (*IBWD*, 7). In this sense, the critical theory test will likely either be overinclusive or reach surprisingly modest conclusions and fail to challenge the legitimacy of a wide range of orders exhibiting inequities in political power and social advantage that seemingly concern Williams and trouble many contemporary realists.

Of central importance is the idea that if the disadvantaged do not have an "independent way" of assessing the instructors' authority, they can reasonably suspect that nothing other than their training gives them reason to "accept what the instructors tell them about the justice of the system" (*TT*, 229). This highlights an issue of great significance: what kinds of independent ways of assessing the instructors' authority does Williams have in mind? At one point, Williams distinguishes between priests, whose claims to have access to an esoteric source of knowledge will likely be unmasked by the critical theory test, and teachers of mathematics or geography, whose claims will not. The salient difference is that in the former case, subjects who seek to uncover independent means of affirming the priests' authority will find none, while there are few reasons to believe teachers of mathematics or geography "would teach these things unless there was a good chance they were true" and "the teaching itself will have suggested, at least in outline, ways in which people may come to know mathematical or geographical truths other than being taught them" (*TT*, 229).

However, in the political situations Williams is concerned with, the advantaged do have reasons to teach things even if they were not true, as doing so helps secure their advantage. If this suspicion is itself sufficient to show that "these particular processes of instruction do *not* have the authority that is claimed for them" (*TT*, 229), then it seems that the critical theory test will impugn all regimes that perpetuate significant power inequalities. In such orders, the disadvantaged ex hypothesi have reason to suspect their instruction.

This is problematic. If all regimes that evince inequalities in power and advantage are denounced, it is hard to endorse Williams's claim that he is not simply "assuming it to be necessarily unjust that power should be unequally distributed" (*TT*, 223). In addition, a test that generates such strong conclusions sits uneasily with Williams's wider political thought. If the critical theory test results in the conclusion that nearly all states, past and present, have been illegitimate orders of manipulation, given the inequalities they sustain or sustained, this suggests that legitimacy is a utopian standard that no political orders will actually meet, cutting directly against the thrust of Williams's realist insistence on legitimacy as the achievable first goal of nascent political order.

Williams cannot have intended the critical theory test to have these implications. In "Human Rights and Relativism," he explicitly states it is possible that, for example, societies ordered around theocratic conceptions of government, with their inevitable power inequalities, will not necessarily be impugned by the critical theory principle: "We may see the members of this society as jointly caught up in a set of beliefs which regulate their lives and which are indeed unsound, but which are shared in ways that move society further away from the paradigm of unjust coercion" (*IBWD*, 71). It is thus clear that condemning a system based on the suggestion that instruction serves the interests of the powerful, as well as the view that this suspicion is *sufficient* to impugn the system, is problematic. Simply put, this would ensure that the critical theory test indicts too many regimes.[50]

A more charitable reading of the critical theory test suggests that Williams is advocating the idea that we can criticize regimes marked by inequalities in power and advantage by mobilizing "the values of truth in a distinctive political interest" (*TT*, 220). On this basis, Paul Sagar suggests that Williams ultimately advocates a "truth-focused method of internal critical evaluation." According to Sagar, what Williams means when he refers to an independent way of assessing instructors' authority is simply whether we have reasons to think that their claims should "be taken as true."[51] This implies that so long as processes of instruction are sufficiently truthful, they will not be impugned, but if they rest on falsehoods, which clearly serve the interests of the advantaged at the expense of the disadvantaged, they will be.

This reading of the critical theory test is certainly less problematic than the one floated earlier. However, in comparison to the aims of much traditional critical theory, it delivers very modest conclusions about when the acceptance of a legitimation story can itself be regarded as a mere expression of the very power relations it is supposed to legitimate. To explain why, it is helpful to take a quick detour through some of the central arguments of *Truth and Truthfulness*. In this book, Williams develops a sustained critique of a group of thinkers he calls the "deniers," who endorse a style of thought that, in his view, "irresponsibly denies the possibility of truth altogether, waves its importance aside, or claims that all truth is 'relative' or suffers from some such disadvantage" (*TT*, 4–5). Against the deniers' outright rejection of truth, Williams lauds the fact that analytical philosophers of language have conclusively shown that "no-one can speak a language unless a large class of statements in that language are recognized to be true" (*TT*, 5). On this basis, there is, he claims, no difficulty in accounting for "everyday" or "plain" truths, such as the simple statement that I am writing this sentence in my kitchen on Wednesday morning.

However, Williams acknowledges that these truths do not touch on the deniers' suspicion about things such as "historical narrative, about social representations, about self-understanding, about psychological and political interpretation" (*TT*, 5). Nonetheless, Williams insists that the existence of plain truths does enable these forms of inquiry to be truthful. Thus, when discussing the complex relationship between truth and historical narrative, Williams grants that a historical interpretation cannot simply be a matter of recounting various facts about the past in a positivistic manner: "facts have to be discovered, and the interests that shape the narrative also shape the inquiry that discovers them" (*TT*, 240). But it does not follow that historical narratives cannot be responsive to the demands of truthfulness. The plain truths that historical narratives highlight are not created by our inquiries: though "facts are not individuated before any inquiry ... that does not mean that the inquiry creates them out of nothing" (*TT*, 257). Geuss employs the example of a constellation to explicate Williams's view of the relation between factual data and interpretation. An accurate exercise in interpretation must capture a series of truths, meaning that it cannot take any form it likes, but the overall picture that we draw with those truths is not predisposed.[52] In the case of historical narratives, Williams thus concludes that while we must accept that "there is no such thing as the 'truth' about the historical past ... this does not mean ... that there are not truths about the past, and it does not mean that interpretations, whatever they may be, need not be responsive to the demands of truthfulness" (*TT*, 258).

This account of interpretation has implications for our view of the truthfulness of the legitimation stories that underpin societies, which are marked by the kinds of inequalities that currently concern us. It suggests that a truth-focused critical theory principle may well undermine legitimation stories that rest on clear falsehoods, deceptions, and myths. For example, thinking in these terms is likely to suggest that rationalizations in terms of race and gender, no matter how widely accepted they are, approximate paradigmatic cases of unmediated coercion because they are untruthful and clearly serve the interests of the advantaged.[53]

However, as we have seen, Williams refers to these sorts of situations as "easy cases." In subtler cases, where legitimation stories do not rest on such egregious empirical falsehoods, but we nonetheless suspect that instructors may problematically benefit at the expense of the disadvantaged, it is hard to see how the kind of truthfulness invoked by Williams's account of interpretation will help us determine whether the acceptance of the system is itself the result of coercive power. For example, at one point in his discussion of these issues, Williams notes that people who attempt to justify forms of present economic inequality no longer invoke, as they traditionally may have done, essentialist differences between men and women or the contrived character traits of the professional and working classes. Rather, they claim either that the economic and social institutions that generate these inequalities are more efficient than their alternatives or that society benefits from the trickle-down effects (and so on) (*TT*, 224). Imagine that the disadvantaged in such societies generally accept these justifications of their plight; "they grumble about it quite a lot ... but in the end they accept it, they bring up their children to accept it, and so on" (*TT*, 222). Will their acceptance be impugned by the critical theory test?

This is the kind of political case that many critical theorists seek to impugn, but, in my view, a truth-focused method of Williams's sort is unlikely to vindicate such claims. To be sure, many commentators hold that when justifications of inequality are "generally accepted" by disadvantaged subjects, this is evidence of the utter pervasiveness of neoliberal ideology. But others, of different political persuasions, contest this analysis, and some of them provide reasoned arguments in support of their position. I do not want to deny that we may have reason to hold that, in the final instance, the former analysis condemning the acceptance of economic equality as itself evidence of the power of the advantaged may be more adequate than the latter. But most of the time when we are confronted with these kinds of debates about the acceptability of inequality, we cannot reasonably claim that anyone who thinks the opposite is simply insensitive to the plain or everyday truths that Williams argues that truthful forms of social inquiry seek to make sense of. It is more plausible (and in my view, politically responsible) to see the criticisms of neoliberal ideology as substantive moves in ongoing political disputes. As such, we ought to accept that reasonable people will disagree about the adequacy of such exercises in political analysis for principled or intellectual reasons and not simply because it is either in their interest or in the interest of the society's most powerful members. In such cases, it is, therefore, very hard to see how a truth-focused method of internal evaluation will reveal that a widespread belief in the acceptability of such economic arrangements is best regarded as a way of sustaining the domination of the powerful. In actual fact, Williams's rendering of the critical theory principle suggests that it is difficult to sustain critiques of neoliberal ideology that take this form.

Clearly, the foregoing argument cannot claim to illustrate decisively that Williams's critical theory test is able to guide our judgment of "subtler cases" because the generalizability of the considerations I have raised is unclear. However, it leads me to suspect that when we leave easy cases that can be refuted on straightforward empirical grounds, the judgment that widespread belief in the legitimacy of the system is problematically formed requires one to endorse various politically and economically controversial positions. This is not something that should surprise political realists, but it suggests that mobilizing the values of truth will actually have quite modest ramifications for our view of which political orders the critical theory principle will impugn.[54]

My own sense is that in more subtle cases, the claim that a belief is produced by the very power it is supposed to justify is pretty resistant to theoretical vindication. Moreover, when we assume that if people came to correctly understand how their beliefs were formed, they would realize that these beliefs do not serve their interests and are therefore suspect, we are required to make some substantive, and therefore controversial, judgments about their "real" interests. The extent to which we can do this without adopting an "outside" perspective on the societies that we examine is unclear. At the very least, if we are to stay true to the spirit of Williams's ethics, we will have to operate with a very minimalist understanding of people's universal interests. (This is another reason to believe that a critical theory principle of Williams's sort will inevitably generate less radical conclusions about the legitimacy of regimes than one might initially suppose.)

Beyond this, we may simply have to engage in various kinds of comparative analysis. For example, it would be a relevant independent way to assess training by examining how a similar training process characterizes other current or past societies without the same power asymmetries or by inspecting whether the training encouraged and enabled significant social mobility across advantaged and disadvantaged groups.[55] However, such judgments are notoriously difficult to come to and often require one to take sides in a number of controversial, substantive issues on which people who are committed to truthfulness will and do disagree.

My argument in this section does not necessarily undermine Williams's account of legitimacy or derail his commitment to the liberalism of fear. However, it should lead us to regard with some skepticism his claim that the critical theory principle "is one of liberalism's most powerful weapons" (*TT*, 220). It certainly can be powerful, but only in a rather limited range of cases. Whether one considers this a deep problem for Williams's political thought ultimately depends on what one hoped his critical theory principle might reveal. There is probably limited scope for denying the legitimacy of many political orders marked by various forms inequality and disadvantage in terms of the critical theory principle alone; applying the standards of truthfulness are likely to only get you so far. Much of the time, we may have to conclude that such societies are legitimate, even if we find them disagreeable.

Conclusion

In chapter 2, I argued that Berlin's value pluralism generates the recognition, contra Berlin's own moralistic declarations about the nature of political theory, that our normative claims about politics must be sensitive to what is unique about politics as a practice that is distinct from morality. As will be clear from the argument of this chapter, even though I have raised some concerns about his critical theory test, I believe that Williams's realist conception of legitimation is a promising way to develop this insight.

It is undeniable that Williams's analysis of why liberalism is worthy of our continued allegiance takes place at an exceedingly high level of generality. A conclusive defense of liberal politics in the terms his work posits would need to display the kind of detailed involvement with history and the social sciences that he counsels but which his political essays do not deliver (*PHD*, 156). However, the big advantage of thinking about these issues in the terms that Williams postulates is that we can avoid having to see our commitment to liberalism as a "triumph of moral understanding" (*TT*, 264). There is, therefore, reason to hope that some of our commitments can stand up to reflection without requiring us to think about politics and morality in the way that Williams's work in moral philosophy forecloses.

Conclusion

Williams was once asked about his motives for doing philosophy. He replied by invoking Hampshire's distinction between two impulses that have historically driven philosophers: curiosity and salvation. He then pregnantly remarked, "I am not into salvation."[1] Neither were Berlin or Hampshire. This book has explained why all three were skeptical of the idea that philosophy might definitively answer the question of how one should live or identify a timeless moral answer to the question of how our political societies should be organized. As a result, their work suggests that the central questions of politics should concern responding to and managing conflict and disagreement in the absence of a consensus on substantive principles of morality.[2]

My discussion of Berlin, Hampshire, and Williams has not taken the form of a defense of a philosophical position that amalgamates the best features of their work while discarding those elements that are problematic. The attempt to extract some kind of shared doctrine from their work in this way, and to illustrate the advantages it has over other doctrines, would be deeply artificial. Despite various shared concerns and similarities, key differences exist between Berlin, Hampshire, and Williams that should not be overlooked. To this end, rather than concluding this book by trying to sketch out and defend some kind of Berlin-Hampshire-Williams master view or recapitulating my arguments about the respective merits and shortcomings of their work, I do three things. First, I highlight three outstanding issues that those who are attracted to the central elements of Berlin's, Hampshire's, and Williams's moral and political thought should address going forward. Second, I elucidate how their work challenges a particular understanding of the "autonomy" of the political proposed by some contemporary realist thinkers, which is not only philosophically problematic but also a source of misunderstanding about the nature of the realist alternative to political moralism. Finally, I explain how my reading of Berlin, Hampshire, and Williams undermines the common refrain that the contemporary realist current is solely negative or critical in orientation.

Future Directions

The foregoing chapters strongly vindicate the claim that Berlin's, Hampshire's, and Williams's work is a vital resource for the burgeoning realist movement in political theory and that several of their commitments align well with, and provide much needed philosophical ballast for, a liberalism of fear.[3] There is much to commend in Berlin's, Hampshire's, and Williams's attempts to detail how a set of negative moral universals are compatible with their skepticism about philosophical ethics at the philosophical level. However, it is clear that those who are sympathetic to their moral and political thought, and who wish to take it forward in political theory, need to reflect hard about the contemporary realities of power and powerlessness and fear and desperation in ways that they did not. While many of the evils that the liberalism of fear traditionally focuses on arise in the domestic political contexts that Berlin, Hampshire, and Williams were chiefly concerned with, as intimated in chapter 6, it is undeniable that many of the other obstinate sources of fear and powerlessness that now confront us can only be made sense of if we think in a moral global vein and address the issues of geopolitics, migration, the inequities of global capitalism, and so on.

The work of Berlin, Hampshire, and Williams does not offer any straightforward recommendations as to how to proceed in this respect. Nonetheless, there are reasons to hope that their general approach to moral and political questions might play an important role in helping us progressively make sense of these issues. Saliently, it suggests that we ought to be skeptical of the idea that such problems can profitably be approached in the way that so many current theories of cosmopolitan justice proceed: that is, by thinking that the task of political philosophy is to articulate substantive principles, usually extracted from domestic politics and applied to the global stage, and to see international political institutions as the mere means by which these principles might be realized at large. Instead, the nonutopian and largely negative approach Berlin, Hampshire, and Williams champion enjoins us to pay attention to the concrete experiences of the powerless and fearful and to be sensitive to the inevitability of moral reminders and political opposition in response to proposed courses of action that seek to mitigate extant cruelties. Their work also rightly suggests that we must think about these issues in political and not just moral terms—that we must reflect in the kinds of "impure" ways I highlighted in chapter 2 and ask how we can work with existing patterns of behavior, instead of insisting that every rational agent has reason to acknowledge the authority of a set of substantive principles that demand an extraordinary transformation of human beings' basic moral sentiments and interests. It also indicates that we cannot simply imagine away the existence of nation-states and their particular interests.[4] The current literature on global justice often seems to regard the invocation that we must take these issues seriously as a pernicious way of excusing the status quo, rather than as a first step in making sense of it (and how we should act to improve it). The kind of approach to political theory that I have explored in this book is therefore likely to have something valuable to contribute to our understanding of these issues.

Additionally, while I have argued that Berlin's, Hampshire's, and Williams's work is an important corrective to much contemporary political theory that seeks to model a rational consensus on a shared ideal of the just society, it is imperative that those sympathetic to their moral and political thought attempt to make better sense of the set of distinctively political goods that their work suggests must be at the heart of any adequate understanding of the ethics of politics. Although Berlin's work on political judgment, Hampshire's attempt to articulate a negative conception of justice, and Williams's account of a realist standard of legitimacy are significant counters to the moralistic tendencies of mainstream political theory, there is considerable scope for more sustained philosophical reflection from a realist perspective on the nature of political goods like security and order and the value of political compromise. Incisive realist work on these issues will have to display a more institutional and concrete form than much of the existent realist literature currently exhibits.

Similarly, the lack of a serious analysis of representative democracy is a genuine lacuna that should be righted. Again, it is not hard to believe that a realist contribution to the contemporary literature on democratic theory would be very welcome. Key recent contributions to this literature in mainstream political philosophy[5] often seem to be addressing a form of political rule that is entirely different from the one actually experienced by democratic citizens.[6] They also bear little relationship to the form of political rule vividly described by contemporary political science.[7] Much normative philosophical work on democracy is thus worryingly vulnerable to critiques advanced by democracy skeptics like Jason Brennan.[8] We sorely need a more historically attuned and politically savvy defense of democratic politics that highlights the evils and cruelties that democratic politics has a real track record of averting, rather than attempting to articulate ever more refined elaborations of the particular moral principles that supposedly ground a commitment to democratic politics, but which no known democratic regime ever actually realizes.

Finally, it is vital that realists consider the kinds of issues that Hampshire draws attention to when he discusses the fallacy of false fixity if they are to escape the common suspicion that realism's nonutopianism is inevitably status quo–affirming. As I have shown, Williams, too, was cognizant of the importance of these concerns, even though his critical theory test is likely to generate quite modest conclusions. The task of unmasking social myths that constrain our sense of what is politically possible is ongoing and important for any approach claiming to articulate a set of normative political standards that enable us to evaluate our political arrangements and political conduct while avoiding the solaces of ideal theory.

Again, it is not obvious how those sympathetic to the body of work that I have examined in this book can think in these terms. Nonetheless, one point is worth noting: that rather than seeking some kind of grand, master diagnosis in the nebulous forces of neoliberalism or Western hegemony, we would do better to adopt the skeptical spirit of Berlin, Hampshire, and Williams and engage in more a piecemeal or pointed analysis that is resistant to overencompassing narratives.

Ethics in Realist Thought

The strand of moral and political thought that I have focused on exemplifies a nuanced view of the role that ethical judgments play in politics that calls into question the more crude renderings of the realist claim that political theorists must acknowledge the autonomy of political considerations. While Berlin, Hampshire, and Williams problematize the idea that it is helpful to see political theory as a kind of applied moral philosophy, their "antimoralism" does not lead them to refrain from making ethical judgments about politics. Some fellow "realists" have suggested that this is problematic.

In the introduction, I touched on Enzo Rossi and Matt Sleat's distinction between "strong" and "weak" variations of the realist claim concerning the autonomy of politics from morality. As Rossi and Sleat parse it, "weak" realist approaches, like the ones explored in this book, recognize that ethical or moral considerations have some kind of role in normative political theory while claiming that it is "important to appreciate the manner in which politics remains a distinct sphere of human activity, with its own concerns, pressures, ends and constraints which cannot be reduced to ethics (nor law, economics, religion, etc.)." In contrast, the "strong" view holds that "it is possible to derive normative political judgments from specifically political values—a position resting on the view that not all values are moral values, plus the more controversial claim that such political values can and should guide politics, whereas moral values are ill-suited to that task."[9]

Are there any reasons to hold that strong versions of realism are preferable to the kind of weaker versions that this book has addressed? I do not think so. Hampshire and Williams articulate standards of evaluation—the principle of adversary argument and the basic legitimation demand—that are cognizant of the "circumstances of politics" and avoid the colonization of political philosophy by moral philosophy. Yet as I have illustrated, some ethical or moral considerations inevitably play a role in determining our judgments of whether these principles are adequately satisfied in concrete circumstances. Williams is especially forthright about this, claiming that "there can be local applications of moral ideas in politics, and these may take, on a limited scale, an enactment or structural form" (*IBWD*, 8). That moral ideas will play such a role follows from the fact that when we ask ourselves what makes sense as an intelligible order of political authority, we partake in "first order discussions using our political, moral, social, interpretative, and other concepts" (*IBWD*, 11). Hampshire also explicitly recognizes that the arguments made in political debate will often appeal to conventional practices and invoke moral principles and substantive principles of justice. This is simply part and parcel of politics.

Neither Hampshire nor Williams hold that such moral ideas will necessarily (or indeed should) trump other salient considerations or that they can fully determine our political judgments. They also insist that we cannot claim the kind of authority for these moral ideas that their, and Berlin's, shared pessimism about the power of moral philosophy rules out. But so long as these conditions are met, it is hard to see why we should want our political judgments to take the "strong" form adduced by Rossi and Sleat. Rejecting the suggestion that political philosophy is a form of applied moral philosophy does not commit one to thinking that ethical considerations have *no role* to play in politics.

Rossi and Sleat refer to Geuss's work as an example of "strong" realism. At one point, Geuss does indeed claim that "ethics is usually dead politics: the hand of a victor in some past conflict reaching out to try to extend its grip on the present and the future."[10] This suggests that ethical claims are really expressions of prior political struggles—nothing more and nothing less. This quote is also invoked by Rossi to support the view that "purely normative political theory" is best understood "as (an at least potential) expression of ideology."[11] I take it that this idea—that all ethical assertions ought to be regarded as ideological in the pejorative sense—is the core motivation behind endorsing a "strong" rather than "weak" understanding of realism. The problem with this, though, is that it is hard to see why we should consider Geuss's claim that "ethics is usually dead politics" as anything but melodrama.[12] Even if some ethical or moral claims are power plays, it is hard to understand why, at least in the absence of some grand philosophical narrative of a Marxian variety—the kind of narrative that Berlin, Hampshire, and Williams would regard with deep suspicion—we ought to see all such claims as nothing but that. In this sense, the basic motivation for supporting "strong" rather than "weak" versions of realism is unclear. Accordingly, there is little reason to support considering the "strong" stance as an attractive way of developing the core realist insight that politics cannot be straightforwardly ordered by moral norms.

Geuss also says that we cannot understand politics until we take the "ethical dimension" of political action seriously. He recognizes that political actors are "generally pursuing certain conceptions of the 'good'" and that if we are to understand what they are doing, we must pay attention to their "value-judgements about the good, the permissible, the attractive, the preferable, that which is to be avoided at all costs."[13] If this is interpreted in "strong" terms, it seems that we should merely observe these judgments—as we might observe the fact that it is Friday—and not bother to interrogate, scrutinize, and possibly affirm them. This is a gratuitous narrowing of the reflective questions that we should ask about such judgments.[14]

Instead of endorsing the reductivism at the heart of "strong" realism, it makes more sense to consider our ethical convictions in the way that Berlin, Hampshire, and Williams explicitly urge us to. That is, to abandon the idea that these beliefs are the "autonomous products of moral reason" rather than "another product of historical conditions." Yet, as Williams argues, even if we think in such terms, the correct response is not to "throw our political convictions away" or to "stare" at them with "ironical amazement" but to think hard about whether they nonetheless stand up to reflection (*IBWD*, 12–13). There is, consequently, a sense in which strong realism is counterfactually moralist: it implies that if moral and political convictions cannot be seen as the autonomous products of moral reason, then all invocations of principle are mere exercises of power waiting to be unmasked. This seems to me to make an error similar, albeit in reverse, to G. A. Cohen's insistence that unless philosophical reflection leads us to a set of a priori principles that are true across all possible worlds, we are merely wrangling over rules of regulation.[15] Just as we should reject the idea that good political judgment is a matter of (inadequately) trying to imitate a set of pure and timeless foundational moral principles in the cave, we should also reject the idea that all invocations of principle made within the cave are more or less well-disguised plays for power.

CONCLUSION

In this sense, Berlin's, Hampshire's, and Williams's work suggests that the challenge is not to find a vantage point from which we can assess politics without invoking moral or ethical considerations but to think realistically about what kinds of ethical claims, and what kind of normative political judgments, it makes sense for us to affirm in a fully disenchanted world. Realists need to be realistic about the fact that politics is replete with ethical judgments and that any realist political position that engages in the normative evaluation of politics will be as well, at least to some extent.

Moreover, the vast majority of the deepest and most engaging works of realist political theory are not neutral on some basic questions in moral philosophy but often directly shaped by a theorist's attitude toward them, a fact that should not be obscured by the realist invocation that we treat politics as politics rather than morality. In this book, I have tried to meet this demand by explaining how Berlin's, Hampshire's, and Williams's political thought is clearly motivated by their moral philosophy, even though it is not merely a programmatic application of their ethical views to politics (precisely because they do not articulate the kinds of ethical "theory" that can be applied in such a way). Commentators who interpret realists as merely urging us to take seriously various factual constraints that call into question the overambitious aspirations of mainstream political theory suppress these deeper motivations. This results in narrow-minded misunderstandings of what engages many realist thinkers.[16]

With these concerns in mind, I also think that we ought to be somewhat skeptical of realist approaches that claim to be neutral on these questions. For example, Andrew Sabl has recently suggested that some versions of realism can sidestep such "foundational questions" and instead think about politics solely in first-order terms.[17] Yet, shortly after saying this, Sabl explains that thinking in exclusively first-order terms is possible because politics can be regarded "as in part, a science." Thus, Sabl's liberal realism is motivated by the idea that we learn a great deal about politics without engaging in ideal theory because "human actors can, over time, develop institutions that are ever better suited to promoting their various ends, and can devise strategies ever more likely to bring about and improve those institutions."[18]

Sabl's distinctive view of liberal realism is stimulating and worth taking seriously.[19] However, even if it does not explicitly address such foundational questions, there are good reasons to deny that it is neutral among competing answers to these foundational questions. In particular, it is hard to see how it does not rest on the claim that there is a basic uniformity of human interests and that these interests are determinate enough to guide our political judgments in the ways that Sabl describes. In this sense, Sabl's account ultimately seems to rely on an optimistic rendering of some kind of Humean ethical position.[20] If that is the case, then conceiving of politics as the kind of a science Sabl alludes to is contentious on both first-order and second-order grounds.[21]

It is clearly not reasonable to insist that every work of realist theory should begin by outlining its basic commitments about ethics and morality, and that is not what I am urging, not least because doing so would get in the way of potentially engaging work. However, keeping in mind that many prescriptive realist visions will not be neutral on the kinds of issues that Sabl's realist liberalism claims to evade is important if we are to grasp the nature of the claims that realist thinkers make.[22]

On the Alleged Negativity of Political Realism

In the introduction, I noted William Galston's remarks that it is not apparent if realism is best seen in "critical" and "cautionary" terms—as a "warning against liberal utopianism"—or as a "coherent affirmative alternative" to political moralism and ideal theory.[23] It should be clear that the strand of realist thought I have examined does not merely offer a criticism of political moralism and ideal theory. I have illustrated that Berlin, Hampshire, and Williams articulate views of how we might theorize about politics in ways that are not merely concerned with pointing out errors of ideal theory and political moralism. Hampshire and Williams certainly suggest more in the way of a positive realist approach than Berlin does, but in all three cases, criticisms and warnings are far from exhaustive of their contributions to political theory.

Nor is it true that their work is solely cautionary. Berlin is admirably clear on this point when he remarks that "men do not live only by fighting evils. They live by positive goals, individual and collective" (*L*, 93). In a number of his most important essays, he consequently expresses his view that wide-ranging negative liberty is the kind of positive goal that is worthy of our endorsement and defense in the modern world. Although Hampshire is principally concerned with articulating the features of a negative conception of justice, he also recognizes that human beings are moved by visions of social justice and conceptions of the good, as he himself was. Likewise, Williams insists "that the conditions of LEG [legitimacy] in modern states present a progressive project" (*IBWD*, 17). One of his most interesting recent readers plausibly argues that pretty stringent forms of egalitarian politics may be required "now and around here" if political orders are to meet the basic legitimation demand.[24]

Yet, when Berlin, Hampshire, and Williams think in this vein, they adopt an intellectual stance that is very different from the idealism of mainstream political philosophy. Rather than seeking to guide our political behavior on the basis of a hopeful sense of the moral values and harmonious social relations that would be realized if human beings were morally well motivated, they urge us to concentrate on what people are actually like and what is actually likely to move them to act. Thinking in this way is not aided by imagining a purportedly realistic utopia in which all citizens act in accordance with an alleged sense of justice. Instead, it requires us to focus on the world as we find it and to take seriously the actual dispositions and motivations people display.

Berlin's, Hampshire's, and Williams's work in moral and political philosophy also counsels us to recognize that it is deceptive to suppose that these positive views are either seamlessly derived from the bare conditions of moral reasoning, the deliverances of a compelling theoretical account of how our political societies must be rightly organized according to moral terms, or baked into the necessities of stable political coexistence. In most cases, Berlin, Hampshire, and Williams also claim that it is specious to suggest we have *chosen* our convictions. As I have illustrated at various junctures in this book, the recognition that we simply have not chosen (most of) our beliefs consequently requires the kinds of questions we ask of our convictions to take a different form to that assumed in most mainstream political philosophy.

Nonetheless, one might question how consoling the work of Berlin, Hampshire, and Williams is and deny that their approach to moral and political philosophy has the potential to affirm all that we need political philosophy to affirm. This anxiety is not perverse. Given their skepticism about systematic moral and political "theory," the alternative ways of approaching politics that Berlin, Hampshire, and Williams advocate do not result in the kind of normative theory that can claim to exhaustively guide our political judgments about what should be done here and now. All three stress that prudence and judgment are ineliminable in politics, and their historical sensitivity leads them to regard as naively hubristic the idea that the prescriptive or evaluative judgments that we endorse will necessarily persist long into the future. They are similarly resolute in their belief that we should have little truck with the idea that meticulous philosophical argument might conclusively deliver a set of substantive principles that political adversaries can be expected to concur with.

In this respect, as in many others, they diverge from Rawls and those who take up the Rawlsian project. Rawls famously claims that philosophical abstraction offers a way in which we can continue public discussion when serious political disagreements have arisen because it enables us to "ascend to get a clearer and uncluttered view of its roots."[25] This is one of the reasons why Rawls is hopeful that our political disputes may be soluble through appeal to a set of shared ideals that we can build into an idealized account of justice that reasonable people will agree on.[26] Berlin, Hampshire, and Williams do not share this hope. One of the most important lessons they impart is that we should not be surprised that some people will fervently disagree with us about questions of political value for reasons that we may consider ill-founded, unreasonable, and even abhorrent. Their work also suggests that there is little reason to be optimistic about the possibility of arguing one's political opponents into a different political view. This skepticism concerning the limits of political philosophy in these respects can seem stark. But it should only generate despair if one sees it as the negation of a reasonable expectation—and it is not at all obvious that it does that.

In any case, I hope that this book might assuage worries about the overwhelmingly critical nature of realism like those Galston voices in at least two ways. First, I have shown that Hampshire and Williams offer competing first-order accounts of how we should think about politics in a realist key. These are not solely critical visions but positive attempts to theorize about politics without merely seeing political theory as a kind of applied moral philosophy. While I have been somewhat skeptical of Hampshire's minimalist proceduralism, I have argued that Williams's distinctively political account of legitimation is more coherent and attractive than has been acknowledged.

Second, I have argued that thinking more realistically about ethics and politics in the terms that Berlin, Hampshire, and Williams advocate is vital if we are to honestly reflect on whether our political convictions can be endorsed in a disenchanted world. As I hope to have illustrated, elements of Berlin's, Hampshire's, and Williams's work can be read in a way that is conducive to thinking through what this might involve. To be sure, approaching the question of the relation between reflection and commitment by drawing on the salient features of Berlin's, Hampshire's, and Williams's work issues a pretty chastened view of what philosophical inquiry might deliver in this respect. Nonetheless, it does hold out the possibility of achieving a more realistic understanding of some of our ethical and political commitments that is not thoroughly debunking and, in a sense, vindicatory. This is not everything that mainstream contemporary political philosophy promises. But, in the end, we would do well to remember that it is not nothing.

Acknowledgments

I have incurred significant debts while writing this book. First, I would like to thank Paul Sagar and Matt Sleat. I discuss political theory more often with them than anyone else, and they both commented on this work with characteristic enthusiasm and encouragement. Their sharp remarks on matters of substance and style have improved nearly every page. I am extremely grateful to them both for their support.

Second, I am indebted to everyone who came to the workshop on the manuscript held in Sheffield in July 2018. First, I would like to thank my departmental colleagues: Alasdair Cochrane, Andrew Leary, Indra Mangule, Clara Sandelind, Matt Sleat, Luke Ulas, and Peter Verovsek. Sheffield is a great place to be a political theorist. My fellow Sheffield theorists are not only smart and interesting but lovely people to hang out with. Three external participants—Derek Edyvane, David Owen, and Mark Philp—also kindly agreed to take part. Mark's comments on the chapters on Berlin were philosophically sophisticated and politically acute, which will not surprise anyone who has read his own contributions to realist political theory. I benefited hugely from his comments and learn something new from his work every time I engage with it. Derek not only helped me see connections between different elements of Hampshire's thought that I would otherwise have missed but also robustly defended Hampshire from any and every criticism of his work that I raised. This has (I hope) made me a much less complacent commentator than I would otherwise have been. I have not acknowledged every single point where Derek has improved my discussion of Hampshire because I have simply lost count. David's knowledge of moral and political philosophy is staggering. He thoughtfully commented on the chapters on Williams, urging me to stress the shortcomings and limitations of Williams's work alongside its salutary features and to think about the broader implications it has for moral and political philosophy.

The portion of this project that addresses Bernard Williams began in the Government Department at the London School of Economics. I am indebted to Paul Kelly, my official supervisor, and the late Geoff Hawthorn, who essentially served as an unofficial second supervisor, for their advice and guidance. I often still reflect on Geoff's kindness in implicitly taking on that role, and taking it so seriously, when he had no obligation to.

Thanks must also go to the following people for reading and commenting on specific parts of this book and earlier pieces of mine, as well as for influencing my thinking on these topics in conversation: the late Carlo Argenton, Mat Coakley, Katrin Flikschuh, Liz Frazer, Leigh Jenco, Chandran Kukathas, Holly Lawford-Smith, Pietro Maffettone, Enzo Rossi, David Schmidtz, and Lea Ypi. I must also thank audiences at the University of Münster, the University of Stirling, and the National University of Singapore, where I presented some of the arguments included here. Rob Jubb deserves special thanks for his comments on the introduction and conclusion, and for many exchanges on the themes addressed in this book over the years. Henry Hardy answered numerous questions about Berlin and also kindly commented on chapters 1 and 2, pushing me to think and write more clearly. Simon Hope and Nakul Krishna also commented on chapter 5, which was invaluable.

I know I am not alone in often finding the peer review process frustrating. Happily, in this instance it worked exactly as I hoped it would. My editor, Chuck Myers, secured two exemplary reports. Both anonymous reviewers read the manuscript with care and attention, and their comments were intelligent, perceptive, thoughtful, and constructive. I am still blown away by their sheer professionalism and would like to thank them for taking such care to explain precisely how they thought the manuscript could be improved. Likewise, I am extremely thankful to Chuck for his support for this project and to Alicia Sparrow and everyone else at the University of Chicago Press for helping bring the book to completion. Elizabeth Ellingboe also deserves huge thanks for her expert copyediting.

Finally, my most serious debts. First, I must thank my parents and siblings for their love and unwavering support over the years. Second, it is simply inconceivable that I could have written this book without Kaj's love, encouragement, partnership, and tolerance. Since I began working on this book we've had a daughter and a son—Amber and Archie. I want to end by sending my love to them both and to Kaj for all that she does for us.

Some parts of this work have appeared previously. An earlier version of a small portion of the introduction appeared in "How to Do Realistic Political

Theory (and Why You Might Want To)," *European Journal of Political Theory* 16, no. 3 (July 2017): 284–86. Earlier parts of chapters 5 and 6 appeared, respectively, as "Contingency, Confidence, and Liberalism in the Political Thought of Bernard Williams," *Social Theory and Practice* 40, no. 4 (October 2014): 545–69, and "Bernard Williams and the Basic Legitimation Demand: A Defence," *Political Studies* 63, no. 2 (June 2015): 466–80. They are reproduced here by permission of the editors and publishers.

Notes

Introduction

1. William Galston, "Realism in Political Theory," *European Journal of Political Theory* 9, no. 4 (2010): 386.

2. Raymond Geuss, *Philosophy and Real Politics* (Princeton, NJ: Princeton University Press, 2008), 8.

3. For that complaint, see Colin Farrelly, "Justice in Ideal Theory: A Refutation," *Political Studies* 55, no. 4 (2007): 844–64, and Amartya Sen, "What Do We Want from a Theory of Justice?," *Journal of Philosophy* 103, no. 5 (2006): 215–38.

4. For these complaints, see Eva Erman and Niklas Moller, "Political Legitimacy in the Real Normative World," *British Journal of Political Science* 45, no. 1 (2015): 215–33; Laura Valentini, "Ideal vs. Non-ideal theory: A Conceptual Map," *Philosophy Compass* 7, no. 9 (2012): 654–64; and Jonathan Leader-Maynard and Alex Worsnip, "Is There a Distinctively Political Normativity?," *Ethics* 128, no. 4 (2018): 756–87.

5. John Rawls, *A Theory of Justice: Revised Edition* (Oxford: Oxford University Press, 1999), 3.

6. In terms that Jeremy Waldron has popularized, their work is therefore suitably cognizant of the "circumstances of politics": "the felt need among the members of a certain group for a common framework or decision or course of action on some matter, even in the face of disagreement about what that framework, decision, or action should be." Jeremy Waldron, *Law and Disagreement* (Oxford: Oxford University Press, 1999), 102.

7. Most significantly, alongside their various fellowships at All Souls, Berlin was elected Chichele Professor of Social and Political Theory at Oxford, where he was also the founding head of Wolfson College. He also served as president of the British Academy. Hampshire held professorships at University College London, Princeton, and Stanford and was warden of Wadham College, Oxford. Williams was Knightbridge Professor of Philosophy at the University of Cambridge, Monroe Deutsch Professor of Philosophy at the University of California, Berkeley, and White's Professor of Moral Philosophy at Oxford and served as provost of King's College, Cambridge.

8. For fuller discussions, see Michael Ignatieff, *Isaiah Berlin: A Life* (London: Vintage, 2000), and Arie Dubnov, *Isaiah Berlin: The Journey of a Jewish Liberal* (New York: Palgrave, 2012).

9. In 1966, the *Sunday Times* described the couple as "the New Left at its most able, generous and sometimes most eccentric." Quoted in Shirley Williams, *Climbing the Bookshelves: The Autobiography of Shirley Williams* (London: Virago, 2009), 137.

10. Williams chaired the 1979 Committee on Obscenity and Film Censorship and also sat on commissions examining the role of British private schools (1965–70), gambling (1976–78), and social justice (1993–94).

11. For such judgments, see, for example, William Galston, *Liberal Pluralism: The Implications of Value Pluralism for Political Theory* (Cambridge: Cambridge University Press, 2002), 5; John Kekes, *The Morality of Pluralism* (Princeton, NJ: Princeton University Press, 1993), 12; and Peter Lassman, *Pluralism* (Cambridge: Polity, 2011), 6–7.

12. "An Oxford Pessimist," *Daily Telegraph*, November, 20 1999, https://www.telegraph.co.uk/culture/4719061/An-Oxford-pessimist.html. Thanks to Nakul Krishna for drawing my attention to Nancy Cartwright's "Philosophy of Social Technology: Get on Board," *Proceedings and Address of the American Philosophical Association*, 89, no. 2 (2015): 98–116, which references the *Telegraph* article.

13. As is well known, Berlin and Hampshire, along with A. J. Ayer, J. L. Austin, Donald Macnabb, A. D. Woozley, and Donald MacKinnon, took part in the All Souls discussion group that is credited with instigating "Oxford Philosophy." (For Berlin's account of the discussion group, see *PI*, 108–9. For more detailed discussion, see Naomi Choi, "Berlin, Analytical Philosophy, and the Revival of Political Philosophy," in *The Cambridge Companion to Isaiah Berlin*, ed. Joshua Cherniss and Steven B. Smith [Cambridge: Cambridge University Press, 2018], 33–52.) While they both endorsed certain elements of "Oxford Philosophy," they also expressed serious misgivings with some of its more restrictive, and reductive, implications, especially its relationship with emotivism. One implication of this study is that while Berlin's and Hampshire's role in the formation of Oxford Philosophy should not be downplayed, their most important intellectual legacy is the kind of Oxford pessimism I am concerned with.

14. Enzo Rossi and Matt Sleat, "Realism in Normative Political Theory," *Philosophy Compass* 9, no. 10 (2014): 695.

15. Two review articles played an important role in bringing political realism to prominence in the field: Marc Stears, "Liberalism and the Politics of Compulsion," *British Journal of Political Science* 37, no. 3 (2007): 533–53, and Galston, "Realism in Political Theory."

16. See, for example, Raymond Geuss, "Did Williams Do Ethics?," *Arion* 19, no. 3 (2012): 141–62, and Janosch Prinz and Enzo Rossi, "Political Realism as Ideology Critique," *Critical Review of International Social and Political Philosophy* 20, no. 3 (2017): 348–65.

17. Julian Korab-Karpowicz, "Political Realism in International Relations," *Stanford Encyclopedia of Philosophy* (Summer 2018 edition), ed. Edward N. Zalta, https://plato.stanford.edu/archives/sum2018/entries/realism-intl-relations/.

18. For an excellent discussion of this point, see Alison McQueen, "The Case for Kinship: Classical Realism and Political Realism," in *Politics Recovered: Realist Thought in Theory and Practice*, ed. Matt Sleat (New York: Columbia University Press, 2018), 243–69.

19. As Mark Philp notes, "the range of human motivations that can be appealed to and elicited in politics cannot be limited a priori to self-interest and it would be a dramatically impoverished realism that assumed egoism as the sole motivation." Mark Philp, "Realism without Illusions," *Political Theory* 40, no. 5 (2012): 636.

20. Rossi and Sleat, "Realism in Normative Political Theory," 689.

21. For an exemplary illustration, see Mark Philp, *Political Conduct* (Cambridge, MA: Harvard University Press, 2007).

22. With this in mind, it is worth stressing that the body of work I focus on in this book does not attempt to offer the kind of "freestanding" political philosophy pursued by Rawls and many

contemporary scholars who work on public reason. For Rawls, *freestanding* is a term of art. He says that a theory of justice is freestanding—which is one feature of a "political" conception of justice (another term of art)—when it involves "so far as possible, no wider commitment to any doctrine." John Rawls, *Political Liberalism* (New York: Columbia University Press, 1996), 13. Rawls proceeds to develop this point with reference to his understanding of what makes a moral conception "general" and "comprehensive." These are also technical terms of Rawls's, and I do not discuss them here in detail. Suffice to say, Rawls's basic point is that a conception of justice is freestanding if it is not reliant on a set of a wider metaphysical, epistemological, or metaethical positions for its justification. (Thus, in the "Reply to Habermas," Rawls claims that his political liberalism "works entirely within the domain of the political" and does not "rely on anything outside it." Rawls, *Political Liberalism*, 374.)

On this view, Berlin's, Hampshire's, and Williams's political thought is unlikely to be classed as "freestanding" and relevantly "political" because it flows from various positions that these thinkers endorse in moral philosophy. Some of the time it is impossible to say, definitively, whether a particular piece of theirs, or a point that they are making, belongs to moral or political philosophy; but unless one is committed to the Rawlsian project, there is no reason to think that this precludes their work from being relevantly "political." For one thing, the body of work that I address in this book shows far greater sensitivity to various commonly understood "platitudes about politics" (to use Williams's formulation; *IBWD*, 13) than moralist political philosophy does, including of a late Rawlsian sort. Moreover, realists tend to be skeptical of the idea that we can offer a freestanding political theory anyway. Moreover, Berlin's, Hampshire's, and Williams's views on moral philosophy and ethics are well placed to offer an explanation, though by no means the only one, of why politics has the peculiar characteristics that realists insist moralist political philosophy overlooks or imagines away.

23. Raymond Geuss, "Thucydides, Nietzsche, and Williams," in *Outside Ethics* (Princeton, NJ: Princeton University Press, 2005), 223.

24. Think, for example, of Carl Schmitt's friend/enemy distinction in *The Concept of the Political: Expanded Edition*, trans. George Schwab (Chicago: University of Chicago Press, 2007).

25. For example, as when Williams remarks that "political difference is of the essence of politics, and political difference is a relation of opposition, rather than, in itself, a relation of intellectual and interpretative disagreement" (*IBWD*, 78).

26. Alison McQueen, *Political Realism in Apocalyptic Times* (Cambridge: Cambridge University Press, 2018), 10–11.

27. McQueen, *Political Realism in Apocalyptic Times*, 11.

28. Galston, "Realism in Political Theory," 396.

29. John Dunn, "Political Obligations and Political Possibilities," in *Political Obligation in its Historical Context: Essays in Political Theory* (Cambridge: Cambridge University Press, 1990), 196.

30. John Rawls's work can be read in such terms. Rawls, *Political Liberalism*, lx.

31. Galston, "Realism in Political Theory," 396.

32. In one of the most comprehensive discussions of ideal theory, Alan Hamlin and Zofia Stemplowska distinguish four ways of understanding the distinction between ideal and nonideal ways of doing political theory: (1) full vs. partial compliance, (2) idealization vs. abstraction, (3) fact-sensitivity vs. fact-insensitivity, and (4) perfect justice vs. local improvements. Alan Hamlin and Zofia Stemplowska, "Theory, Ideal Theory, and the Theory of Ideals," *Political Studies Review* 10, no. 1 (2012): 48–62. Yet nearly everyone agrees that Rawls is the originator of the debate;

see in particular his discussions in *A Theory of Justice* and *The Law of Peoples* (Cambridge, MA: Harvard University Press, 1999). Other key contributions include G. A. Cohen, *Rescuing Justice and Equality* (Cambridge, MA: Harvard University Press, 2008); David Estlund, "Human Nature and the Limits (if Any) of Political Philosophy," *Philosophy & Public Affairs* 39, no. 3 (2011): 207–37; Farrelly, "Justice in Ideal Theory"; Gerald Gaus, *The Tyranny of the Ideal: Justice in a Diverse Society* (Princeton, NJ: Princeton University Press, 2016); Robert Jubb, "The Tragedies of Non-ideal Theory," *European Journal of Political Theory* 11, no. 3 (2012): 229–46; David Miller, "Political Philosophy for Earthlings," in *Political Theory: Methods and Approaches*, ed. David Leopold and Marc Stears (Oxford: Oxford University Press, 2008), 29–48; David Miller, "A Tale of Two Cities; or, Political Philosophy as Lamentation," in *Justice for Earthlings: Essays in Political Philosophy* (Cambridge: Cambridge University Press, 2013), 228–49; Liam Murphy, *Moral Demands in Nonideal Theory* (Oxford: Oxford University Press, 2003); Onora O'Neill, *Towards Justice and Virtue* (Cambridge: Cambridge University Press, 1996); Ingrid Robeyns, "Ideal Theory in Theory and Practice," *Social Theory and Practice* 34, no. 3 (2008): 341–62; David Schmidtz, "Nonideal Theory: What It Is and What It Needs to Be," *Ethics* 121, no. 4 (2011): 772–96; Sen, "What Do We Want"; Amartya Sen, *The Idea of Justice* (London: Penguin, 2010); A. John Simmons, "Ideal and Nonideal Theory," *Philosophy & Public Affairs* 38, no. 1 (2010): 5–36; Zofia Stemplowska, "What's Ideal about Ideal Theory?," *Social Theory and Practice* 34, no. 3 (2008): 319–40; Zofia Stemplowska and Adam Swift, "Ideal and Nonideal Theory," in *The Oxford Handbook of Political Philosophy*, ed. David Estlund (Oxford: Oxford University Press, 2012), 373–92; Adam Swift, "The Value of Philosophy in Nonideal Circumstances," *Social Theory and Practice* 34, no. 3 (2008): 363–87; Laura Valentini, "On the Apparent Paradox of Ideal Theory," *Journal of Political Philosophy* 17, no. 3 (2009): 332–55; and Valentini, "Ideal vs. Non-ideal Theory." Finally, the Winter 2016 edition of *Social Philosophy and Policy*, "Ideal Theory for a Political World" (33, no. 1/2), contains a wide array of important essays on the issue.

33. Following Rawls, ideal theorists refer to this as the assumption of full or strict compliance.

34. As Gerald Gaus puts it, advocates of ideal theory hold that the first task of political theory is to identify "the institutional structures and patterns of interaction of an achievable ideally just social world" because it is only when we have sight of such an ideal that "we can rest assured that our efforts to secure justice have at least moved us in the right direction." Gaus, *Tyranny of the Ideal*, 4.

35. Rawls, *Theory Of Justice*, 8, and Simmons, "Ideal and Nonideal Theory," 7.

36. Rawls, *Law of Peoples*, 138.

37. Jacob Levy, "There Is No Such Thing as Ideal Theory," *Social Philosophy and Policy* 33, no. 1/2 (2016): 313–14.

38. Rawls says this about his assumption that the "basic structure is that of a closed society" (a society that is "self-contained and [has] no relations with other societies"). Rawls, *Political Liberalism*, 12. However, the attempt to abstract away from distractions captures the motivating theoretical claim at the heart of ideal theory.

39. Levy, "There Is No Such Thing," 333. Alison McQueen rightly argues that in this sense there is a deep *conceptual* motivation behind the realist critique of political moralism. As she puts it, realists argue that by insisting on the priority of the moral over the political and understanding "the purpose of politics as the elimination of conflict and disagreement," moralists operate with a fatally misconceived conception of politics. McQueen, "Case for Kinship," 250. This explains why realism is not merely a variant of nonideal theory. Although there are some similarities between realism and nonideal theory, nonideal theorists are concerned with the problem

of implementing or applying an ideal theory in nonideal circumstances. As such, they are solely focused on questions of feasibility. Realists, on the other hand, stress that political moralism has an impoverished, overly sanitized understanding of politics (and often also morality) and hold that correcting for this has more important normative implications than the nonideal theorists acknowledge. For further discussion, see Matt Sleat, "Realism, Liberalism and Ideal Theory: or, Are There Two Ways to Do Realistic Political Theory?," *Political Studies* 64, no. 1 (2016): 27–41, and Edward Hall and Matt Sleat, "Ethics, Morality, and the Case for Realist Political Theory," *Critical Review of International Social and Political Philosophy* 20, no. 3 (March 2017): 276–90.

40. Galston, "Realism in Political Theory," 408.

41. Robert Jubb, "The Real Value of Equality," *Journal of Politics* 77, no. 3 (2015): 680.

42. See, in particular, Erman and Moller, "Political Legitimacy in the Real Normative World." In their survey article, Rossi and Sleat did, in my view, unfortunately, flag the possibility of distinguishing between strong and weak variations of the realist claim concerning the autonomy of the political, giving some credence to the kind of misreading Erman and Moller advocate. Rossi and Sleat claim that "the strong version insists that it is possible to derive normative political judgments from specifically political values—a position resting on the view that not all values are moral values, plus the more controversial claim that such political values can and should guide politics, whereas moral values are ill-suited to that task." On the weaker view, "there is not such a stark contrast between politics and morality, and indeed morality may have a role to play in providing a source of political normativity, yet it remains important to appreciate the manner in which politics remains a distinct sphere of human activity, with its own concerns, pressures, ends and constraints which cannot be reduced to ethics (nor law, economics, religion, etc.)." Rossi and Sleat, "Realism in Normative Political Theory," 690. The version of political realism I focus on in this book is unapologetically of the "weak" kind, and in the conclusion I explain why I am perplexed by the idea that a "strong" version of the sort Rossi and Sleat describe could be found either coherent or attractive.

43. Hall and Sleat, "Ethics, Morality," 279.

44. Duncan Bell, "Introduction: Under an Empty Sky—Realism and Political Theory," in *Political Thought and International Relations: Variations on a Realist Theme*, ed. Duncan Bell (Oxford: Oxford University Press, 2009), 1.

45. I am sometimes inclined to think that the term *antimoralist* might be more appropriate, especially with regard to Berlin, Hampshire, and Williams considered together. Yet this would rob this way of approaching political theory I am concerned with of the strong historical lineage of thinkers associated with realist political thought whom they do draw on in different ways, including Thucydides, Machiavelli, Hobbes, Hume, Nietzsche, Weber, and Schmitt.

46. Martha Nussbaum, "Perfectionist Liberalism and Political Liberalism," *Philosophy & Public Affairs* 39, no. 1 (2011): 2.

47. Jeremy Waldron, *Political Political Theory: Essays on Institutions* (Cambridge, MA: Harvard University Press, 2016), 3. Berlin didn't actually entirely neglect the first of these questions, as we will see. The claim that Berlin paid too little attention to institutions is also developed, but in a much less hostile way, by Ira Katznelson in "Isaiah Berlin's Modernity," *Social Research* 66, no. 4 (1999): 1099–1100.

48. Waldron, *Political Political Theory*, 288.

49. Hampshire's work is more seriously treated in the philosophy of mind where it has, perhaps most notably, influenced the work of Richard Moran. See Richard Moran, *Authority and Estrangement: An Essay on Self-Knowledge* (Princeton, NJ: Princeton University Press, 2001), esp. 36–65.

50. Galen Strawson, "Towards a Common Justice," *The Observer*, November 12, 1989, 46.

51. On the face of it, the fact that Berlin penned this obituary is rather surprising, given that Berlin died in 1997. In fact, Berlin initially drafted an obituary for Hampshire in 1965—in what one can only assume was an act of friendship and not gleeful anticipation—and redrafted it on a number of subsequent occasions before his own death. See Henry Hardy, "Isaiah Berlin's Obituary of Stuart Hampshire," Isaiah Berlin Virtual Library, June 20, 2013, http://berlin.wolf.ox.ac.uk/lists/bibliography/joint-text.pdf.

52. Isaiah Berlin, "Sir Stuart Hampshire," Obituary, *The Times*, June 16, 2004, http://www.thetimes.co.uk/tto/opinion/obituaries/article2082485.ece.

53. Berlin, "Sir Stuart Hampshire."

54. William Frankena, Review of *Morality and Conflict*, by Stuart Hampshire, *Ethics* 95, no. 3 (April 1985): 740.

55. In the obituary she wrote for the *Guardian*, Jane O'Grady claims that Williams was "arguably the greatest British philosopher of his era." Jane O'Grady, "Professor Sir Bernard Williams," Obituary, *Guardian*, June 13, 2003, https://www.theguardian.com/news/2003/jun/13/guardianobituaries.obituaries. This is not to say that Williams's approach to philosophy is widely imitated or that his ethical and political views are widely endorsed. As Alasdair MacIntyre has recently written, "The vast majority of those now at work in academic moral philosophy continue to write as though Williams never existed." MacIntyre insists this is "a more interesting fact about them than it is about Williams." Alasdair MacIntyre, *Ethics in the Conflicts of Modernity: An Essay on Desire, Practical Reasoning, and Narrative* (Cambridge: Cambridge University Press, 2016), 152.

56. For example, in his monograph on Williams, Mark Jenkins remarks that the absence of "more in the way of a politics" is a notable lacuna in his corpus. Mark Jenkins, *Bernard Williams* (Chesham: Acumen, 2006), 188. Martha Nussbaum, rather prematurely, also noted Williams's "increasing withdrawal from politics and even political thinking in later life" in her remembrance of Williams. Martha Nussbaum, "Tragedy and Justice," *Boston Review*, October/November 2003, http://bostonreview.net/archives/BR28.5/nussbaum.html.

57. Alex Voorhoeve, "Bernard Williams: A Mistrustful Animal," in *Conversations on Ethics*, ed. Alex Voorhoeve (Oxford: Oxford University Press, 2009), 203.

58. This is significant because many realists explicitly reject liberalism. Raymond Geuss, for example, derides Williams's political thought, despite his positive assessment of Williams's work in ethics, for "paddling about in the tepid and slimy puddle created by Locke, J. S. Mill, and Isaiah Berlin." Geuss, "Did Williams Do Ethics?," 150.

Chapter One

1. Joshua Cherniss and Henry Hardy, "Isaiah Berlin," *Stanford Encyclopedia of Philosophy* (Winter 2017 edition), ed. Edward N. Zalta, https://plato.stanford.edu/entries/berlin.

2. For example, Eva Erman and Niklas Moller have recently claimed that "political realism . . . is in fact a relativist outlook." On this ground, they charge realists with endorsing excessively pessimistic and undemanding accounts of "what we may rightfully demand of political rule." Eva Erman and Niklas Moller, "Political Legitimacy for Our World: Where Is Political Realism Going?," *Journal of Politics* 80, no. 2 (2018): 535, 525.

3. Joseph Raz, *The Morality of Freedom* (Oxford: Oxford University Press, 1986), 395.

4. Berlin sometimes claims that because no such standard exists, men cannot "rationally choose between competing values" (*AC*, 69). In the next chapter, I will show that this is an

overstatement. The key point that follows from Berlin's belief in incommensurability is a chastened view of the power of philosophical ethics. The point is not that value conflict can *never* be rationally resolved or that reasonable decisions can never be made but that there cannot be a theory or decision procedure that satisfactorily resolves such disputes in *every* case.

5. Kekes, *Morality of Pluralism*, 46.

6. John Gray, *Isaiah Berlin: An Interpretation of His Thought* (Princeton, NJ: Princeton University Press, 1996), 79–80.

7. Gray, *Isaiah Berlin*, 79.

8. Berlin goes so far as to say that these visions of life "form wholes" (*A*, 208). He also sometimes intimates that value conflict derives from the conflicting ideals of human life expressed by outlooks (*L*, 212; *CTH*, 33). This implies that value pluralism is ultimately a result of a pluralism of such outlooks. Yet it is hard to determine conclusively Berlin's considered view of the consummate sources of value conflict and incommensurability (or, indeed, if he had a settled final view)—he simply never sets out his commitments definitively.

9. For a particularly clear and influential liberal view that refuses to see conflicts between freedom and equality in these terms, see Ronald Dworkin's *Sovereign Virtue: The Theory and Practice of Equality* (London: Harvard University Press, 2002), 120–83. For a pluralist/realist reply, see Bernard Williams, "From Freedom to Liberty: The Construction of a Political Value," *IBWD*, 75–96. For further discussion, see my "How to Do Realistic Political Theory (and Why You Might Want To)," *European Journal of Political Theory* 16, no. 3 (July 2017): 283–303.

10. At points, most notably when addressing Herder's political thought, Berlin suggests that this is explained by the fact that forms of life are organic wholes (*TCE*, 235). As Michele Moody-Adams argues, there is reason to be skeptical of this idea when it is taken too literally. Michele Moody-Adams, *Fieldwork in Familiar Places: Morality, Culture, and Philosophy* (Cambridge, MA: Harvard University Press, 2002), esp. 13–106. Yet the suggestion that the *vitality* of a distinct outlook's valuable elements in some way depends on the wider way of life that they form a part of is distinguishable from the more extreme versions of this focus on "organic wholes."

11. Jonathan Riley, "Interpreting Berlin's Liberalism," *American Political Science Review* 95, no. 2 (June 2001): 286.

12. For a thoughtful philosophical mediation, see Williams's discussion of the Jacobin leader Saint-Just's attempt to implement Roman ideals of civic virtue in French society (*MSH*, 135–52).

13. Claude Galipeau, *Isaiah Berlin's Liberalism* (Oxford: Clarendon Press, 1994), 81.

14. In this respect, there is a sense in which Berlin affirms a version of what is now called *moral antirealism*: "the denial of the thesis that moral properties—or facts, objects, relations, events, etc. (whatever categories one is willing to countenance)—exist mind-independently." Richard Joyce, "Moral Anti-realism," *Stanford Encyclopedia of Philosophy* (Winter 2016 edition), ed. Edward N. Zalta, https://plato.stanford.edu/entries/moral-anti-realism/. However, Berlin insists that values can be objective, which is something most moral antirealists deny. As is often the case, in this regard his value pluralism defies easy categorization.

15. Thus, Robert Talisse claims that, like the monists, Berlin endorses the ontological claim that "values are like pieces of a jigsaw puzzle" but merely insists "that there are more pieces than can be fit together in a single good picture." Robert Talisse, *Pluralism and Liberal Politics* (New York: Routledge, 2012), 32. Glen Newey also claims that value pluralists like Berlin endorse a "realist claim about the metaphysical structure of value." Glen Newey, "Value Pluralism in Contemporary Liberalism," *Dialogue* 37, no. 3 (1998): 499. Some versions of value pluralism may be consistent with such understandings of moral realism, but Berlin's is not.

16. See also Stuart Hampshire, "Nationalism," in *Isaiah Berlin: A Celebration*, ed. Edna Margalit and Avishai Margalit (London: Hogarth Press, 1991), 129.

17. See also John Gray, *Two Faces of Liberalism* (Cambridge: Polity, 2000), 41; William Galston, *The Practice of Liberal Pluralism* (New York: Cambridge University Press, 2005), 6; and Kekes, *Morality of Pluralism*, 58.

18. As Mark Bode notes, this phenomenological approach cannot exclude "the *logical* possibility that an advance in philosophical understanding... might prove the monistic structure of value." Mark Bode, "Everything Is What It Is, and Not Another Thing: Knowledge and Freedom in Isaiah Berlin's Thought," *British Journal for the History of Philosophy* 19, no. 2 (2011): 324. See also Gray, *Isaiah Berlin*, 99.

19. The idea is that translating diverse values into a common measure of value, like utility, requires us to think about our values and commitments in ways that fail to do justice to our moral experiences. As an example, Galston describes a person "who opposes the construction of a dam on the grounds that the species of animal thereby destroyed has intrinsic value." Such a person would, clearly, find it problematic to see this belief of theirs as nothing but a want or preference to be satisfied in the way that utilitarianism suggests they should. Galston, *Liberal Pluralism*, 33.

20. Kekes, *Morality of Pluralism*, 58.

21. Alex Zakaras, "Isaiah Berlin's Cosmopolitan Ethics," *Political Theory* 32, no. 4 (2004): 498–99.

22. For this allegation, see, in particular, George Kateb, "Can Cultures Be Judged? Two Defenses of Cultural Pluralism in Isaiah Berlin's Work," *Social Research* 66, no. 4 (1999): 1029, and Leo Strauss, "Relativism," in *The Rebirth of Classical Political Rationalism: An Introduction to the Thought of Leo Strauss* (Chicago: University of Chicago Press, 1989), 12–26.

23. Berlin claims that modern historical relativism sees men as being "wholly bound by tradition or culture or class or generation to particular attitudes or scales of value which cause other outlooks or ideals to seem strange and, at times, even unintelligible" (*CTH*, 85).

24. Chris Gowans, "Moral Relativism," *Stanford Encyclopedia of Philosophy* (Winter 2016 edition), ed. Edward N. Zalta, https://plato.stanford.edu/entries/moral-relativism/.

25. Miranda Fricker, "Styles of Moral Relativism—A Critical Family Tree," in *The Oxford Handbook of the History of Ethics*, ed. Roger Crisp (Oxford: Oxford University Press, 2015), 794.

26. Gowans, "Moral Relativism."

27. Strauss, "Relativism," 15.

28. Crowder illustrates how difficult this is. George Crowder, *Isaiah Berlin: Liberty and Pluralism* (Cambridge: Polity, 2004), 132–34.

29. Moody-Adams, *Fieldwork in Familiar Places*, 2.

30. Some of Berlin's claims about the objectivity of morality are simply unhelpful. He claims that Herderian pluralism holds that "objective standards of judgement . . . are derived from understanding the life purposes of individual societies, and are themselves objective historical structures" (*TCE*, 106–7). Yet this does not distinguish pluralism from relativism in any plausible sense and bears little relation to any of the normal ways that the term *objective* is used in moral argument. Likewise, in "The Pursuit of the Ideal," Berlin states that when he talks of a "world of objective value," he means "those ends that men pursue for their own sakes, to which other things are means" (*CTH*, 11–12). This suggests that moral objectivity is a matter of valuing something for noninstrumental reasons that will not do. In what follows, I focus on Berlin's statements about moral objectivity that have more prima facie plausibility.

31. H. L. A. Hart, *The Concept of Law* (Oxford: Clarendon Press, 2012), 192–93. Hart focuses on five truisms: (1) human vulnerability, (2) approximate equality, (3), limited altruism, (4) limited resources, and (5) limited understanding and strength of will. Hart, *Concept of Law*, 194–200. These truisms reveal the needs for prohibitions restricting the use of violence in killing or inflicting bodily harm, a system of mutual forbearance and compromise, some kind of regulation of property, and sanctions to guarantee obedience.

32. Kekes, *Morality of Pluralism*, 38–39.

33. This is how Berlin parses the point in one of his exchanges with Beata Polanowska-Sygulska (*UD*, 41). In the introduction to *Five Essays on Liberty*, he also writes that we now understand human beings to be "endowed with a nucleus of needs and goals, a nucleus common to all men," and that "the notion of such a nucleus in such limit enters into our conception of the central attributes and functions in terms of which we think of men and societies" (*L*, 54). At one point, Berlin even intimates that certain human interests are just as basic as the fact that we are three-dimensional (*SR*, 15).

34. Kekes, *Morality of Pluralism*, 42.

35. Gray, *Isaiah Berlin*, 104; Gray, *Two Faces of Liberalism*, 66; Zakaras, "Isaiah Berlin's Cosmopolitan Ethics," 514.

36. Gray, *Two Faces of Liberalism*, 67; Galipeau, *Isaiah Berlin's Liberalism*, 119. As George Crowder notes, Jonathan Riley's claim that Berlin's account of basic needs and human rights has distinctively liberal political consequences is untenable for this reason. Crowder, *Isaiah Berlin*, 134.

37. Isaiah Berlin and Steven Lukes, "Isaiah Berlin in Conversation with Steven Lukes," *Salmagundi*, no. 120 (Fall 1998): 105; *CTH*, 318.

38. The majority of the time, as in the quotations above, Berlin claims that such similarity relates to the common core (what I have called *shared basic needs*) (*POI*, 12). However, in his letter to Hendrik Hoetink (June 15, 1983), which is a very revealing meditation on these issues in general and which I therefore draw on in my exposition in other respects, Berlin implies that a family resemblance between outlooks is sufficient to explain this kind of understanding and communication. Thus, he claims that if outlook "A has something in common with B, B with C, C with D, etc. I can move along this line and finally end up with Z, which shares nothing in common with A or B or C, but which is intelligible to us. Thus, there is no need to postulate a 'natural man' stripped of all his acquired characteristics." *A*, 209. The "family resemblance" reading is independently plausible and would succeed in going some way toward distinguishing his pluralism from his understanding of relativism. However, it is incompatible with his endorsement of the minimum content of natural law because this implies there will be some shared content (even if only in a very thin sense), not merely the kind of lineage Berlin's posits in his letter to Hoetink.

39. George Crowder and Henry Hardy, "Appendix: Berlin's Universal Values—Core or Horizon?," in *The One and the Many*, ed. George Crowder and Henry Hardy (New York: Prometheus Books, 2007), 294–95.

40. In this regard, Berlin was deeply influenced by his reading of Vico and Herder (*CIB*, 7; *CTH*, 82, 85).

41. Berlin frequently stresses that many of the basic concepts and categories we use are value-laden, most clearly in his discussions of free will and determinism (*L*, 94–165, 252–70). However, this is irrelevant to the issues I am examining about the objective nature of morality because it merely repudiates naively positivist views. When discussing comprehensibility in terms of the human horizon and the possibility of moral objectivity, Berlin must be committed to a much stronger position of the sort I detail above.

42. My reading has something in common with that of Alex Zakaras, who also interprets Berlin as holding that outlooks that fall within the human horizon "reveal different and unfamiliar forms of human flourishing which, taken together, constitute a range of real possibilities within which good lives can be lived." Yet I am unsure why Zakaras deems that this reveals that Berlin's view is "mildly teleological." Zakaras, "Isaiah Berlin's Cosmopolitan Ethics," 503, 500. It makes more sense to stress that Berlin believes that our understanding of moral objectivity is conditioned by generic features of human nature and that this places some constraints on our understanding of which forms of life are in principle capable of being objectively valuable. This does not imply a moving *toward* anything.

43. The other advantage of this reading is that it enables us to understand why Berlin holds that "variety is an independent value" (*CTH*, 59–60). Relativists cannot consider moral variety valuable but must merely treat it as a brute fact about the world. Berlin, on the other hand, can praise it because it reveals the myriad ways in which human nature can develop.

44. Alex Zakaras, "A Liberal Pluralism: Isaiah Berlin and John Stuart Mill," *Review of Politics* 75, no.1 (2013): 89.

45. James Griffin, "First Steps in an Account of Human Rights," *European Journal of Philosophy* 9, no. 3 (2001): 313.

46. Admittedly, the action-guiding nature of the basic needs and interests I am referring to cannot be explained by the unique role they play in constituting a particular local social world, as Williams suggests is typically the case with "thick" concepts (*ELP*, 140–56).

47. Michael Ignatieff makes a related point: "Either you maintain that fascists are human only too human, and you therefore absorb into your account of human nature some measure of the de Maistrean vision of human beings as innately and naturally violent; or you maintain that all human beings know what inhumanity consists in, in which case fascists cease to qualify as normal human beings." Michael Ignatieff, "Understanding Fascism?," in *Isaiah Berlin: A Celebration*, 145. See also Kateb, "Can Cultures Be Judged?," 1030.

48. Philipp Meyer, *The Son* (London: Simon & Schuster, 2013); Jonathan Lear, *Radical Hope: Ethics in the Face of Cultural Devastation* (London: Harvard University Press, 2006).

49. Lear, *Radical Hope*, 20.

50. Lear, *Radical Hope*, 21.

51. Of course, there is nothing to stop Berlinian value pluralists from referring to those outlooks and ends that we can imaginatively "enter into" as being objective if they wish to. However, this is a very idiosyncratic way of rendering that term. As Gerald Gaus notes, when philosophers employ the language of objectivity, they normally mean not only that something is widely desired or pursued but that it is "worthy of being so desired or pursued." Accordingly, "congeniality to humanity is not objectivity." Gerald Gaus, *Contemporary Theories of Liberalism* (London: Sage, 2003), 30. In making this point, I am not criticizing Berlin and his followers for failing to offer a theoretical account of what is *worthy* of being so desired and pursued. (That would be problematic precisely because most value pluralists reject the forms of ethical theory that purport to deliver these ultimate ethical truths.) But given that most moral and political philosophers do think about objectivity in the way that Gaus describes, Berlin's use of the term is misleading.

52. Berlin acknowledges that a belief in "subhumanity" is intelligible. In a letter to Michael Ignatieff, dated June 7, 1991, he writes, "The idea of subhumans is a piece of odious nonsense; but it cannot be said to be beyond the pale, unintelligible. That is roughly what I think the Dominicans thought about the South American Indians in the sixteenth century when Jesuits opposed them, and said that they were human beings. Some Catholic orders thought that these were not

creatures for whom Christ had died—that is certainly an allegation of subhumanity. But that is not unintelligible, merely appalling, from the point of view of semi-universally accepted human values. From that there is no great distance to the racialism of Gobineau and the Nazi horrors" (A, 419). This strengthens my claim that there is a tension in Berlin's response to relativism between his claims about intelligibility and his commitment to universal human values such as those outlined in his account of the minimum content of natural law.

53. Michele Moody-Adams notes that "every society in some way confines some persons or groups to its margins," creating what she calls "internal outsiders." Some, like slave societies, endorse claims about subhumanity, while others less extremely consign persons to the margins based on their "economic status, gender, physical appearance, behaviour, sexual preference, or age." Moody-Adams, *Fieldwork in Familiar Places*, 68. These less extreme kinds of marginalization may not deny people's common humanity, but Moody-Adams's analysis suggests that denials of common humanity are, in their own way, comprehensible developments of this all-too-common feature of social life. This buttresses my point that failing to uphold some people's basic needs is not an uncommon feature of comprehensible outlooks.

54. As Gerald Gaus remarks: "In the course of history many have found appealing the values of personal self-assertion (even if this leads to oppressing others); national self-assertion (even if this leads to oppressing other nations); fighting for one's values (even if this decreases the possibility of international peace); religious unity (even if this means religious persecution); a meritocratic society in which the able get what they deserve and the incompetent lose out (even if this means that the basic needs of the incompetent are not met); a society of great artistic or intellectual achievement (even if this means that resources are spent on these activities that could have gone to meeting the basic needs of citizens)." Gaus, *Contemporary Theories of Liberalism*, 66. Gaus's target is John Gray, but the point also applies to Berlin.

55. Jan-Werner Müller, "Value-Pluralism in Twentieth-Century Anglo-American Thought," in *Modern Pluralism: Anglo-American Debates since 1880*, ed. Mark Bevir (Cambridge: Cambridge University Press, 2012), 92.

56. I believe these considerations refute the reconstruction of Berlin's position that Jonathan Riley defends in "Isaiah Berlin's 'Minimum of Common Moral Ground,'" *Political Theory* 41, no. 1 (2013): 61–89. Riley stresses Berlin's belief that views like Nazism are "perverted by their truly absurd belief that some people are subhumans" and takes this to prove that such outlooks do not fall within the human horizon, as Berlin understands it (75). I do not deny that a belief in subhumanity is absurd, but I do not think that Berlin's considerations about the human horizon can explain why it is for the reasons outlined above. Riley consistently conflates Berlin's belief in the minimum content of natural law with his understanding of the human horizon. (See Riley, "Interpreting Berlin's Liberalism"; Jonathan Riley, "Defending Cultural Pluralism: Within Liberal Limits," *Political Theory* 30, no. 1 (Feb. 2002): 68–96; Riley, "Isaiah Berlin's 'Minimum of Common Moral Ground.'") This leads Riley to suggest, implausibly, that "a normal human gives moral priority to the survival of all other normal humans." Riley, "Isaiah Berlin's 'Minimum of Common Moral Ground,'" 74. Berlin's account of the human horizon cannot deliver that verdict (nor, it seems, can a plausible understanding of history). Berlin's focus on natural law delivers a different claim: that human beings often *should* consider this a priority.

57. Crowder, *Isaiah Berlin*, 120–21.

58. Sometimes Berlin implies that the core and horizon are synonymous. For example, he writes, "What I mean by the 'human horizon' is a horizon which for the most part, at a great many times, in a great many places, has been what human beings have consciously or unconsciously

lived under, against which values, conduct, life in all its aspects have appeared to them" (*CTH*, 316).

59. As Berlin puts it, "One of my deepest beliefs is that one of the causes of continuous change in human history is the fact that it is precisely the fulfilment (or partial fulfilment) of some human aspiration that itself transforms the aspirant, and breeds, in time, new needs, new goals, new outlooks, that are *ex hypothesi* unpredictable" (*CTH*, 311).

60. In this regard, there is a link between this argument and Crowder's attempt to align pluralism with the capabilities approach. Crowder, *Isaiah Berlin*, 155. I am skeptical about this attempted alignment for the same reason.

61. This strikes me as the basic implication, even if it is not the exact point, that Crowder makes against Gray's "cultural" reading of Berlin's value pluralism. Though Crowder admits that the cultural view does appear in Berlin's texts, he insists that "despite what Berlin himself sometimes says, his better view is that it is primarily *goods* (and sub-goods) that are plural . . . rather than cultures." Crowder, *Isaiah Berlin*, 135–36.

62. Clearly, we would have to judge that such practices are central or necessary features of the outlook, rather than peripheral features or simple failures to live up to central values.

63. Similarly, John Gray claims that "universal evils do not always override particular loyalties" and that "there is nothing unreasonable in putting the claims of one's way of life over those of universal evils." Gray, *Two Faces of Liberalism*, 67.

64. This judgment is compatible with the idea that we should refrain from blaming the members of such groups. Per Miranda Fricker, if someone was "not in a position to grasp the moral status or significance X, then they cannot be blamed for the relevant action or omission." Miranda Fricker, "The Relativism of Blame and Bernard Williams's Relativism of Distance," *Proceedings of the Aristotelian Society* 84 (2010): 152.

Chapter Two

1. See, for example, Galston, "Realism in Political Theory," 396, 407; Philp, "Realism without Illusions," 634; Stears, "Liberalism and the Politics of Compulsion," 541.

2. Ronald Dworkin, "Do Liberal Values Conflict?," in *The Legacy of Isaiah Berlin*, ed. Ronald Dworkin, Mark Lilla, and Robert. B. Silvers (New York: New York Review of Books, 2001), 76; Hampshire, "Nationalism," 133; Joshua Cherniss, "Isaiah Berlin's Thought and Legacy: Critical Reflections on a Symposium," *European Journal of Political Theory* 12, no. 1 (2013): 10.

3. Graeme Garrard, "Strange Reversals: Berlin on the Enlightenment and the Counter-Enlightenment," in Crowder and Hardy, *The One and the Many*, 143.

4. Berlin discusses the distinction between the negative and the positive conceptions of liberty in a number of different ways in his corpus. For example, he also often claims that the extent of one's negative liberty is a matter of determining how many doors one can walk through or how many roads are open for one to take (*CIB*, 150; *UD*, 87, 100). He also frequently insists that positive liberty is ultimately a matter of self-rule or self-direction (*L*, 177–78). In one way or another, all these ways of making the distinction hark back to the way of carving up the conceptual space noted above. On his view, one of the most salient differences between the two ways of thinking about liberty is that proponents of negative liberty "want to curb authority as such," while advocates of positive conceptions of liberty want authority "placed in their own hands" (*L*, 212).

5. Joshua Cherniss holds that if any passage best encapsulates Berlin's view of the value of freedom it is his claim that "the essence of liberty has always lain in the ability to choose as you wish to

choose, because you wish so to choose, uncoerced, unbullied, not swallowed up in some vast system; and in the right to resist, to be unpopular, to stand up your convictions merely because they are your convictions. That is true freedom, and without it there is neither freedom of any kind, nor even the illusion of it" (*FIB*, 103–4). As Cherniss notes, "This may be identified with negative liberty ... but it also involves 'positive' elements: actualizing one's desires, making choices *for oneself*, living a life based on convictions one experiences as one's own." Joshua Cherniss, *A Mind in Its Time: The Development of Isaiah Berlin's Thought* (Oxford: Oxford University Press, 2013), 189.

Berlin was greatly influenced by Kant's insistence on treating people as ends in themselves, and that cannot be understood solely in "negative" terms. Thus, in his well-known letter to George Kennan, he writes that "one thing which no utilitarian paradise, no promise of eternal harmony in the future within which some vast organic whole will makes us accept is the use of human beings as mere means" (*L*, 339). For further discussion of this point, see Cherniss, *A Mind in Its Time*, 88–112, and Joshua Cherniss, "Against 'Engineers of Human Souls': Paternalism, 'Managerialism,' and the Development of Isaiah Berlin's Liberalism," *History of Political Thought* 35, no. 3 (2014): 565–88.

6. For an overview of some of the most important early criticisms of Berlin's distinction, see Ian Harris, "Berlin and His Critics" (*L*, 349–66). For a response to some of these, see Berlin's introduction to *Five Essays on Liberty* (*L*, 3–54) and Crowder, *Isaiah Berlin*, 76–94.

7. For an admirably clear argument to this effect, see Katrin Flikschuh, *Freedom: Contemporary Liberal Perspectives* (Cambridge: Polity, 2007), 22–28. Some critics are scathing about Berlin's work as history. See, for example, Robert Edward Norton, "The Myth of the Counter-Enlightenment," *Journal of the History of Ideas* 68, no. 4 (2007): 635–58, and a number of the essays in *Isaiah Berlin and the Enlightenment*, ed. Laurence Brockliss and Ritchie Robertson (Oxford: Oxford University Press, 2016). More charitably, one might say, as Ian Harris does, that "Berlin wrote history that was formed by, and which was a vehicle for, his philosophical views." Cited by Henry Hardy in the editor's preface to *PIRA*, xix. Either way, as Cherniss notes, "the reader searching for scrupulously and exactly accurate historical reconstruction should not consult Berlin" (*PIRA*, xxxiv).

8. Flikschuh, *Freedom*, 23.

9. At the end of "Two Concepts," Berlin also claims that pluralism "entails" a measure of negative liberty (*L*, 216). In my view, it makes more sense to hold that negative conceptions of liberty are typically compatible with a belief in value pluralism while some positive conceptions are not. This, however, does not show that pluralism *entails* a commitment to negative liberty. I address this claim later in this chapter when discussing the relationship between value pluralism and liberal forms of politics.

10. Cohen, *Rescuing Justice and Equality*, 20–21. Cohen defends this view by arguing that "a principle can respond to a fact (that is, be grounded in) a fact, only because it is also a response to a more ultimate principle that is not a response to fact" (229). For example, Cohen claims that we may endorse the principle (P) "keep your promises" because we believe the fact (F) that people can only successfully pursue their projects when promises are kept. Yet if we ask why (F) grounds (P), we have to appeal to a more fundamental fact-independent principle (P1) that we should help people pursue their projects. According to Cohen, only a principle such as (P1) can enable (F) to support (P), and (P1's) validity is independent of the truth of (F). This is taken to show that the grounding of fundamental principles is independent of any facts and that if we affirm an ultimate principle, our support of it is applicable across any set of facts.

11. Swift, "Value of Philosophy," 382.

12. Cohen, *Rescuing Justice and Equality*, 291.

13. I borrow this phrase from Elizabeth Anderson, "Moral Bias and Corrective Practices: A Pragmatist Perspective," *Proceedings and Address of the American Philosophical Association* 89 (2015): 21.

14. Cohen's defenders might reply by saying that when choosing between competing conceptions of liberty in this way, we still appeal to further principles (such as principles that urge us to avoid the horrors generated by the kinds of authoritarian politics Berlin detested) and that they may be fact-insensitive. Perhaps. However, as David Miller notes, much of the time if we follow Cohen's recursive logic, we are going to end up thinking in quasi-utilitarian terms and holding that a fact supports a principle because "following the principle satisfies human wants or avoids human pain." Miller, "Political Philosophy for Earthlings," 36. If this is right, what looks like a startling metaethical thesis may simply turn out to show that our ultimate principles are rather banal and uncontroversial.

15. Berlin and Lukes, "Isaiah Berlin in Conversation," 98.

16. Eric MacGilvrey, "Republicanism and the Market in 'Two Concepts of Liberty,'" in *Isaiah Berlin and the Politics of Freedom: "Two Concepts of Liberty" 50 Years Later*, ed. Bruce Baum and Robert Nichols (London: Routledge, 2013), 123.

17. Rawls, *Political Liberalism*, 197.

18. Rawls, *Political Liberalism*, 57. See also John Rawls, *Justice as Fairness: A Restatement* (Cambridge, MA: Harvard University Press, 2003), 36n26, 154. Rawls is a much fairer reader of Berlin than Berlin is of Rawls. Berlin's discussion of Rawls in his interview with Steven Lukes shows that he had a uncharitable understanding of Rawls's work in general. Berlin and Lukes, "Isaiah Berlin in Conversation," 113.

19. For example, Jeremy Waldron remarks that Berlin thought that "Enlightenment social design was arrogant and monistic, seeking a fatuous reconciliation of all values and a comprehensive solution of all conflicts in a glittering work of reason." Waldron, *Political Political Theory*, 282–83. This is, at best, partially correct.

20. Galston, "Realism in Political Theory," 407.

21. For example, Rawls claims that the exercise of political power is "fully proper only when it is exercised in accordance with a constitution the essentials of which all citizens as free and equal may reasonably be expected to endorse in the light of principles and ideals acceptable to their common human reason." Rawls, *Political Liberalism*, 137.

22. Galston, *Liberal Pluralism*, 7.

23. William Galston, "Moral Pluralism and Liberal Democracy: Isaiah Berlin's Heterodox Liberalism," *Review of Politics* 71, no. 1 (2009): 96. Elsewhere, Galston insists that the moral particularism he favors is "compatible with the existence of right answers in specific cases; there may be compelling reasons to conclude that certain trade-offs among competing goods are preferable to others." Galston, *Liberal Pluralism*, 7.

24. George Crowder, "Pluralism and Liberalism," *Political Studies* 42, no. 2, (1994), 293—305.

25. Isaiah Berlin and Bernard Williams, "Pluralism and Liberalism: A Reply," *Political Studies* 42, no. 2 (1994): 307. Similarly, John Gray asserts that value pluralists do not deny that values can never be compared but hold that "their value can only be compared in particular contexts." Gray, *Two Faces of Liberalism*, 42.

26. Cherniss, "Isaiah Berlin's Thought and Legacy," 10.

27. Rawls, *Law of Peoples*, 90. Simmons, "Ideal and Nonideal Theory," 34.

28. Joshua Cherniss, "'The Sense of Reality': Berlin on Political Judgement and Political Leadership," in *The Cambridge Companion to Isaiah Berlin*, ed. Joshua Cherniss and Steven B.

Smith (Cambridge: Cambridge University Press, 2018), 53–78; Ryan Patrick Hanley, "Political Science and Political Understanding: Isaiah Berlin on the Nature of Political Inquiry," *American Political Science Review* 98, no. 2 (2004): 330.

29. Steven Smith, *Modernity and Its Discontents: Making and Unmaking the Bourgeois from Machiavelli to Bellow* (New Haven, CT: Yale University Press, 2017), 288.

30. Berlin describes Weizmann in the following terms: "His method of argument was, as a rule, neither a demonstration founded on statistical or other carefully documented evidence, nor emotional rhetoric, nor sermon addressed to the passions; it consisted in painting a very vivid, detailed, coherent, concrete picture of a given situation or course of events; and his interlocutors, as a rule, felt that this picture, in fact, coincided with reality and conformed to their own experience of what men and events were like, of what had happened, or might happen or, on the contrary, could not happen; of what could and what could not be done" (*PI*, 54–55). Berlin goes on to note that this kind of "concreteness" in thinking is especially common in England (*PI*, 55).

31. In the concluding paragraph of his essay on Franklin Roosevelt, Berlin remarks that Roosevelt's political career not only showed that "it is possible to be politically effective and yet benevolent and human" but also that "the promotion of social justice and individual liberty does not necessarily mean the end of all efficient government; that power and order are not identical with a straightjacket of doctrine, whether economic and political; that it is possible to reconcile individual liberty . . . with the indispensable minimum of organising and authority" (*PI*, 31).

32. To anticipate a possible misunderstanding: this is not because I think Berlin believes that there exists a distinct set of political values that conflict with moral values, as one might be inclined to think, given his belief in distinct spheres of value that I discussed in chapter 1. As noted in the introduction, Berlin consistently insists that political philosophy is "but ethics applied to society" (*CTH*, 2) and denies that moral philosophy is one thing and political philosophy another (*CIB*, 58). This point is made especially clearly in his essay on Machiavelli. According to Berlin, Machiavelli does not distinguish distinctively moral from distinctively political values, but rather between two different moralities or "ideals of life"—the pagan and the Christian (*AC*, 44–45).

33. When making this point in "Does Political Theory Still Exist?," Berlin principally had some forms of positivism and Marxism in mind (*CC*).

34. Janos Kis, "Berlin's Two Concepts of Positive Liberty," *European Journal of Political Theory* 12, no. 1 (2013): 43.

35. Cherniss, "Isaiah Berlin's Thought and Legacy," 13; Gray, *Isaiah Berlin*, 97–98.

36. This is one of several instances in which, as Michael Kenny notes, "the mis-match between the grandeur of his moral understanding and the banality of some of his political prescription is rather striking." Michael Kenny, "Isaiah Berlin's Contribution to Modern Political Theory," *Political Studies* 48, no. 5 (2000): 1030.

37. As Berlin was fond of remarking, "there is no a priori reason for supposing that the truth, when discovered, will necessarily prove interesting" (*CTH*, 20).

38. Henry Hardy reports that these notes were hastily written for a friend who asked Berlin how he might treat this theme in a lecture he was due to give (*L*, xxx).

39. In "Marxism in the Nineteenth Century," Berlin, relatedly, remarks that the history of political thought has been marked by two camps—roughly, the pluralist and monist. The former recognizes that politics inevitably "involves clashes and the constant need for conciliation, adjustment, balance, an order that is always in a condition of imperfect equilibrium, which is required to be maintained by conscious effort." The latter clings to the forlorn hope that "health consists in unity, peace, the elimination of the very possibility of disagreement, the recognition

of only one end or set of non-conflicting ends as being alone rational, with the corollary that rational disagreement can affect only means" (*SR*, 121).

40. Philp, "Realism without Illusions," 635. Similarly, Stears claims that "politics takes place in the face of inevitable *dis*agreement, and, indeed, it is best understood as a functional response to that disagreement" and that "the mechanisms that are employed in order to respond to that disagreement are themselves inherently coercive. They are mechanisms through which either elites or more widely dispersed social groups seek to enforce their will, or realize their desires, at the same time as to maintain stability and order of a certain sort." Stears, "Liberalism and the Politics of Compulsion," 545.

41. Rawls, *Political Liberalism*, 8.

42. Rawls, *Justice as Fairness*, 5.

43. George Klosko, "Rawls's Public Reason and American Society," in *Reflections on Rawls: An Assessment of His Legacy*, ed. Shaun Young (Farnham: Ashgate, 2009), 30. For a detailed discussion of the empirical literature that he claims supports this judgment, see George Klosko, *Democratic Procedures and Liberal Consensus* (New York: Oxford University Press, 2004), 81–115. Most saliently perhaps, Klosko claims that between 20 and 25 percent of the American population are authority-minded, believe in transcendent truth, and reason from sacred texts, thereby endorsing modes of reasoning that are "inimical" to Rawlsian public reason. Klosko, *Democratic Procedures*, 111.

44. Fabian Freyenhagen, "Taking Reasonable Pluralism Seriously: An Internal Critique of Political Liberalism," *Politics, Philosophy, and Economics* 10, no. 3 (2011): 328–29.

45. Galston, "Realism in Political Theory," 407.

46. In particular, see Jeremy Waldron's "Isaiah Berlin's Neglect of Enlightenment Constitutionalism" in *Political Political Theory*, 274–89.

47. Waldron, *Political Political Theory*, 4–8.

48. Berlin consistently holds that the ability to make choices is, in some sense, an essential element of humanity. For example, he claims that making choices of one's own, rather than being chosen for, is "an inalienable ingredient in what makes human beings human" (*L*, 52). Yet it is important to distinguish between Berlin's account of the significance of "basic liberty" and his defense of negative liberty. This distinction is most fully articulated in Berlin's reply to Robert Kocis, where Berlin states that he endorses Kant's view that the ability to make choices is "a *sine qua non* of being a fully developed human being" (*CTH*, 305) but explicitly distinguishes this from his doctrine of negative freedom (*CTH*, 309). We therefore need to distinguish between basic liberty—the choice between alternatives—and negative liberty—the extent to which people are unimpeded in pursuing their choices. For useful discussions, see Cherniss, *A Mind in Its Time*, 189–98, Cherniss, "Against 'Engineers of Human Souls,'" 578–81, and Gray, *Isaiah Berlin*, 51–52.

49. Gray, *Isaiah Berlin*, 21. (For a similar argument, see Gaus, *Contemporary Theories of Liberalism*, 49.) Some commentators continue to persist with the attempt to derive a defense of liberalism from recognition of the truth of value pluralism. For example, in *Isaiah Berlin: Liberty and Pluralism*, George Crowder claims that value pluralism imposes hard choices on agents as they must decide how to act without making recourse to an overarching philosophical standard. Crowder claims, "To cope well with these choices, we need to develop certain dispositions of character, or virtues. Those virtues overlap the character traits distinctively promoted by liberal forms of politics, in particular the exercise of personal autonomy" (164). On this basis, Crowder's attempts to align liberalism and pluralism proceed by treating autonomy as a supreme value. There are several problems with this argument. First, despite his protestations to the contrary, it is hard to see how

this view is not merely a kind of monism. After all, Crowder ends up valuing one of many ways of life—autonomous lives—over all others. Second, Crowder seems to beg the question by supposing that there exists some kind of universal standard of "coping well" that we can appeal to here, but it is hard to see how such an understanding will not, inevitably, be rooted in a particular outlook. For further, to my mind, convincing criticism of Crowder's attempt to make a logical case for liberal implications of value pluralism, see Ella Myers, "From Pluralism to Liberalism: Rereading Isaiah Berlin," *Review of Politics* 72, no. 4 (2010): 621, and Zakaras, "A Liberal Pluralism," 92.

50. In one of his interviews with Jahanbegloo, Berlin admits as much, remarking, "Pluralism and liberalism are not the same or even overlapping concepts. There are liberal theories which are not pluralistic. I believe in both liberalism and pluralism, but they are not logically connected" (*CIB*, 44). See also *UD*, 84–86, 214.

51. Myers, "From Pluralism to Liberalism," 623–24. Similarly, Joshua Cherniss claims that Berlin's commitment to liberalism is importantly grounded in his "humanism." Cherniss, "Isaiah Berlin's Thought and Legacy," 14.

52. I do not want to contend that the account of moral psychology I go on to develop here can be referred to as Berlin's "position" on this issue. However, it is *a* position that Berlin explicitly expresses at various junctures and that is implicit in many of his remarks that bear on this issue. It is also congenial to the spirit of value pluralism and plausible in its own terms.

53. Zakaras, "Isaiah Berlin's Cosmopolitan Ethics," 510; Jason Ferrell, "Isaiah Berlin as Essayist," *Political Theory* 40, no. 5 (October 2012): 614.

54. Gray, *Isaiah Berlin*, 188–89.

55. Cherniss, "Isaiah Berlin's Thought and Legacy," 12.

56. Galipeau, *Isaiah Berlin's Liberalism*, 112.

57. According to this view, rather than holding that the ability to choose our ends and values enables us to express our agency in some fundamental manner—as Berlin suggests in his more expansive and moralistic moods—one can merely note that the ability to see through one's choices is likely to matter a great deal to people and that such choices should, therefore, only be frustrated for very good countervailing reasons.

58. Galston, *Liberal Pluralism*, 57–58.

59. Galston, *Liberal Pluralism*, 63. See also John Horton, "Realism, Liberalism, and a Political Theory of Modus Vivendi," *European Journal of Political Theory* 9, no. 4 (2010): 439.

60. David Hume, "Of the First Principles of Government," "Of the Origin of Government," and "Idea of a Perfect commonwealth," in *Essays: Moral, Political, and Literary*, ed. Eugene F. Miller (Indianapolis: Liberty Fund, 1987), 32–36, 37–41, 512–29. As we will see in part 2, Stuart Hampshire's account of procedural justice broadly endorses this Humean idea.

61. David Caute essentially sees Berlin's political thought in this light in *Isaac and Isaiah: The Punishment of a Cold War Heretic* (London: Yale University Press, 2013).

Chapter Three

1. To be clear, I am not suggesting that Hampshire's work ought to be assimilated with the agonist current in contemporary political theory associated with the work of Bonnie Honig and Chantal Mouffe. See, in particular, Bonnie Honig, *Political Theory and the Displacement of Politics* (Ithaca, NY: Cornell University Press, 1993), and Chantal Mouffe, *On the Political* (Abingdon: Routledge, 2005). While there are certainly some areas of overlap, Hampshire works within a philosophical tradition distinct from Honig and Mouffe and does not endorse the same kind

of political conclusions that they do. As a result, the attempt to identify him too closely with the strand of agonist thought that their work represents is problematic. His is a different kind of agonism, differently grounded.

2. In this regard, as noted in chapter 1, Berlin and Hampshire are united in endorsing what I have called the *mutual dependence condition*.

3. Jane O'Grady, "Sir Stuart Hampshire," Obituary, *Guardian*, June 16, 2004, https://www.theguardian.com/news/2004/jun/16/guardianobituaries.obituaries. See also *MC*, 114.

4. As he puts it, "A way of life is a complicated thing, marked out by many details of style and manner, and also by particular activities and interests, which a group of people of similar dispositions in a similar social situation may share; so that the group may become an imitable human type who transmit many of their habits and ideals to their descendants, provided that social change is not too rapid" (*MC*, 91).

5. This line of argument is closely related to Hampshire's broader epistemological notion of the "inexhaustibility of description." This thesis holds that "any situation which confronts me, and which is not a situation in a game, has an inexhaustible set of discriminable features over and above those which I explicitly notice at the time because they are of immediate interest to me. Secondly, the situation has features over and above those which are mentionable in the vocabulary that I possess and use" (*MC*, 106). In *Thought and Action*, Hampshire develops the implications of this notion in detail.

6. A similar thought recurs when Hampshire insists that if someone has "left the most primitive level of self-consciousness, and therefore has the freedom of reflection, he cannot easily see himself as guided by any established morality that is already complete" (*TA*, 222).

7. Hampshire denies that arguments in moral and political theory can aspire to the kind of proof that many other domains of inquiry aspire to. In moral and political theory, arguments are always "matters of opinion, of rationally confident opinion, and they are supported by reasons, more or less compelling, which obviously never amount to proofs" (*IE*, 89).

8. In his early work, Hampshire pushes these insights in a psychoanalytic direction, drawing on his engagement with Spinoza. He argues there that once we accept that our interests, actions, and ways of classifying the world are largely inherited and "passively learnt," we can consider ourselves "more free" whenever we are able to detach ourselves from these habits and achieve a kind of reflective self-consciousness (*TA*, 213). The clearest account of Hampshire's take on Spinoza's thought in this regard occurs in his "Spinoza and the Idea of Freedom," *SS*, 175–99.

9. Hampshire claims that Kantian deontology and utilitarianism are the prime examples of moral theories that fail to do justice to the role of imaginative thought in a person's life (*IE*, 47).

10. In a letter to Henry Hardy on April 2, 1991, Berlin remarks that he does not believe in the existence of "absolute evil" in the way that Hampshire does (*A*, 410).

11. Paul Sheehy, "Interview: Stuart Hampshire," *Philosophy Now*, August/September 2000, https://philosophynow.org/issues/28/Sir_Stuart_Hampshire.

12. As will be apparent from the argument of chapter 1, I do not think that Berlin actually offers the view that Hampshire imputes to him, but this claim nonetheless reveals something significant about Hampshire's own position.

13. For further discussion, see Derek Edyvane, "Richly Imaginative Barbarism: Stuart Hampshire and the Normality of Conflict," *Theoria: A Journal of Social and Political Theory* (forthcoming).

14. In an interview, Hampshire insists that "we are always and ought to be in conflict. The development of our lives, of forms of civilisation, depend upon this experimental settlement,

compromising, and negotiating of contrary impulses and interests. Therefore, it's not just the case of someone following the natural order of things, but the course that allows for originality, imagination, the things we need in human life in general." Sheehy, "Interview: Stuart Hampshire."

15. Lorna Finlayson, "*With radicals like these, who needs conservatives?* Doom, Gloom, and Realism in Political Theory," *European Journal of Political Theory* 16, no. 3 (2017): 268–69.

16. Finlayson, "*With radicals like these*," 271.

17. To be fair, Finlayson admits that her reading may better map onto various survey articles addressing the realist turn—notably William Galston's—rather than the theorists such articles focus on. Finlayson, "*With radicals like these*," 277n5.

18. Joshua Cohen, "Pluralism and Proceduralism," *Chicago-Kent Law Review* 69 (1994): 593.

19. Gerald Gaus, "Should Philosophers 'Apply Ethics'?," *Think* 3, no. 9 (2005): 67.

Chapter Four

1. As I will show in chapter 6, Bernard Williams attempts something similar with his account of the basic legitimation demand. Both Hampshire and Williams, therefore, avoid attempting to outline various first-order beliefs or propositions that ought to command the assent of all rational agents and instead proceed by identifying a set of norms they claim are inherent in existing political practices.

2. Some commentators hold that this account is damagingly circular. For example, John Horton argues that Hampshire suggests agents should realize that procedural justice is the appropriate response to conflicts in the city because they balance pros and cons in situations of intrapersonal conflict. However, Horton claims that this way of responding to intrapersonal conflict is, itself, explained by our internalization of the public method of responding to conflicts. John Horton, "Proceduralism as Thin Universalism: Stuart Hampshire's 'Procedural Justice,'" in *Principles and Political Order: The Challenge of Diversity*, ed. Bruce Haddock, Peri Roberts, and Peter Sutch (London: Routledge, 2006), 139. John Haldane makes a similar claim in his review of *Justice Is Conflict, Journal of Applied Philosophy* 18, no. 1 (2001): 93.

Derek Edyvane rebuts this reading, stressing that Hampshire never repudiates his claim that justice in the soul shadows justice in the city. According to Edyvane, Hampshire's claim is that if an agent is faced with practical conflict and asks by what model she is supposed to proceed, she looks "at what is 'out there' in the world, observes that the procedures of adversary argument are appropriate (or just) in the political context and accordingly applies that model to her internal processes of thought, once again thinking it the appropriate (rational) model of conflict negotiation." Derek Edyvane, "Justice as Conflict: The Question of Stuart Hampshire," *Contemporary Political Theory* 7, no. 3 (2008): 324.

3. Horton, "Proceduralism as Thin Universalism," 140–41.

4. I am not concerned with the accuracy of Hampshire's interpretation of Rawls. For my purposes, Hampshire's remarks on Rawls matter because they teach us something significant about Hampshire's own position. Rawlsians have attempted to offer a response to Hampshire's critique of Rawls: see Cohen, "Pluralism and Proceduralism." Cohen succeeds in correcting some errors in Hampshire's interpretation of Rawls, but Cohen's interpretation of Hampshire rests on a mistaken understanding of Hampshire's own view (as I noted in chapter 3). In addition, Cohen insists that Hampshire's account of procedural justice is, at heart, a defense of *democratic* political procedures. This is simply untrue.

5. Stuart Hampshire, "Liberalism: The New Twist," *New York Review of Books*, August 1993, http://www.nybooks.com/articles/1993/08/12/liberalism-the-new-twist/.

6. John Rawls, "The Idea of an Overlapping Consensus," *Oxford Journal of Legal Studies* 7, no. 1 (1987): 14n22.

7. For a bleak account of the terrible things that human beings in such situations are not merely capable of doing but also clearly sometimes enjoy, see Jonathan Glover, *Humanity: A Moral History of the Twentieth Century* (London: Penguin, 1999).

8. I owe this way of framing the point to Derek Edyvane.

9. In the same way that Hampshire claims, as we saw in the last chapter, that the sentiments of people who fail to immediately *feel* the universal evils can be "distracted from natural feeling by some theory that explains them away" (JC, xii).

10. Jonathan Floyd neglects this aspect of Hampshire's work when he claims that Hampshire merely counsels us to abide by currently existing institutions and consequently criticizes this view because of the existence of institutions like slavery in the past. Jonathan Floyd, *Is Political Philosophy Impossible? Thoughts and Behaviour in Normative Political Theory* (Cambridge: Cambridge University Press, 2017), 69.

11. Hampshire holds that certain strains of socialist thinking embody this insight as they are driven by the desire to redraw the boundary between "natural and man made evils" (JC, 84).

12. This is basically Jonathan Floyd's reading. Floyd, *Is Political Philosophy Impossible?*, 68. Tom Spragens suggests something similar in "Justice, Consensus, and Boundaries: Assessing Political Liberalism," *Political Theory* 31, no. 4 (August 2003): 595.

13. David Archard, "Just Rules?," *Res Publica* 7, no. 2 (May 2001): 208.

14. For discussion, see Simon May, "Principled Compromise and the Abortion Controversy," *Philosophy & Public Affairs* 33, no. 4 (2005): 318, and Fabian Wendt, *Compromise, Peace, and Public Justification: Political Morality beyond Justice* (London: Palgrave, 2016), 16. This is why moral compromise differs from cases of moral correction. As May puts it, "If an agent is persuaded to correct her political position, she comes to see it as morally inferior on its own merits to the new alternative. Moral correction involves the recognition that one's earlier commitments were mistaken. But if the agent comes to accept an alternative as a moral compromise, she still views her initial position as morally superior." May, "Principled Compromise," 318.

15. Wendt, *Compromise, Peace, and Public Justification*, 23–24.

16. Richard Bellamy, *Liberal and Pluralism: Towards a Politics of Compromise* (London: Routledge, 2001), 101.

17. Bellamy, *Liberal and Pluralism*, 105, 111, 124; Amy Gutmann and Dennis Thompson, *The Spirit of Compromise: Why Governing Demands It and Campaigning Undermines It* (Princeton, NJ: Princeton University Press, 2012), 109–16; Phillippe Van Parjis, "What Makes a Good Compromise?," *Government and Opposition* 47, no. 3 (January 2012): 472; Andrew Sabl, *Ruling Passions: Political Offices and Democratic Ethics* (Princeton, NJ: Princeton University Press, 2002), 20.

18. Wendt, *Compromise, Peace, and Public Justification*.

19. Matt Matravers and Susan Mendus, "The Reasonableness of Pluralism," in *The Culture of Toleration in Diverse Societies*, ed. Catriona McKinnon and Dario Castiglione (Manchester: Manchester University Press, 2003), 39.

20. Chandran Kukathas, *The Liberal Archipelago: A Theory of Diversity and Freedom* (Oxford: Oxford University Press, 2003), 75.

21. Although I do not have the space to develop this point here, it strikes me that the ways of attempting to justify compromising that are developed in the mainstream political philosophy

literature are afflicted by a more general failing. To wit, if moral conflict and disagreement are as pervasive as these thinkers accept, why believe that conflicting parties will agree that some other value, be it reciprocity, respect, or public justification generates reasons to compromise? Won't we also disagree about the priority of this value? Or contest its concrete implications?

22. Edyvane, "Justice as Conflict," 335.

23. Here thanks are due to a very useful set of comments from one of my anonymous readers for the press.

24. Ronald Dworkin offers a good example of such a view when he claims that "people are members of a genuine political community only when . . . they accept that they are governed by common principles, not just by rules hammered out in political compromise." Ronald Dworkin, *Law's Empire* (London: Harvard University Press, 1986), 211.

25. For such an argument, see May, "Principled Compromise."

26. Alin Fumurescu, *Compromise: A Political and Philosophical History* (Cambridge: Cambridge University Press, 2013), 266.

Chapter Five

1. As many of Williams's admirers have noted. Thus, when commenting on *Ethics and the Limits of Philosophy*, Adrian Moore writes that Williams's work has "a kind of clarity. But it does not have the kind of clarity that makes for easy reading. Williams never belabours the obvious; and he rarely makes explicit what he takes to be implicit in something he has already said. His writing is therefore extremely dense. It leaves an enormous amount of work for the reader." Adrian Moore, "Commentary on the Text," *ELP*, 204. Similarly, Susan Wolf notes that "the casual reader will have difficulty seeing what holds all the parts together" while "to the close reader many of the arguments will seem clipped or even occasionally left out altogether." Susan Wolf, "The Deflation of Moral Philosophy," *Ethics* 97, no. 4 (1987): 822. H. L. A. Hart agrees. "It is true that Williams writes without unexplained technicalities and often with clarity and wit," Hart says, but "nonetheless much that he writes needs, as well as deserves, to be read more than once. Often this is because the slant of his attention and the insights he offers are novel; sometimes it is because he writes in an extraordinarily condensed, almost epigrammatic, style which leaves important implications to be worked out by the reader." H. L. A. Hart, "Who Can Tell Right From Wrong?," *New York Review of Books*, July 17, 1986, https://www.nybooks.com/articles/archives/1986/jul/17/who-can-tell-right-from-wrong/.

2. Bernard Williams, "Replies," in *World, Mind, and Ethics: Essays on the Ethical Philosophy of Bernard Williams*, ed. J. E. J. Altham and Ross Harrison (Cambridge: Cambridge University Press, 1995), 186.

3. He remarks that the project "operates, so to speak, in the right corner of the field." Bernard Williams, "History, Morality, and the Test of Reflection," in *The Sources of Normativity*, by Christine Korsgaard (Cambridge: Cambridge University Press, 1996), 213.

4. For further discussion, see Paul Sagar, "Minding the Gap: Bernard Williams and David Hume on Living an Ethical Life," *Journal of Moral Philosophy* 11 (2014): 615–38.

5. In response to Martha Nussbaum, Williams accepts that a less foundationalist reading of Aristotle is possible while still insisting that "the modern world has left behind the elements necessary to make his [Aristotle's] style of ethical theory as a whole plausible" precisely because it undercuts our belief in the kind of harmony that Aristotelian approaches imply. Williams, "Replies," 201.

6. Here, I draw on Adrian Moore's very useful reconstruction of Williams's argument (*PHD*, xvi–xvii).

7. For a useful discussion, see A. W. Moore, "Realism and the Absolute Conception," in *Bernard Williams*, ed. Alan Thomas (Cambridge: Cambridge University Press, 2007), 24–46.

8. Importantly, Williams claims that his "aim in introducing the notion of the absolute conception was . . . the idea . . . that when we reflect on our conceptualization of the world, we might be able to recognize from inside it that some of our concepts and ways of representing the world are more dependent than others on our own perspective, our peculiar and local ways of apprehending things. In contrast, we might be able to identify some concepts and styles of representation which are minimally dependent on our own or any other creature's peculiar ways of apprehending the world" (*PHD*, 185).

9. Williams, "Replies," 208.

10. John Skorupski, "Internal Reasons and the Scope of Blame," in Thomas, *Bernard Williams*, 100. On this score, Williams claims that he finds it "hard to resist Nietzsche's plausible interpretation, that the desire of philosophy to find a way in which morality can be guaranteed to get beyond merely *designating* the vile and recalcitrant, to transfixing them or getting them inside, is only a fantasy of *ressentiment*, a magical project to make a wish and its words into a coercive power." Williams, "Replies," 216.

11. There is dispute concerning the extent to which the internal reasons thesis excludes Kantian approaches. Christine Korsgaard forcefully argues that Kant is not an externalist because if "we can be motivated by considerations stemming from pure practical reason, then that capacity belongs to the subjective motivational sets of every rational being." Christine Korsgaard, "Skepticism about Practical Reason," *Journal of Philosophy* 83, no. 1 (1986): 21. Williams concedes as much in his "Replies," 220n3, and *MSH*, 175. However, he nonetheless denies that universally binding practical reasons of a Kantian sort exist, as we have seen. Regardless of the particular claims about Kantian approaches, Williams's internal reasons thesis rules out intuitionist approaches that presume "you can directly intuit the demands of morality . . . [and] write these demands into every agent's deliberative route by an intuitive fiat." Skorupski, "Internal Reasons," 84. In this regard, this aspect of Williams's work problematizes forms of moralist political philosophy that proceed by outlining a set of, supposedly universal, obligations and duties without asking if the presumed audience can reasonably be expected to recognize their force.

12. In the introduction he wrote to Berlin's *Concepts and Categories*, Williams remarks that Berlin's value pluralism captures a truth about value "revealed in the only way in which it could be revealed, historically. The truthfulness that is required is a truthfulness to that historical experience of human nature" (*CC*, xviii).

13. David Owen, "Realism in Ethics and Politics: Bernard Williams, Political Theory, and the Critique of Morality," in Sleat, *Politics Recovered*, 81–86.

14. Williams, "Replies," 207.

15. Williams, "Replies," 208.

16. Bernard Williams, "*Sources of the Self: The Making of Modern Identity*, by Charles Taylor," in *Essays and Reviews: 1959–2002*, ed. Michael Wood (Oxford: Princeton University Press, 2014), 310.

17. Bernard Williams, "Why Philosophy Needs History," in Wood, *Essays and Reviews*, 410.

18. Thomas Nagel, *The Last Word* (Oxford: Oxford University Press, 1997), 5.

19. Or as Wittgenstein puts it, "to be sure there is justification; but justification comes to an end." Ludwig Wittgenstein, *On Certainty* (Oxford: Blackwell, 1993), 27e.

20. Williams, "Why Philosophy Needs History," 410.

21. Quentin Skinner, "Modernity and Disenchantment: Some Historical Reflections," in *Philosophy in an Age of Pluralism: The Philosophy of Charles Taylor in Question*, ed. James Tully and Daniel Weinstock (Cambridge: Cambridge University Press, 1994), 45.

22. Skinner, "Modernity and Disenchantment," 44.

23. Paul Kelly, "Rescuing Political Theory from the Tyranny of History," in *Political Philosophy versus History? Contextualism and Real Politics in Contemporary Political Thought*, ed. Jonathan Floyd and Marc Stears (Cambridge: Cambridge University Press, 2011), 21.

24. Williams, "Replies," 208.

25. Jenkins, *Bernard Williams*, 186.

26. John Cottingham, "The Good Life and the Radical Contingency of the Ethical," in *Reading Bernard Williams*, ed. Daniel Calcutt (London: Routledge, 2008), 35.

27. Cottingham, "The Good Life," 37.

28. Richard Rorty, *Contingency, Irony, and Solidarity* (Cambridge: Cambridge University Press, 1989), 73–74.

29. Rorty, *Contingency, Irony, and Solidarity*, 45.

30. Bernard Williams, "*Contingency, Irony and Solidarity* by Richard Rorty," in *Essays and Reviews*, 299.

31. Williams, "*Contingency, Irony and Solidarity*," 301.

32. Miranda Fricker, "Confidence and Irony," in *Morality, Reflection, and Ideology*, ed. Edward Harcourt (Oxford: Oxford University Press, 2000), 89.

33. Fricker, "Confidence and Irony," 111.

34. Cottingham, "The Good Life," 36.

35. Friedrich Nietzsche, *Untimely Meditations*, ed. Daniel Breazeale (Cambridge: Cambridge University Press, 2005), 146.

36. Hence Williams's insistence that his skepticism about "morality" and certain models of philosophical justification does not necessarily imply a more wide-ranging skepticism about ethical considerations in general. He is adamant that "more is to be feared and learned from a partial scepticism in ethics, one that casts suspicion on tracts of our moral sentiments and opinions, because of their psychological origins and our actual historical situation." Bernard Williams, "The Need to Be Sceptical," in *Essays and Reviews*, 317.

37. Cottingham, "The Good Life," 36

Chapter Six

1. For Williams, the kind of authority he focuses on is an identifying criterion of politics through history (*IBWD*, 69). Mark Philp gives an admirably concise summation of the central idea at work when he writes that politics "involves at least some claim to authority . . . [while] brute force determines outcomes but it does so coercively, not authoritatively." On this view, "it is therefore integral to political rule to invoke at least some claim to authority and thereby to legitimacy . . . which implies some recognition of this on the part of citizens." Philp, *Political Conduct*, 55–56.

2. This is why Williams *is not* committed to claiming that all politics is by definition legitimate. For this misreading, see Matt Sleat, "Bernard Williams and the Possibility of a Realist Political Theory," *European Journal of Political Theory* 9, no. 4 (2010): 485–603; Matt Sleat, *Liberal Realism: A Realist Theory of Liberal Politics* (Manchester: Manchester University Press, 2013),

112–31; and Paul Raekstad, "Realism, Utopianism, and Radical Values," *European Journal of Philosophy* 26, no. 1 (2018): 145–68. Paul Sagar expresses Williams's point clearly when he claims that the justification offered to legitimate the exercise of power "is presented as something the victim group is expected to be able to recognise as making a claim on them, and is engaged with as such, even if only to be rejected. Absent this, there is only unmediated coercion, and that is what politics is in the first instance supposed to replace, to be an attempted solution to.... The point is ... that the locus of political power offers what it is doing as not *just* coercion, but as something that *ought to be accepted* by the victims, and in the right kind of way by their own lights, even if it isn't." Paul Sagar, "From Scepticism to Liberalism? Bernard Williams, the Foundations of Liberalism, and Political Realism," *Political Studies* 64, no. 2 (2014): 371.

3. Thus, Williams avoids the pitfalls that afflict philosophical views that model legitimate states as kinds of voluntary association. As Raymond Geuss remarks, such accounts are "obsessed with trying to square the circle by presenting as 'voluntary' something which is self-evidently deeply non-voluntary." Raymond Geuss, *History and Illusion in Politics* (Cambridge: Cambridge University Press, 2001), 29.

4. A. John Simmons, "Justification and Legitimacy," *Ethics* 109, no. 4 (1999): 769. Although Simmons's distinction between justification and legitimacy makes his view more complex, his account remains unconvincing because legitimacy ceases to be a meaningful standard of political evaluation: no political society has been, or will be, legitimate. This does not accord with our considered use of the term.

5. Bernard Williams, interview in *Cogito*, reprinted as "Bernard Williams," in *Key Philosophers in Conversation: The Cogito Interviews*, ed. Andrew Pyle (London: Routledge, 1999), 158.

6. John Horton, "Political Legitimacy, Justice, and Consent," *Critical Review of International Social and Political Philosophy* 15, no. 2 (2012): 135.

7. Philp, "Realism without Illusions," 633.

8. Sleat, "Bernard Williams," 495.

9. Williams writes that a subject is "anyone who is in its [the state's] power, whom by its own lights it can rightfully coerce" (*IBWD*, 4) and that the state must offer a justification to each subject because if it does not "there will be people whom they are treating merely as enemies in the midst of their citizens, as the ancient Spartiates, consistently, treated the helots whom they had subjugated" (*IBWD*, 135). To this end, Williams claims that "at least ideally" states must have something to say "to each person whom they constrain" (*IBWD*, 135).

10. See Freyenhagen, "Taking Reasonable Pluralism Seriously," 335.

11. Jonathan Floyd, "From Historical Contextualism, to Mentalism, to Behaviourism," in Floyd and Stears, *Political Philosophy versus History?*, 44.

12. Floyd, "From Historical Contextualism," 47.

13. Michael Freeden, "Interpretative Realism and Prescriptive Realism," *Journal of Political Ideologies* 17, no. 1 (2012): 6.

14. Sleat, "Bernard Williams," 500.

15. Sleat, "Bernard Williams," 496.

16. As Mark Philp has pointed out, the coercion of those who deny that the legitimation story makes sense could be part of a strategy that seeks to secure a more wide-ranging legitimacy in the long run, and such coercion is different to the acts of a state that thinks that such problems can be solved by war or genocide.

17. Thanks to Geoff Hawthorn and Paul Sagar for discussions of this point.

18. Horton, "Political Legitimacy," 131.

19. Floyd, "From Historical Contextualism," 46.

20. For further discussion, see Sagar, "From Scepticism to Liberalism?" Williams is adamant that in many cases various utopian alternatives to liberalism "do not even reach the threshold of offering a serious political consideration" (*IBWD*, 92) because they do not engage with the basic features of modernity.

21. This makes sense of Williams's remark that "it is obvious that in many states most of the time the question of legitimate authority can be sufficiently taken for granted for people to get on with other kinds of political agenda" (*IBWD*, 62).

22. Philp, "Realism without Illusions," 634.

23. Charles Larmore, "What Is Political Philosophy?," *Journal of Moral Philosophy* 10, no. 3 (2013): 291.

24. Charles Larmore, "The Truth in Political Realism," in Sleat, *Politics Recovered*, 43.

25. As Williams puts it, if something makes sense to me, this is "a matter of my reasons, my desires, my on-going projects, and I do not choose all of them" (*SP*, 334).

26. Freeden, "Interpretative Realism," 6–7.

27. Philp, *Political Conduct*, 71.

28. Philp, *Political Conduct*, 72.

29. Philp, *Political Conduct*, 72–73.

30. In the postscript to *Ethics and the Limits of Philosophy*, Williams insists that despite his critique of the morality system, belief in the meaningfulness of individual lives, in truth, and in the value of truthfulness is possible (*ELP*, 198–99). His writings on what we can broadly refer to as moral psychology develop a picture of agency in which something akin to a notion of authenticity is central. This seems to imply a politics that gives people a kind of prima facie presumption to live their lives in accordance with their most deeply held projects and commitments. In Williams's early ethical thought, there is, consequently, a sense in which a defense of liberalism might be developed by focusing on the kind of authentic lives wide-ranging political freedom might make possible. The only sustained discussion of this, as far as I am aware, is Nakul Krishna's unpublished manuscript, "Liberalism and Authenticity in the Philosophy of Bernard Williams." Interestingly though, in his late political work, Williams refrains from defending liberalism in these terms and instead offers a broadly negative defense of liberal political institutions that focuses on the evils and domination they guard against. This is not accidental.

31. Voorhoeve, "Bernard Williams," 200.

32. It is tempting to think that by endorsing such claims, Williams assumes the truth of a certain liberal conception of the person. However, he is careful to insist that the reason we can reflectively hold that liberalism makes sense "is not, though it is often thought to be, because some liberal conception of the person, which delivers the morality of liberalism, is or ought to be seen to be correct" because this conception is itself "a product of the same forces that lead to a situation in which the BLD is satisfied only by a liberal state" (*IBWD*, 8).

33. According to the gloss I am applying to this term here, which is not explicit in "The Idea of Equality," we might say that this "weak principle" makes particular sense to us because of the disenchanted conditions in which we find ourselves.

34. Judith Shklar, "The Liberalism of Fear," in *Political Thought and Political Thinkers*, ed. Stanley Hoffman (Chicago: University of Chicago Press, 1998), 8–9.

35. Shklar, "Liberalism of Fear," 9.

36. Shklar, "Liberalism of Fear," 8.

37. Shklar, "Liberalism of Fear," 10–11.

38. Shklar, "Liberalism of Fear," 14.

39. Shklar, "Liberalism of Fear," 18. See also Bernard Yack, introduction to *Liberalism without Illusions: Essays on the Liberal Theory and Political Vision of Judith N. Shklar*, ed. Bernard Yack (Chicago: University of Chicago Press, 1996), 3–4.

40. Shklar, "Liberalism of Fear," 19.

41. Matt Sleat, "Making Sense of Our Political Lives—The Political Philosophy of Bernard Williams," *Critical Review of International Social and Political Philosophy* 10, no. 3 (2007): 396.

42. Robert Jubb, "Realism in Analytical Political Theory," in *Methods in Analytical Political Theory*, ed. Adrian Blau (Cambridge: Cambridge University Press, 2017), 120.

43. John Gray, "Agonistic Liberalism," *Enlightenment's Wake* (Abingdon: Routledge, 1995), 117.

44. As noted in chapter 2, nonliberals may insist that because liberalism is so imperfect in these respects, this claim cannot ring true. Williams's work suggests that they need to offer a realistic judgment to the effect that viable alternatives will be as good at ensuring order and the conditions of cooperation in the modern world.

45. Thanks to David Owen for pressing me to consider this issue.

46. In this referenced passage, Williams is addressing the question whether the refusal of the "happy slaves" to complain that their liberty is frustrated by the state is relevant to our understanding of their political liberty, but the point can be generalized in the way I suggest.

47. If resistance and dissent are not manifest, it does not necessarily follow that legitimacy in Williams's sense obtains. As Paul Sagar has recently argued, drawing on James Scott's work on domination and Lisa Wedeen's study of Syria under Hafez al-Assad, even if regimes display some external trappings of legitimacy, insofar as subjects acquiesce to power in various ways, it is often the case that disadvantaged subjects are under no illusion about the fact that they are simply being dominated. Paul Sagar, "Legitimacy and Domination," in Sleat, *Politics Recovered*, 122–24. Nonetheless, it is hard to shake the thought that there will be cases in which such attitudes do not obtain but where we may suspect that subjects' beliefs about the acceptability of their regimes are problematically formed. This is where a critical theory principle of some kind must come into play.

48. Raymond Geuss, *The Idea of a Critical Theory* (Cambridge: Cambridge University Press, 1981), 62–66.

49. In what follows, I focus on the adequacy of the particular formulation of the critical theory test that Williams articulates in *Truth and Truthfulness*, rather than considering more generally whether an "internalist" approach in the spirit of Williams's can explain what is wrong with political orders marked by significant inequalities in power and advantage without making recourse to external, prepolitical moral considerations.

50. As an anonymous reviewer for the press has helpfully noted, if disadvantaged subjects do become suspicious of the processes of instruction for the reasons discussed above, we do not necessarily have to conclude that the claim to political authority is groundless; instead, the instructors will have to accept that the political order needs a different and better legitimation. Yet for a "better legitimation" to emerge, it must be possible to explain how a general acceptance of inequity can be legitimated, even though the disadvantaged will have reasons to suspect that the order serves the interests of the advantaged.

51. Sagar, "Legitimacy and Domination," 120.

52. Geuss, "Did Williams Do Ethics?," 147–48.

53. For useful discussion, see Sagar, "Legitimacy and Domination," 127–36.

54. In my view, Sagar's essay implicitly suggests as much. He discusses two hypothetical cases taken from Williams and argues that a minimalist critical theory can impugn them. In the first, a group of villagers defer to the authority of a local priest because the priest and his fellow religious instructors have generated a set of beliefs about their own authority that the villagers unwittingly endorse. The second is a "total" patriarchal society where members of each gender take highly unequal gender norms for granted. However, as I have shown, Williams insists that internalized sexist beliefs are easy cases for the critical theory principle and claims that it is not hard to see why subjects would come to reject the authority of religious instructors who claim to have unique access to an esoteric source of knowledge. For this reason, I am not convinced that Sagar's development of Williams's view reveals how we can deal with subtler cases either. (I am not sure that Sagar would consider this a problem: his intention is to rebut the common claim that "internalist" views cannot explain what is wrong with the kinds of cases he addresses, and he convincingly argues that we do not need to make recourse to various "external" moral convictions to explain what is problematic about such cases.)

55. Thanks are due to one of my reviewers for the press for making this point.

Conclusion

1. Voorhoeve, "Bernard Williams," 197–98.

2. Certainly, no plausible view will hold that the conflictual nature of morality is the sole reason that politics has the character that realists insist on. Mark Philp convincingly notes four further causes of political conflict: the possibility of class antagonism and factionalism; struggles that arise when individuals compete with one another over social goods; the conflicts that can arise between the rulers and the ruled (especially when those with power use political office to further their own interests); and finally, the conflict that may exist between different units of sovereignty. Philp, *Political Conduct*, 62–64.

3. A number of readers place Berlin squarely in the liberalism of fear camp. See, for example, Jonathan Allen, "A Liberal-Pluralist Case for Truth Commissions," in Crowder and Hardy, *The One and the Many*, 245; Joshua Cherniss, "Isaiah Berlin," in *The Edinburgh Companion to Political Realism*, ed. Robert Schuett and Miles Hollingworth (Edinburgh: Edinburgh University Press, 2018); Garrard, "Strange Reversals," 155; and Jan-Werner Müller, "Fear and Freedom: On Cold War Liberalism," *European Journal of Political Theory* 7, no. 1 (2008): 45–64. Hampshire is also interpreted in these terms by Peter Lassman in "Pluralism and Pessimism: A Central Theme in the Political Thought of Stuart Hampshire," *History of Political Thought* 30, no. 2 (2009): 335. As we saw in chapter 6, Williams expressly committed himself to the liberalism of fear.

4. This point is well made in Duncan Bell, "Security and Poverty: On Realism and Global Justice," in Sleat, *Politics Recovered*, 305.

5. For example, Thomas Christiano, *The Constitution of Equality: Democratic Authority and Its Limits* (Oxford: Oxford University Press, 2010); David Estlund, *Democratic Authority: A Philosophical Framework* (Princeton, NJ: Princeton University Press, 2009); Niko Kolodny, "Rule Over None I: What Justifies Democracy?," *Philosophy & Public Affairs* 42, no. 3 (2014): 195–229; and Niko Kolodny, "Rule Over None II: Social Equality and the Justification of Democracy," *Philosophy & Public Affairs* 42, no. 4 (2014): 287–336.

6. The insistence that any adequate view of democratic politics must squarely accept something that reflective inhabitants of democratic regimes grasp—that we do not have the ability to make our rulers act as we would like them to, even though they are in some sense accountable

to us—is a fundamental theme of John Dunn's work. See, in particular, *Western Political Theory in the Face of the Future* (Cambridge: Cambridge University Press, 1993), 1–28, and *Breaking Democracy's Spell* (New Haven, CT: Yale University Press, 2014).

7. In *Democracy for Realists: Why Elections Do Not Produce Responsive Government* (Princeton, NJ: Princeton University Press, 2016), Christopher H. Achen and Larry M. Bartels contend that a realistic understanding of democratic politics enjoins us to accept that citizens do not *determine* the policies of democratic regimes in any of the ways that traditional democratic theorists suggest they do. Moreover, they claim that most citizens support a party "not because its policy positions are closest to their own, but rather because 'their kind' of person belongs to that party" (307). As such, they stress that the outcomes of elections are "mostly just erratic reflections of the current balance of partisan loyalties in a given political system" (16) and that these loyalties should be understood in nonrational terms of social identity.

8. Jason Brennan, *Against Democracy* (Princeton, NJ: Princeton University Press, 2016).

9. Rossi and Sleat, "Realism in Normative Political Theory," 690.

10. Raymond Geuss, "Moralism and Realpolitik," in *Politics and the Imagination* (Princeton, NJ: Princeton University Press, 2009), 42.

11. Enzo Rossi, "Justice, Legitimacy, and (Normative) Authority for Political Realists," *Critical Review of International Social and Political Philosophy* 15, no. 2 (2012): 149–50.

12. At one point, Geuss attributes something akin to this view to Williams, claiming that Williams endorsed the idea that "politics should replace ethics." Geuss, "Did Williams Do Ethics?," 143–44. I have found no evidence of this assertion in Williams's corpus. As we have seen, Williams does insist that politics is not simply a branch of morality and should not be theorized in such terms, but this is a very different point.

13. Geuss, *Philosophy and Real Politics*, 2.

14. To be clear, I am not convinced that Geuss's work does, in fact, express the kind of "strong" realism Rossi and Sleat impute to him. However, the "strong" understanding is detectible in various discussions of political realism at the moment, so it is worth responding to.

15. Cohen, *Rescuing Justice and Equality*, 229–343.

16. For this error, see Valentini, "Ideal vs. Non-ideal Theory," 659.

17. Andrew Sabl, "Realist Liberalism: An Agenda," *Critical Review of International Social and Political Philosophy* 20, no. 3 (2017): 366.

18. Sabl, "Realist Liberalism," 367.

19. It expresses the interesting distinction between "dry" and "wet" realist approaches that tracks how thoroughly realists reject the standard liberal demand that political orders be rationally justified to their members. As Sabl puts it, "Wet realists long for a society that could justify itself with thoroughly good reasons, or could mostly do so, while stressing that such a project must grapple with more conflict, and will be realized less perfectly, than ideal liberals admit." Dry realists, on the other hand, "reject the idea of rational justification altogether, or think it largely beside the point. They think that all institutions and practices rest not primarily on reasons and justifications but on power, subrational passions and sentiments, irreducibly partial viewpoints, or social norms and habits. And they see many, perhaps most, political and moral arguments as post-hoc rationalizations for individual or group interests." Andrew Sabl, review of *Liberal Realism: A Realist Theory of Liberal Politics*, by Matt Sleat, *Perspectives on Politics* 13, no. 4 (2015): 1141.

20. This is not surprising; Sabl is the author of *Hume's Politics: Co-ordination and Crisis in the History of England* (Princeton, NJ: Princeton University Press, 2012).

21. Williams's reply to Simon Blackburn's review of *Ethics and the Limits of Philosophy* is informative in this respect. Blackburn accused Williams of downplaying the attractions of Humean approaches that he said were, more or less, unscathed by Williams's critique of the morality system. Simon Blackburn, "Making Ends Meet," *Philosophical Books* 27, no. 4 (1986): 193–203. In his response, Williams acknowledged that while Hume's work in moral philosophy was of great importance, he thought that Hume endorsed an unrealistic view of the basic uniformity of the moral sentiments and interests of mankind and, therefore, was insufficiently responsive to the "problems raised by moral diversity." Bernard Williams, "Reply to Simon Blackburn," *Philosophical Books* 27, no. 4 (1986): 206. In this regard, Williams later noted, "I once had a great admiration for Hume. Now I think that he suffered from a somewhat terminal degree of optimism." Bernard Williams, "Seminar with Bernard Williams," *Ethical Perspectives* 6 (1999): 256. For more detailed discussions of the relationship between Hume and Williams in this regard, see Sagar, "Minding the Gap," and Paul Russell, "Hume's Optimism and Williams's Pessimism: From a Science of Man to Genealogical Critique," in *New Essays on Bernard Williams' "Ethics and the Limits of Philosophy,"* ed. Sophie Grace Chappell and Marcel van Ackeren (London: Routledge, 2019), 37–52.

22. A notable exception may be "descriptive" accounts of modus vivendi that merely seek to explain whether a particular political settlement successfully secures peace and order in a way that its subjects freely accept; see John Horton, "What Might It Mean for Political Theory to Be More Realistic?," *Philosophia* 45 (2017): 487–501. Yet it is precisely because such views eschew prescription that they may be genuinely ecumenical toward different underlying ethical views. That other versions of modus vivendi that seek to do more than merely describe political settlements in this way are not similarly ecumenical is a point well made by Horton in "John Gray and the Political Theory of Modus Vivendi," in *The Political Theory of John Gray*, ed. John Horton and Glen Newey (Oxford: Routledge, 2007), 43–57.

23. Galston, "Realism in Political Theory," 408. Peter Jones has commented more resentfully about realism in these terms, dismissing the "entirely negative character" of realism as "particularly irritating." As Jones sees it, realists are very happy to point out the faults of moralist liberalism, but they then "either walk away from the issues that contemporary liberals are trying to resolve or pretend that those issues do not exist." Peter Jones, "The Political Theory of Modus Vivendi," *Philosophia* 45 (2017): 444.

24. Jubb, "Real Value of Equality." This is because Jubb alleges that without a threshold of egalitarian concern, modern states will not be able to explain why they rightfully rule over their worse off members.

25. Rawls, *Political Liberalism*, 46.

26. For good discussion of this point, see Jubb, "Realism," 121–22.

Bibliography

Achen, Christopher H., and Larry M. Bartels. *Democracy for Realists: Why Elections Do Not Produce Responsive Government*. Princeton, NJ: Princeton University Press, 2016.

Allen, Jonathan. "A Liberal-Pluralist Case for Truth Commissions." In *The One and the Many: Reading Isaiah Berlin*, edited by George Crowder and Henry Hardy, 213–50. London: Prometheus Books, 2007.

Anderson, Elizabeth. "Moral Bias and Corrective Practices: A Pragmatist Perspective." *Proceedings and Address of the American Philosophical Association* 89 (2015): 21–47.

Archard, David. "Just Rules?" *Res Publica* 7, no. 2 (May 2001): 205–13.

Bell, Duncan. "Introduction: Under an Empty Sky—Realism and Political Theory." In *Political Thought and International Relations: Variations on a Realist Theme*, edited by Duncan Bell, 1–25. Oxford: Oxford University Press, 2009.

———. "Security and Poverty: On Realism and Global Justice." In *Politics Recovered: Realist Thought in Theory and Practice*, edited by Matt Sleat, 296–319. New York: Columbia University Press, 2017.

Bellamy, Richard. *Liberal and Pluralism: Towards a Politics of Compromise*. London: Routledge, 2001.

Berlin, Isaiah. *Affirming: Letters 1975–1997*. Edited by Henry Hardy and Mark Pottle. London: Chatto and Windus, 2015.

———. *Against the Current: Essays in the History of Ideas*. Edited by Henry Hardy. 1979. Reprint, London: Pimlico, 1997.

———. *Concepts and Categories: Philosophical Essays*. Edited by Henry Hardy. 1978. Reprint, London: Pimlico, 1999.

———. *The Crooked Timber of Humanity: Chapters in the History of Ideas*. Edited by Henry Hardy. 1990. Reprint, Princeton, NJ: Princeton University Press, 2013.

———. *Freedom and Its Betrayal*. Edited by Henry Hardy. 2002. Reprint, London: Pimlico, 2003.

———. *Karl Marx: His Life and Environment*. 1939. Reprint, Oxford: Oxford University Press, 1978.

———. *Liberty*. Edited by Henry Hardy. Oxford: Oxford University Press, 2002.

———. *Personal Impressions*. Edited by Henry Hardy. London: Hogarth Press, 1980.

———. *Political Ideas in the Romantic Age: Their Rise and Influence on Modern Thought*. Edited by Henry Hardy. London: Chatto and Windus, 2006.

———. *The Power of Ideas*. Edited by Henry Hardy. 2000. Reprint, London: Pimlico, 2001.
———. *The Roots of Romanticism*. Edited by Henry Hardy. London: Chatto and Windus, 1999.
———. *Russian Thinkers*. Edited by Henry Hardy. 1978. Reprint, London: Penguin, 1988.
———. *The Sense of Reality: Studies in Ideas and Their History*. Edited by Henry Hardy. London: Chatto and Windus, 1996.
———. "Sir Stuart Hampshire." Obituary. *The Times*, June 16, 2004. http://www.thetimes.co.uk/tto/opinion/obituaries/article2082485.ece.
———. *Three Critics of the Enlightenment: Vico, Hamann, Herder*. Edited by Henry Hardy. London: Pimlico, 2000.
———. *Unfinished Dialogue*. With Beata Polanowska-Sygulska. New York: Prometheus Books, 2006.
Berlin, Isaiah, and Steven Lukes. "Isaiah Berlin in Conversation with Steven Lukes." *Salmagundi*, no. 120 (Fall 1998): 52–134.
Berlin, Isaiah, and Bernard Williams. "Pluralism and Liberalism: A Reply." *Political Studies* 42, no. 2 (1994): 306–9.
Blackburn, Simon. "Making Ends Meet." *Philosophical Books* 27, no. 4 (1986): 193–203.
Bode, Mark. "Everything Is What It Is, and Not Another Thing: Knowledge and Freedom in Isaiah Berlin's Thought." *British Journal for the History of Philosophy* 19, no. 2 (2011): 305–26.
Brennan, Jason. *Against Democracy*. Princeton, NJ: Princeton University Press, 2016.
Brockliss, Laurence, and Ritchie Robertson. *Isaiah Berlin and the Enlightenment*. Oxford: Oxford University Press, 2016.
Cartwright, Nancy. "Philosophy of Social Technology: Get on Board." *Proceedings and Address of the American Philosophical Association* 89, no. 2 (2015): 98–116.
Caute, David. *Isaac and Isaiah: The Punishment of a Cold War Heretic*. London: Yale University Press, 2013.
Cherniss, Joshua. "Against 'Engineers of Human Souls': Paternalism, 'Managerialism,' and the Development of Isaiah Berlin's Liberalism." *History of Political Thought* 35, no. 3 (2014): 565–88.
———. "Isaiah Berlin." In *The Edinburgh Companion to Political Realism*, edited by Robert Schuett and Miles Hollingworth. Edinburgh: Edinburgh University Press, 2018.
———. "Isaiah Berlin's Thought and Legacy: Critical Reflections on a Symposium." *European Journal of Political Theory* 12, no. 1 (2013): 5–23.
———. *A Mind in Its Time: The Development of Isaiah Berlin's Thought*. Oxford: Oxford University Press, 2013.
———. "'The Sense of Reality': Berlin on Political Judgement and Political Leadership." In *The Cambridge Companion to Isaiah Berlin*, edited by Joshua Cherniss and Steven B. Smith, 53–78. Cambridge: Cambridge University Press, 2018.
Cherniss, Joshua, and Henry Hardy. "Isaiah Berlin." *Stanford Encyclopedia of Philosophy* (Winter 2017 edition), edited by Edward N. Zalta. https://plato.stanford.edu/entries/berlin.
Choi, Naomi. "Berlin, Analytical Philosophy, and the Revival of Political Philosophy." In *The Cambridge Companion to Isaiah Berlin*, edited by Joshua Cherniss and Steven B. Smith, 33–52. Cambridge: Cambridge University Press, 2018.
Christiano, Thomas. *The Constitution of Equality: Democratic Authority and Its Limits*. Oxford: Oxford University Press, 2010.
Cohen, G. A. *Rescuing Justice and Equality*. Cambridge, MA: Harvard University Press, 2008.
Cohen, Joshua. "Pluralism and Proceduralism." *Chicago-Kent Law Review* 69 (1994): 589–618.

Cottingham, John. "The Good Life and the Radical Contingency of the Ethical." In *Reading Bernard Williams*, edited by Daniel Calcutt, 24–42. London: Routledge, 2008.

Crowder, George. *Isaiah Berlin: Liberty and Pluralism*. Cambridge: Polity, 2004.

———. "Pluralism and Liberalism." *Political Studies* 42, no. 2 (1994): 293–305.

Crowder, George, and Henry Hardy. "Appendix: Berlin's Universal Values—Core or Horizon?" In *The One and the Many*, edited by George Crowder and Henry Hardy, 293–98. New York: Prometheus Books, 2007.

Daily Telegraph. "An Oxford Pessimist." November 20, 1999. https://www.telegraph.co.uk/culture/4719061/An-Oxford-pessimist.html.

Dubnov, Arie. *Isaiah Berlin: The Journey of a Jewish Liberal*. New York: Palgrave, 2012.

Dunn, John. *Breaking Democracy's Spell*. New Haven, CT: Yale University Press, 2014.

———. "Political Obligations and Political Possibilities." In *Political Obligation in Its Historical Context: Essays in Political Theory*, 243–300. Cambridge: Cambridge University Press, 1990.

———. *Western Political Theory in the Face of the Future*. Cambridge: Cambridge University Press, 1993.

Dworkin, Ronald. "Do Liberal Values Conflict?" In *The Legacy of Isaiah Berlin*, edited by Ronald Dworkin, Mark Lilla, and Robert. B. Silvers, 73–90. New York: New York Review of Books, 2001.

———. *Law's Empire*. London: Harvard University Press, 1986.

———. *Sovereign Virtue: The Theory and Practice of Equality*. London: Harvard University Press, 2002.

Edyvane, Derek. "Justice as Conflict: The Question of Stuart Hampshire." *Contemporary Political Theory* 7, no. 3 (2008): 317–40.

———. "Richly Imaginative Barbarism: Stuart Hampshire and the Normality of Conflict." *Theoria: A Journal of Social and Political Theory* (forthcoming).

Erman, Eva, and Niklas Moller. "Political Legitimacy for Our World: Where Is Political Realism Going?" *Journal of Politics* 80, no. 2 (2018): 525–38.

———. "Political Legitimacy in the Real Normative World." *British Journal of Political Science* 45, no. 1 (2015): 215–33.

Estlund, David. *Democratic Authority: A Philosophical Framework*. Princeton, NJ: Princeton University Press, 2009.

———. "Human Nature and the Limits (if Any) of Political Philosophy." *Philosophy & Public Affairs* 39, no. 3 (2011): 207–37.

Farrelly, Colin. "Justice in Ideal Theory: A Refutation." *Political Studies* 55, no. 4 (2007): 844–64.

Ferrell, Jason. "Isaiah Berlin as Essayist." *Political Theory* 40, no. 5 (October 2012): 602–28.

Finlayson, Lorna. "*With radicals like these, who needs conservatives?* Doom, Gloom, and Realism in Political Theory." *European Journal of Political Theory* 16, no. 3 (2017): 264–82.

Flikschuh, Katrin. *Freedom: Contemporary Liberal Perspectives*. Cambridge: Polity, 2007.

Floyd, Jonathan. "From Historical Contextualism, to Mentalism, to Behaviourism." In *Political Philosophy versus History? Contextualism and Real Politics in Contemporary Political Thought*, edited by Jonathan Floyd and Marc Stears, 38–64. Cambridge: Cambridge University Press, 2011.

———. *Is Political Philosophy Impossible? Thoughts and Behaviour in Normative Political Theory*. Cambridge: Cambridge University Press, 2017.

Frankena, William. Review of *Morality and Conflict*, by Stuart Hampshire. *Ethics* 95, no. 3 (April 1985): 740–43.

Freeden, Michael. "Interpretative Realism and Prescriptive Realism." *Journal of Political Ideologies* 17, no. 1 (2012): 1–11.
Freyenhagen, Fabian. "Taking Reasonable Pluralism Seriously: An Internal Critique of Political Liberalism." *Politics, Philosophy, and Economics* 10, no. 3 (2011): 323–42.
Fricker, Miranda. "Confidence and Irony." In *Morality, Reflection, and Ideology*, edited by Edward Harcourt, 87–112. Oxford: Oxford University Press, 2000.
———. "The Relativism of Blame and Bernard Williams's Relativism of Distance." *Proceedings of the Aristotelian Society* 84 (2010): 151–77.
———. "Styles of Moral Relativism—A Critical Family Tree." In *The Oxford Handbook of the History of Ethics*, edited by Roger Crisp, 793–817. Oxford: Oxford University Press, 2015.
Fumurescu, Alin. *Compromise: A Political and Philosophical History*. Cambridge: Cambridge University Press, 2013.
Galipeau, Claude. *Isaiah Berlin's Liberalism*. Oxford: Clarendon Press, 1994.
Galston, William. *Liberal Pluralism: The Implications of Value Pluralism for Political Theory*. Cambridge: Cambridge University Press, 2002.
———. "Moral Pluralism and Liberal Democracy: Isaiah Berlin's Heterodox Liberalism." *Review of Politics* 71, no. 1 (2009): 85–99.
———. *The Practice of Liberal Pluralism*. New York: Cambridge University Press, 2005.
———. "Realism in Political Theory." *European Journal of Political Theory* 9, no. 4 (2010): 385–411.
Garrard, Graeme. "Strange Reversals: Berlin on the Enlightenment and the Counter-Enlightenment." In *The One and the Many*, edited by George Crowder and Henry Hardy, 141–58. New York: Prometheus Books, 2007.
Gaus, Gerald. *Contemporary Theories of Liberalism*. London: Sage, 2003.
———. "Should Philosophers 'Apply Ethics'?" *Think* 3, no. 9 (2005): 63–68.
———. *The Tyranny of the Ideal: Justice in a Diverse Society*. Princeton, NJ: Princeton University Press, 2016.
Geuss, Raymond. "Did Williams Do Ethics?" *Arion* 19, no. 3 (2012): 141–62.
———. *History and Illusion in Politics*. Cambridge: Cambridge University Press, 2001.
———. *The Idea of a Critical Theory*. Cambridge: Cambridge University Press, 1981.
———. "Moralism and Realpolitik." In *Politics and the Imagination*, 31–42. Princeton, NJ: Princeton University Press, 2009.
———. *Philosophy and Real Politics*. Princeton, NJ: Princeton University Press, 2008.
———. "Thucydides, Nietzsche, and Williams." In *Outside Ethics*, 219–33. Princeton, NJ: Princeton University Press, 2005.
Glover, Jonathan. *Humanity: A Moral History of the Twentieth Century*. London: Penguin, 1999.
Gowans, Chris. "Moral Relativism." *Stanford Encyclopedia of Philosophy* (Winter 2016 edition), edited by Edward N. Zalta. https://plato.stanford.edu/entries/moral-relativism/.
Gray, John. *Enlightenment's Wake*. Abingdon: Routledge, 1995.
———. *Isaiah Berlin: An Interpretation of His Thought*. Princeton, NJ: Princeton University Press, 1996.
———. *Two Faces of Liberalism*. Cambridge: Polity, 2004.
Griffin, James. "First Steps in an Account of Human Rights." *European Journal of Philosophy* 9, no. 3 (2001): 306–27.
Gutmann, Amy, and Dennis Thompson. *The Spirit of Compromise: Why Governing Demands It and Campaigning Undermines It*. Princeton, NJ: Princeton University Press, 2012.

Haldane, John. Review of *Justice Is Conflict*, by Stuart Hampshire. *Journal of Applied Philosophy* 18, no. 1 (2001): 91–93.

Hall, Edward. "How to Do Realistic Political Theory (and Why You Might Want To)." *European Journal of Political Theory* 16, no. 3 (July 2017): 283–303.

Hall, Edward, and Matt Sleat. "Ethics, Morality, and the Case for Realist Political Theory." *Critical Review of International Social and Political Philosophy* 20, no. 3 (March 2017): 276–90.

Hamlin, Alan, and Zofia Stemplowska. "Theory, Ideal Theory, and the Theory of Ideals." *Political Studies Review* 10, no. 1 (2012): 48–62.

Hampshire, Stuart. *Freedom of Mind: And Other Essays*. Oxford: Clarendon Press, 1972.

———. *Innocence and Experience*. 1989. Reprint, London: Penguin, 1992.

———. *Justice Is Conflict*. 1999. Reprint, Princeton, NJ: Princeton University Press, 2000.

———. "Liberalism: The New Twist." *New York Review of Books*, August 1993. http://www.nybooks.com/articles/1993/08/12/liberalism-the-new-twist/.

———. *Morality and Conflict*. Oxford: Basil Blackwell, 1983.

———. "Nationalism." In *Isaiah Berlin: A Celebration*, edited by Edna Margalit and Avishai Margalit, 127–34. London: Hogarth Press, 1991.

———. *Spinoza and Spinozism*. Oxford: Clarendon Press, 2005.

———. *Thought and Action*. London: Chatto and Windus, 1960.

———. "Uncertainty in Politics." *Encounter* (January 1957): 34–37.

Hanley, Ryan Patrick. "Political Science and Political Understanding: Isaiah Berlin on the Nature of Political Inquiry." *American Political Science Review* 98, no. 2 (2004): 327–39.

Harris, Ian. "Berlin and His Critics." In *Liberty*, edited by Henry Hardy, 349–66. Oxford: Oxford University Press, 2002.

Hart. H. L. A. *The Concept of Law*. Oxford: Clarendon Press, 2012.

———. "Who Can Tell Right from Wrong?" *New York Review of Books*, July 17, 1986. https://www.nybooks.com/articles/1986/07/17/who-can-tell-right-from-wrong/.

Honig, Bonnie. *Political Theory and the Displacement of Politics*. Ithaca, NY: Cornell University Press, 1993.

Horton, John. "John Gray and the Political Theory of Modus Vivendi." In *The Political Theory of John Gray*, edited by John Horton and Glen Newey, 43–57. Oxford: Routledge, 2007.

———. "Political Legitimacy, Justice, and Consent." *Critical Review of International Social and Political Philosophy* 15, no. 2 (2012): 129–48.

———. "Proceduralism as Thin Universalism: Stuart Hampshire's 'Procedural Justice.'" In *Principles and Political Order: The Challenge of Diversity*, edited by Bruce Haddock, Peri Roberts, and Peter Sutch, 128–46. London: Routledge, 2006.

———. "Realism, Liberalism, and a Political Theory of Modus Vivendi." *European Journal of Political Theory* 9, no. 4 (2010): 431–48.

———. "What Might It Mean for Political Theory to Be More Realistic?" *Philosophia* 45 (2017): 487–501.

Hume, David. "Idea of a Perfect Commonwealth." In *Essays: Moral, Political, and Literary*, edited by Eugene F. Miller, 512–29. Indianapolis: Liberty Fund, 1987.

———. "Of the First Principles of Government." In *Essays: Moral, Political, and Literary*, edited by Eugene F. Miller, 32–36. Indianapolis: Liberty Fund, 1987.

———. "Of the Origin of Government." In *Essays: Moral, Political, and Literary*, edited by Eugene F. Miller, 37–41. Indianapolis: Liberty Fund, 1987.

Ignatieff, Michael. *Isaiah Berlin: A Life*. London: Vintage, 2000.

———. "Understanding Fascism?" In *Isaiah Berlin: A Celebration*, edited by Edna Margalit and Avishai Margalit, 135–45. London: Hogarth Press, 1991.

Jahanbegloo, Ramin. *Conversations with Isaiah Berlin: Recollections of a Historian of Ideas*. 1991. Reprint, London: Orion, 1993.

Jenkins, Mark. *Bernard Williams*. Chesham: Acumen, 2006.

Jones, Peter. "The Political Theory of Modus Vivendi." *Philosophia* 45 (2017): 443–61.

Joyce, Richard. "Moral Anti-realism." *Stanford Encyclopedia of Philosophy* (Winter 2016 edition), edited by Edward N. Zalta. https://plato.stanford.edu/entries/moral-anti-realism/.

Jubb, Robert. "Realism in Analytical Political Theory." In *Methods in Analytical Political Theory*, edited by Adrian Blau, 112–30. Cambridge: Cambridge University Press, 2017.

———. "The Real Value of Equality." *Journal of Politics* 77, no. 3 (2015): 679–91.

———. "The Tragedies of Non-ideal Theory." *European Journal of Political Theory* 11, no. 3 (2012): 229–46.

Kateb, George. "Can Cultures Be Judged? Two Defenses of Cultural Pluralism in Isaiah Berlin's Work." *Social Research* 66, no. 4 (1999): 1009–38.

Katznelson, Ira. "Isaiah Berlin's Modernity." *Social Research* 66, no. 4 (1999): 1079–1101.

Kekes, John. *The Morality of Pluralism*. Princeton, NJ: Princeton University Press, 1993.

Kelly, Paul. "Rescuing Political Theory from the Tyranny of History." In *Political Philosophy versus History? Contextualism and Real Politics in Contemporary Political Thought*, edited by Jonathan Floyd and Marc Stears, 13–37. Cambridge: Cambridge University Press, 2011.

Kenny, Michael. "Isaiah Berlin's Contribution to Modern Political Theory." *Political Studies* 48, no. 5 (2000): 1026–39.

Kis, Janos. "Berlin's Two Concepts of Positive Liberty." *European Journal of Political Theory* 12, no. 1 (2013): 31–48.

Klosko, George. *Democratic Procedures and Liberal Consensus*. New York: Oxford University Press, 2004.

———. "Rawls's Public Reason and American Society." In *Reflections on Rawls: An Assessment of His Legacy*, edited by Shaun Young, 23–44. Farnham: Ashgate, 2009.

Kolodny, Niko. "Rule Over None I: What Justifies Democracy?" *Philosophy & Public Affairs* 42, no. 3 (2014): 195–229.

———. "Rule Over None II: Social Equality and the Justification of Democracy." *Philosophy & Public Affairs* 42, no. 4 (2014): 287–336.

Korab-Karpowicz, Julian. "Political Realism in International Relations." *Stanford Encyclopedia of Philosophy* (Summer 2018 edition), edited by Edward N. Zalta. https://plato.stanford.edu/archives/sum2018/entries/realism-intl-relations/.

Korsgaard, Christine. "Skepticism about Practical Reason." *Journal of Philosophy* 83, no. 1 (1986): 5–25.

Krishna, Nakul. "Liberalism and Authenticity in the Philosophy of Bernard Williams." Unpublished Manuscript.

Kukathas, Chandran. *The Liberal Archipelago: A Theory of Diversity and Freedom*. Oxford: Oxford University Press, 2003.

Larmore, Charles. "The Truth in Political Realism." In *Politics Recovered: Realist Thought in Theory and Practice*, edited by Matt Sleat, 27–48. New York: Columbia University Press, 2017.

———. "What Is Political Philosophy?" *Journal of Moral Philosophy* 10, no. 3 (2013): 276–306.

Lassman, Peter. *Pluralism*. Cambridge: Polity, 2011.

———. "Pluralism and Pessimism: A Central Theme in the Political Thought of Stuart Hampshire." *History of Political Thought* 30, no. 2 (2009): 315–35.

Leader-Maynard, Jonathan, and Alex Worsnip. "Is There a Distinctively Political Normativity?" *Ethics* 128, no. 4 (2018): 756–87.
Lear, Jonathan. *Radical Hope: Ethics in the Face of Cultural Devastation*. London: Harvard University Press, 2006.
Levy, Jacob. "There Is No Such Thing as Ideal Theory." *Social Philosophy and Policy* 33, no. 1/2 (2016): 312–33.
MacGilvrey, Eric. "Republicanism and the Market in 'Two Concepts of Liberty.'" In *Isaiah Berlin and the Politics of Freedom: "Two Concepts of Liberty" 50 Years Later*, edited by Bruce Baum and Robert Nichols, 114–28. London: Routledge, 2013.
MacIntyre, Alasdair. *Ethics in the Conflicts of Modernity: An Essay on Desire, Practical Reasoning, and Narrative*. Cambridge: Cambridge University Press, 2016.
Matravers, Matt, and Susan Mendus. "The Reasonableness of Pluralism." In *The Culture of Toleration in Diverse Societies*, edited by Catriona McKinnon and Dario Castiglione, 38–53. Manchester: Manchester University Press, 2003.
May, Simon. "Principled Compromise and the Abortion Controversy." *Philosophy & Public Affairs* 33, no. 4 (2005): 317–48.
McQueen, Alison. "The Case for Kinship: Classical Realism and Political Realism." In *Politics Recovered: Realist Thought in Theory and Practice*, edited by Matt Sleat, 243–69. New York: Columbia University Press, 2018.
———. *Political Realism in Apocalyptic Times*. Cambridge: Cambridge University Press, 2018.
Meyer, Philipp. *The Son*. London: Simon & Schuster, 2013.
Miller, David. "Political Philosophy for Earthlings." In *Political Theory: Methods and Approaches*, edited by David Leopold and Marc Stears, 29–48. Oxford: Oxford University Press, 2008.
———. "A Tale of Two Cities; or, Political Philosophy as Lamentation." In *Justice for Earthlings: Essays in Political Philosophy*, 228–49. Cambridge: Cambridge University Press, 2013.
Moody-Adams, Michele. *Fieldwork in Familiar Places: Morality, Culture, and Philosophy*. Cambridge, MA: Harvard University Press, 2002.
Moore, A. W. "Realism and the Absolute Conception." In *Bernard Williams*, edited by Alan Thomas, 24–46. Cambridge: Cambridge University Press, 2007.
Moran, Richard. *Authority and Estrangement: An Essay on Self-Knowledge*. Princeton, NJ: Princeton University Press, 2001.
Mouffe, Chantal. *On the Political*. Abingdon: Routledge, 2005.
Müller, Jan-Werner. "Fear and Freedom: On Cold War Liberalism." *European Journal of Political Theory* 7, no. 1 (2008): 45–64
———. "Value-Pluralism in Twentieth-Century Anglo-American Thought." In *Modern Pluralism: Anglo-American Debates since 1880*, edited by Mark Bevir, 81–104. Cambridge: Cambridge University Press, 2012.
Murphy, Liam. *Moral Demands in Nonideal Theory*. Oxford: Oxford University Press, 2003.
Myers, Ella. "From Pluralism to Liberalism: Rereading Isaiah Berlin." *Review of Politics* 72, no. 4 (2010): 599–625.
Nagel, Thomas. *The Last Word*. Oxford: Oxford University Press, 1997.
Newey, Glen. "Value Pluralism in Contemporary Liberalism." *Dialogue* 37, no. 3 (1998): 493–522.
Nietzsche, Friedrich. *Untimely Meditations*. Edited by Daniel Breazeale. Cambridge: Cambridge University Press, 2005.
Norton, Robert Edward. "The Myth of the Counter-Enlightenment." *Journal of the History of Ideas* 68, no. 4 (2007): 635–58.

Nussbaum, Martha. "Perfectionist Liberalism and Political Liberalism." *Philosophy & Public Affairs* 39, no. 1 (2011): 3–45.

———. "Tragedy and Justice." *Boston Review*, October/November 2003. http://bostonreview.net/archives/BR28.5/nussbaum.html.

O'Grady, Jane. "Professor Sir Bernard Williams." Obituary. *Guardian*, June 13, 2003. https://www.theguardian.com/news/2003/jun/13/guardianobituaries.obituaries.

———. "Sir Stuart Hampshire." Obituary. *Guardian*, June 16, 2004. https://www.theguardian.com/news/2004/jun/16/guardianobituaries.obituaries.

O'Neill, Onora. *Towards Justice and Virtue*. Cambridge: Cambridge University Press, 1996.

Owen, David. "Realism in Ethics and Politics: Bernard Williams, Political Theory, and the Critique of Morality." In *Politics Recovered: Realist Thought in Theory and Practice*, edited by Matt Sleat, 73–92. New York: Columbia University Press, 2017.

Philp, Mark. *Political Conduct*. Cambridge, MA: Harvard University Press, 2007.

———. "Realism without Illusions." *Political Theory* 40, no. 5 (2012): 629–49.

Prinz, Janosch, and Enzo Rossi. "Political Realism as Ideology Critique." *Critical Review of International Social and Political Philosophy* 20, no. 3 (2017): 348–65.

Raekstad, Paul. "Realism, Utopianism, and Radical Values." *European Journal of Philosophy* 26, no. 1 (2018): 145–68.

Rawls, John. "The Idea of an Overlapping Consensus." *Oxford Journal of Legal Studies* 7, no. 1 (1987): 1–25.

———. *Justice as Fairness: A Restatement*. Cambridge, MA: Harvard University Press, 2003.

———. *The Law of Peoples*. Cambridge, MA: Harvard University Press, 1999.

———. *Political Liberalism*. New York: Columbia University Press, 1996.

———. *A Theory of Justice: Revised Edition*. Oxford: Oxford University Press, 1999.

Raz, Joseph. *The Morality of Freedom*. Oxford: Oxford University Press, 1986.

Riley, Jonathan. "Defending Cultural Pluralism: Within Liberal Limits." *Political Theory* 30, no. 1 (Feb. 2002): 68–96.

———. "Interpreting Berlin's Liberalism." *American Political Science Review* 95, no. 2 (June 2001): 283–95.

———. "Isaiah Berlin's 'Minimum of Common Moral Ground.'" *Political Theory* 41, no.1 (2013): 61–89.

Robeyns, Ingrid. "Ideal Theory in Theory and Practice." *Social Theory and Practice* 34, no. 3 (2008): 341–62.

Rorty, Richard. *Contingency, Irony, and Solidarity*. Cambridge: Cambridge University Press, 1989.

Rossi, Enzo. "Justice, Legitimacy, and (Normative) Authority for Political Realists." *Critical Review of International Social and Political Philosophy* 15, no. 2 (2012): 149–64.

Rossi, Enzo, and Matt Sleat. "Realism in Normative Political Theory." *Philosophy Compass* 9, no. 10 (2014): 689–701.

Russell, Paul. "Hume's Optimism and Williams's Pessimism: From a Science of Man to Genealogical Critique." In *New Essays on Bernard Williams' "Ethics and the Limits of Philosophy,"* edited by Sophie Grace Chappell and Marcel van Ackeren, 37–52. London: Routledge, 2019.

Sabl, Andrew. *Hume's Politics: Co-ordination and Crisis in the History of England*. Princeton, NJ: Princeton University Press, 2012.

———. "Realist Liberalism: An Agenda." *Critical Review of International Social and Political Philosophy* 20, no. 3 (2017): 366–84.

———. Review of *Liberal Realism: A Realist Theory of Liberal Politics*, by Matt Sleat. *Perspectives on Politics* 13, no. 4 (2015): 1141–43.

———. *Ruling Passions: Political Offices and Democratic Ethics*. Princeton, NJ: Princeton University Press, 2002.

Sagar, Paul. "From Scepticism to Liberalism? Bernard Williams, the Foundations of Liberalism, and Political Realism." *Political Studies* 64, no. 2 (2014): 368–84.

———. "Legitimacy and Domination." In *Politics Recovered: Realist Thought in Theory and in Practice*, edited by Matt Sleat, 114–39. New York: Columbia University Press, 2017.

———. "Minding the Gap: Bernard Williams and David Hume on Living an Ethical Life." *Journal of Moral Philosophy* 11 (2014): 615–38.

Schmidtz, David. "Nonideal Theory: What It Is and What It Needs to Be." *Ethics* 121, no. 4 (2011): 772–96.

Schmitt, Carl. *The Concept of the Political: Expanded Edition*. Translated by George Schwab. Chicago: University of Chicago Press, 2007.

Sen, Amartya. *The Idea of Justice*. London: Penguin, 2010.

———. "What Do We Want from a Theory of Justice?" *Journal of Philosophy* 103, no. 5 (2006): 215–38.

Sheehy, Paul. "Interview: Stuart Hampshire." *Philosophy Now: A Magazine of Ideas*, August/September 2000. https://philosophynow.org/issues/28/Sir_Stuart_Hampshire.

Shklar, Judith. "The Liberalism of Fear." In *Political Thought and Political Thinkers*, edited by Stanley Hoffman, 3–20. Chicago: University of Chicago Press, 1998.

Simmons, A. John. "Ideal and Nonideal Theory." *Philosophy & Public Affairs* 38, no. 1 (2010): 5–36.

———. "Justification and Legitimacy." *Ethics* 109, no. 4 (1999): 739–71.

Skinner, Quentin. "Modernity and Disenchantment: Some Historical Reflections." In *Philosophy in an Age of Pluralism: The Philosophy of Charles Taylor in Question*, edited by James Tully and Daniel Weinstock, 37–48. Cambridge: Cambridge University Press, 1994.

Skorupski, John. "Internal Reasons and the Scope of Blame." In *Bernard Williams*, edited by Alan Thomas, 73–103. Cambridge: Cambridge University Press, 2007.

Sleat, Matt. "Bernard Williams and the Possibility of a Realist Political Theory." *European Journal of Political Theory* 9, no. 4 (2010): 485–603.

———. *Liberal Realism: A Realist Theory of Liberal Politics*. Manchester: Manchester University Press, 2013.

———. "Making Sense of Our Political Lives—The Political Philosophy of Bernard Williams." *Critical Review of International Social and Political Philosophy* 10, no. 3 (2007): 389–98.

———. "Realism, Liberalism, and Ideal Theory: or, Are There Two Ways to Do Realistic Political Theory?" *Political Studies* 64, no. 1 (2016): 27–41.

Smith, Steven. *Modernity and Its Discontents: Making and Unmaking the Bourgeois from Machiavelli to Bellow*. New Haven, CT: Yale University Press, 2017.

Spragens, Tom. "Justice, Consensus, and Boundaries: Assessing Political Liberalism." *Political Theory* 31, no. 4 (August 2003): 589–601.

Stears, Marc. "Liberalism and the Politics of Compulsion." *British Journal of Political Science* 37, no. 3 (2007): 533–53.

Stemplowska, Zofia. "What's Ideal about Ideal Theory?" *Social Theory and Practice* 34, no. 3 (2008): 319–40.

Stemplowska, Zofia, and Adam Swift. "Ideal and Nonideal Theory." In *The Oxford Handbook of Political Philosophy*, edited by David Estlund, 373–92. Oxford: Oxford University Press, 2012.

Strauss, Leo. "Relativism." In *The Rebirth of Classical Political Rationalism: An Introduction to the Thought of Leo Strauss*, 12–26. Chicago: University of Chicago Press, 1989.

Strawson, Galen. "Towards a Common Justice." *The Observer*, November 12, 1989.

Swift, Adam. "The Value of Philosophy in Nonideal Circumstances." *Social Theory and Practice* 34, no. 3 (2008): 363–87.

Talisse, Robert. *Pluralism and Liberal Politics*. New York: Routledge, 2012.

Valentini, Laura. "Ideal vs. Non-ideal Theory: A Conceptual Map." *Philosophy Compass* 7, no. 9 (2012): 654–64.

———. "On the Apparent Paradox of Ideal Theory." *Journal of Political Philosophy* 17, no. 3 (2009): 332–55.

Van Parjis, Phillippe. "What Makes a Good Compromise?" *Government and Opposition* 47, no. 3 (January 2012): 466–80.

Voorhoeve, Alex. "Bernard Williams: A Mistrustful Animal." In *Conversations on Ethics*, edited by Alex Voorhoeve, 195–214. Oxford: Oxford University Press, 2009.

Waldron, Jeremy. *Law and Disagreement*. Oxford: Oxford University Press, 1999.

———. *Political Political Theory: Essays on Institutions*. Cambridge, MA: Harvard University Press, 2016.

Wendt, Fabian. *Compromise, Peace, and Public Justification: Political Morality beyond Justice*. London: Palgrave, 2016.

Williams, Bernard. "*Contingency, Irony and Solidarity* by Richard Rorty." In *Essays and Reviews: 1959–2002*, edited by Michael Wood, 295–300. Oxford: Princeton University Press, 2014.

———. "A Critique of Utilitarianism." In *Utilitarianism: For and Against*, with J. J. C. Smart. 1973. Reprint, Cambridge: Cambridge University Press, 2007.

———. *Descartes: The Project of Pure Enquiry*. 1978. Reprint, London: Routledge, 2005.

———. *Ethics and the Limits of Philosophy*. 1985. Reprint, London: Routledge, 2006.

———. "History, Morality, and the Test of Reflection." In *The Sources of Normativity*, by Christine Korsgaard, 210–18. Cambridge: Cambridge University Press, 1996.

———. *In the Beginning Was the Deed: Realism and Moralism in Political Argument*. Edited by Geoffrey Hawthorn. Princeton, NJ: Princeton University Press, 2005.

———. *Making Sense of Humanity and Other Philosophical Papers 1982–1993*. 1995. Reprint, Cambridge: Cambridge University Press, 1998.

———. *Morality: An Introduction to Ethics*. 1972. Reprint, Cambridge: Cambridge University Press, 1993.

———. *Moral Luck: Philosophical Papers 1973–1980*. 1981. Reprint, Cambridge: Cambridge University Press, 1999.

———. "The Need to Be Sceptical." In *Essays and Reviews: 1959–2002*, edited by Michael Wood, 311–17. Oxford: Princeton University Press, 2014.

———. *Philosophy as a Humanistic Discipline*. Edited by A. W. Moore. Princeton, NJ: Princeton University Press, 2006.

———. "Replies." In *World, Mind, and Ethics: Essays on the Ethical Philosophy of Bernard Williams*, edited by J. E. J. Altham and Ross Harrison, 185–224. Cambridge: Cambridge University Press, 1995.

———. "Reply to Simon Blackburn." *Philosophical Books* 27, no. 4 (1986): 203–8.

———. "Seminar with Bernard Williams." *Ethical Perspectives* 6 (1999): 243–65.

———. *The Sense of the Past: Essays in the History of Philosophy*. Edited by Myles Burnyeat. Princeton, NJ: Princeton University Press, 2006.

———. *Shame and Necessity*. 1993. Reprint, Berkeley: University of California Press, 2008.

———. "*Sources of the Self: The Making of Modern Identity*, by Charles Taylor." In *Essays and Reviews: 1959–2002*, edited by Michael Wood, 301–10. Oxford: Princeton University Press, 2014.

———. "Tribute." In *The Book of Isaiah: Personal Impressions of Isaiah Berlin*, edited by Henry Hardy, 21–25. Woodbridge: Boydell, 2009.

———. *Truth and Truthfulness: An Essay in Genealogy*. Princeton, NJ: Princeton University Press, 2002.

———. "Why Philosophy Needs History." In *Essays and Reviews: 1959–2002*, edited by Michael Wood, 405–12. Oxford: Princeton University Press, 2014.

Williams, Shirley. *Climbing the Bookshelves: The Autobiography of Shirley Williams*. London: Virago, 2009.

Wittgenstein, Ludwig. *On Certainty*. Oxford: Blackwell, 1993.

Wolf, Susan. "The Deflation of Moral Philosophy." *Ethics* 97, no. 4 (1987): 821–33.

Yack, Bernard. Introduction to *Liberalism without Illusions: Essays on the Liberal Theory and Political Vision of Judith N. Shklar*, edited by Bernard Yack, 1–15. Chicago: University of Chicago Press, 1996.

Zakaras, Alex. "Isaiah Berlin's Cosmopolitan Ethics." *Political Theory* 32, no. 4 (2004): 495–518.

———. "A Liberal Pluralism: Isaiah Berlin and John Stuart Mill." *Review of Politics* 75, no. 1 (2013): 69–96.

Index

Note: when an entry refers to one of the primary theorists examined here, the name appears in parentheses.

Achen, Christopher H., 208n7
adversary argument, principle of (Hampshire): compromise and, 105–6; egalitarian norms required by, 103–4; as hearing the other side, 91–92; locally existing institutions and, 94–95; political audibility of demands and, 97–99
Archard, David, 101
Archilochus, 13
Archimedean point (Williams), 118
Aristotle: on human nature and moral philosophy, Hampshire's engagement with, 72–76, 104; phronesis, account of, 56; rationality of ethical life, skeptical implications of (Williams), 118–19
Attlee, Clement, 4
Austin, J. L., 182n13
authenticity (Williams), 133
authoritarianism: monism and (Berlin), 47–48; positive conception of freedom and (Berlin), 50
authority: legitimacy and (Williams), 145 (*see also* basic legitimation demand [BLD] [Williams]; legitimacy [Williams]); value pluralism and (Berlin), 60–62
Ayer, A. J., 182n13

Bartels, Larry M., 208n7
basic legitimation demand (BLD) (Williams): account of, 139–43, 199n1; consensus critique of, 145–48; core violations of human rights established by, 153; incorporation and, 144–45; "might is not right" axiom of, 150–52; normative content of, challenge to, 148–50; scope of, criticism of, 144–45; universal consent and, 146–47; Williams's politics, alleged unrealism of as challenge to, 150–51
Berlin, Isaiah: as empiricist, 27; examining basic presuppositions of political theory as chief task of, 22; the fox and the hedgehog, distinction between, 13; introduction to, 3–7; "liberal rationalist," claim to be, 52; obituary of Hampshire, 16–17; reasons for addressing, 14–15. *See also* Berlin-Hampshire-Williams
Berlin-Hampshire-Williams: ethical judgments by, realism and, 170–74; "freestanding" political thought not pursued by, 183n22; ideal/philosophical ethics, rejection of, 3–10; outstanding issues left by, 169–70; positive realist approach of, 12, 174–76; as Thucydidean realists, 10; as value pluralists, 5
Blackburn, Simon, 209n21
BLD. *See* basic legitimacy demand (BLD) (Williams)
Bode, Mark, 188n18
Brennan, Jason, 169
Burke, Edmund, 100

Carr, E. H., 8
Cherniss, Joshua, 192–93n5, 193n7, 197n51
Churchill, Winston, 4
Cohen, G. A., 1; fundamental principles, 50–51, 172; grounding of fundamental principles, 193n10
Cohen, Joshua, 194n14, 199n4
Collingwood, R. G., 22
compromise: Berlin on, 59–60; as a direct subsidiary requirement of procedural justice

compromise (cont.)
  (Hampshire), 104; fairness and (Hampshire), 17, 103–4, 106; Hampshire on, 60; moralist scorn for, undermining of (Hampshire), 111–12; perpetuity of conflict as reason to value (Hampshire), 107–9; reasons to, dilemma in establishing (Hampshire), 105–7, 112
confidence (Williams): historical analysis/consideration as a key to, 129–33; in relation to ethical commitments and beliefs, 128–33
conflict (Hampshire): gaps in Williams and Berlin influenced Hampshire's thinking on, 84; as a healthy sign of human thought and moral imagination, 71, 85–87, 111; perpetuity of as reason to value compromise, 107–9; political conflict not transcended by management of, 95; positive role of in generating values, 84–85; the principle of adversary argument and, 92; procedural justice as (see procedural justice [Hampshire])
conflict, defending political convictions in the face of, 100
Cottingham, John, 134, 136
critical theory principle (Williams): critical theory test, the disadvantaged/inequality and, 159–63, 165; definition of, 141; power of, doubts about, 165–66; truth-focused, historical narratives based on falsehoods and, 164; truth-focused, subtle cases and, 164–65
Crowder, George: "cultural" reading of Berlin's value pluralism, rejection of, 192n61; mutual dependence condition, rejection of, 43; pluralism and liberalism, attempt to align, 196–97n49; pluralism and the capabilities approach, attempt to align, 192n60; reconstruction of Berlin in a rejoinder to the value-twisting argument, 41–42; Riley's claim, rejection of, 189n36; value pluralist decisions are non-rational, argument that, 54; values that fall within the human horizon, 34

Dancy, Jonathan, 64
democratic theory, need for realist contributions to, 169–70
Dick, Philip K., 37
Dunn, John, 7, 208n6
Dworkin, Ronald, 1, 53, 62, 143, 201n24

Edyvane, Derek, 108–9, 199n2
Enlightenment: approval of thinkers of (Berlin), 52–53; negative narrative of (Williams), 154
Erman, Eva, 186n2
ethical reflection, value of (Williams), 125
ethics: Aristotle's attempt to find an Archimedean point, rejection of (Williams), 118–19; confidence (rather than knowledge or certainty) as the basis of ethical conviction (Williams) (see confidence [Williams]); external justification of ethical life, absence of (Williams), 122–23; historical reflection on commitments and beliefs (Williams), 131–33; imagination as part of human nature and (Hampshire), 76–77, 78–79; Kant's rational agency as an Archimedean point, rejection of (Williams), 120–21; knowledge in, thick concepts and, 122–23; morality as a threat to (Williams), 126–28; nonobjectivity and the application of beliefs, 123–24; objective foundation for/Archimedean point, rejection of (Williams), 118–23; propositions as true/false as basis for objectivity of, rejection of (Williams), 122–23; real and notional confrontations, distinction between (Williams), 124; realism and, 170–74; science and, difference between (Williams), 122–23; "single-criterion" theories (Kantian and utilitarian), rejection of (Hampshire), 77–78; "the superior power of the negative" in (Hampshire), 85
evil: absolute, difference between Berlin and Hampshire on, 198n10; domination as (Hampshire), 94; justice as a negative virtue and (Hampshire), 80–82; poverty as a persisting (Hampshire), 100; similarity to Berlin's minimum content of natural law, 80

fact/value distinction, 2, 36–37
fairness (Hampshire): compromise and, 17, 103–4, 106; procedural justice and, 17, 91, 94–96, 106–7, 156
fallacy of false fixity (Hampshire), 98–99, 101, 170
Finlayson, Lorna, 87
Floyd, Jonathan, 145, 147–48, 200n10, 200n12
Frankena, William, 16–17
Freeden, Michael, 145, 150–51
freedom, two conceptions of (Berlin). See liberty (Berlin)
Freyenhagen, Fabian, 62
Fricker, Miranda, 135, 192n64
Fumurescu, Alin, 111–12

Galston, William: majority of realists as "critical and cautionary," 12, 174; moral particularism favored by, 194n23; translating values into a common measure of value (utility) as problematic, 188n19; value pluralism and institutions that appeal to negotiation and bargaining, 62; value pluralism and liberalism, link between, 66–67; value pluralism and the impossibility of identifying ultimate values, 53–54
Gaus, Gerald, 88, 184n34, 190n51, 191n54
Geuss, Raymond: anti-liberal approach championed by, 8; ethics-first approach, realist rejection of, 1; liberalism, deriding Williams for his,

186n58; "politics should replace ethics" attributed to Williams by, 208n12; as realist political theorist, 7; relation between factual data and interpretation, explication of Williams's view of, 163; as strong realist, 171–72; "Thucydidean realism," 9–10
"good," Aristotle on, 72–73
Gray, John, 7, 63–65, 156, 192n63, 194n25
Griffin, James, 36–37

Haldane, John, 199n2
Hamlin, Alan, 183n32
Hampshire, Stuart: Berlin's obituary of, 16; intelligence officer, work as, 4, 43, 74, 78, 81; introduction to, 3–7. *See also* Berlin-Hampshire-Williams
Hardy, Henry, 34, 195n38
Harris, Ian, 193n7
Hart, H. L. A., 30–31, 189n31, 201n1
Hegel, Georg Wilhelm Friedrich, 157
Heraclitus, 86
Herder, Johann Gottfried, 35, 187n10
historical reflection/understanding (Williams): confidence and, 129–33; contingency and, 134–35; ethical commitments and, 131–33; Skinner's concern regarding, 132–33; truth and, 163–64
Hobbes, Thomas, 8, 143
Honig, Bonnie, 7–8, 197–98n1
Horton, John, 92–93, 199n2
human horizon (Berlin): comprehensible human values must fall within, 34–35; discussion of the concept, 37–40
human nature: account of (Berlin), 27; controversial account of (Hampshire), 110–11; moral philosophy and, Hampshire vs. Aristotle on, 72–76; recognition of basic needs as compatible with value pluralism (Berlin), 31–32; rejection of ahistorical models of (Berlin), 26; underdetermines questions about the good life, 5
human rights: core violations of (Williams), 152–53; existence of asserted (Berlin), 32
Hume, David, 82, 100, 132, 209n21

ideal theory, 11–12, 183–84n32
Ignatieff, Michael, 190n47
imagination (Hampshire): conflict as the inevitable result of, 85; diversity and, 75–76; moral judgments and, 78–79, 84–85
"inexhaustibility of description" (Hampshire), 78, 198n5
international relations (IR) realism, 8

Jahanbegloo, Ramin, 32
Jenkins, Mark, 133, 186n56
Jones, Peter, 209n23
Jubb, Robert, 156

justice: fairness and, distinction between (Hampshire), 91; as a negative virtue (Hampshire), 81–82, 91, 103; procedural (*see* procedural justice [Hampshire])

Kaltenbrunner, Ernst, 4
Kant, Immanuel: Berlin, influence on, 22, 193n5; ethics of, rejection of (Hampshire), 77–78; as progenitor of nationalism, Berlin's claim regarding, 16; rational agency as an objective grounding for ethics, rejection of (Williams), 120–21; the Romantics and, 27; view of making choices, endorsement of (Berlin), 196n48
Katznelson, Ira, 185n47
Kenny, Michael, 195n36
Klosko, George, 62, 196n43
Korab-Karpowicz, Julian, 8
Korsgaard, Christine, 202n11

Larmore, Charles, 148–50
Lear, Jonathan, 37–38
legitimacy (Williams): basic legitimation demand (*see* basic legitimation demand [BLD] [Williams]); critical theory principle (*see* critical theory principle [Williams]); of hierarchical structures, 153–54
Levy, Jacob, 12
liberalism: Berlin's defense of, 65–67; critics of, 67–68; of fear (Shklar), 154–55, 158; history of itself, lack of knowledge of (Williams), 129–30; realist version of (Williams), 143; Rorty and, 134–35; value pluralism (Berlin) and, 63–68; a value pluralism view of, 58; Williams's defense of, 67, 151–58, 166; Williams's defense of, problematic elements of, 155–56
liberal state: atrocities committed abroad, problem posed by, 157–58; legitimacy of (Williams), 147–48
liberty (Berlin): negative and positive conceptions of freedom, distinction between, 24, 48–49; negative conception of freedom, liberalism and, 63–64; negative conception of freedom, social evils generated by, 51; negative conception of freedom and basic liberty, distinction between, 196n48; positive conception of freedom, dangers of, 48–49, 51
Locke, John, 150

Machiavelli, Niccolò, 8, 59, 195n32
MacIntyre, Alasdair, 186n55
MacKinnon, Donald, 182n13
Macnabb, Donald, 182n13
Marx, Karl, 157
May, Simon, 200n14
McQueen, Alison, 10, 184n39
Meyer, Philipp, 37

Miller, David, 194n14
Moller, Niklas, 186n2
monism (Berlin): attraction of a priori assumptions, 28; "barbarous consequences" of in practice, 47–48; basic conception and implication of, 22–23; conflicting values, ignoring of, 27; failure to establish the truth of, 28; as one of two camps in the history of political thought, 195–96n39; politics as instrumental with antecedently discovered ends, 57–58
Moody-Adams, Michele, 187n10, 191n53
Moore, Adrian, 123, 201n1
moral antirealism (Berlin), 187n14
moralist vs. realist approach to political theory/philosophy, 1–3, 7–14; conflict and diversity as constructive (Hampshire), 88–89; impure considerations, necessity of confronting (Berlin), 51–52; legitimacy and (Williams), 141–42, 148–50; moral claims, multiplicity of (Hampshire), 74, 78–79; morality as a threat to ethical life (Williams), 126–28; political conflict and, 60–62; principles that can finally resolve disputes as a delusion (Hampshire), 100; "theory" as guide for judgments, rejection of (Berlin), 52–57; thin conception of procedural justice, critique of Rawls and (Hampshire), 96–97; utopianism and, 52; value pluralism and, 46; ways of life preclude reductive theorization (Hampshire), 82–83
morality: averting evils as the central presupposition of (Hampshire), 80 (see also evil); common core/natural element of (Hampshire), 79–82; common core of (Berlin), 31; conflict and, inseparability of (Hampshire), 71, 113; conflict and negation in, place of (Hampshire), 84–85; distinction between universal/convergent and distinctive/divergent moral claims (Hampshire), 79; of impartiality, rejection of (Williams), 121; pagan and Christian, distinction between (Berlin), 26; reason to be moral, argument that some people have no (Williams), 125; Romantics and Kant, disagreement between, 27; as a threat to ethical life (Williams), 126–28, 136; "three-tiered conception of" (Hampshire), 75; two faces of (Hampshire), 83–84; ways of life and holistic justifications (Hampshire), 82–83
moral philosophy: central/essential task of (Williams), 125, 137; essential task of (Berlin), 22; Hampshire and/vs. Aristotle on, 72–76; historical considerations to be taken seriously in (Williams), 130; two ways of approaching (Williams), 126
moral psychology: choosing between values and, 64; Hampshire's silence on, 109–10; Williams's, 205n30

moral relativism: central intuition behind, 29; of distance (Williams), 124; nonobjectivism distinguished from (Williams), 123–24; as self-refuting (Williams), 29; value pluralism and (see value pluralism leads to moral relativism, denial of [Berlin])
moral universalism, 130
Morgenthau, Hans, 8
Mouffe, Chantal, 7–8, 197–98n1
Müller, Jan-Werner, 40
mutual dependence condition, outlooks and, 25, 42–43

Nagel, Thomas, 130
naturalism (Hampshire), 94–95
natural law, minimum content of (Berlin), 21–22, 27, 30–32, 36–41, 43–44, 66; Hampshire's conception of evil and, 80
Nazis: Berlin on, 37, 40–41; entering into the outlook of, 37; as example of rule without legitimacy, 150–51; Hampshire on, 81, 102; Riley on Berlin on, 191n56
New Deal, Berlin's praise for, 51
Newey, Glen, 187n15
Nietzsche, Friedrich, 129, 133, 136, 157, 202n10
"no-shopping principle" (Hampshire), 25, 43
Nozick, Robert, 1
Nussbaum, Martha, 14–15, 186n56

objectivity of values: as consistent with value pluralism (Berlin), 27, 29–30, 34, 187n14; the human horizon and (Berlin), 37–39; moral objectivity, implications of a belief in, 29; unhelpful claims about (Berlin), 188n30
outlooks (Berlin): common values shared by different, 31–33; constrained by universal features of human nature, 32–34 (see also human horizon [Berlin]); as a dimension along which human nature can develop, 35; evaluation of, 35; implications of, 24–25; minimum content of natural law and, 43–44; multiplicity of, late Renaissance acknowledgment of, 26; mutual dependence condition and, 25, 42–43. See also ways of life (Hampshire)
Oxford Pessimists, 5

philosophy: ability to tell us how to live, skepticism about (Williams), 118, 124; Spinoza on the purpose of, 108; task of (Williams), 127. See also political theory/philosophy
Philp, Mark: on coercion in politics, 60; on coercion of those who deny that the legitimation story makes sense, 204n16; political conflict, further causes of, 207n2; political ethics, work in, 8; politics and brute force, distinction between, 203n1; as realist political theorist, 7

Plato, 86
pluralism: as one of two camps in the history of political thought (Berlin), 195n39; resolvable, 61–62; value (*see* value pluralism [Berlin]; value pluralism [Hampshire]; value pluralism [William])
political compromise. *See* compromise
political institutions (Hampshire): maintaining allegiance to by continuously forging political compromises, 89; protection from evil as the first job of, 89
political judgment (Berlin): the sense of reality and, 55–56; "theory" as guide for, rejection of, 52–57
political theory/philosophy: central tasks of (Williams), 137; challenging presuppositions as central task of (Berlin), 22; conflict as central to (Hampshire), 86–89, 112; as ethics applied to society (Berlin), 61; examination of social myths to unveil fallacies of false fixity as a role of (Hampshire), 99; historical considerations to be taken seriously (Williams), 130; historical turning points that challenge the presuppositions of, 26–27; ideal theory, impurity of, value pluralism and (Berlin), 47–52; moralist vs. realist approach to (*see* moralist vs. realist approach to political theory/philosophy); "rival elaborations of a moral text," rejection of political thought as (Williams), 62
politics: central purpose of (Hampshire), 89, 113; first question of (Williams), 139–43; irrelevance of to political moralists, 2; legitimacy, question of (*see* legitimacy [Williams]); of monism (Berlin), 57–58; moralist despondency about, rejection of (Hampshire), 112–13; questions of authority and legitimacy, 60–62; of value pluralism (Berlin), 57–63; Williams's alleged misunderstanding of, 150–51
practical reason: limits of (Hampshire), 73; the personal in (Williams), 120–21; procedural justice and (Hampshire), 92, 94; requirements for formulating reasons that defend a policy (Hampshire), 103
procedural justice (Hampshire): adversary argument, principle of (*see* adversary argument, principle of [Hampshire]); argument for basic, 91–97, 113–14; compromise and (*see* compromise); as a duty but not absolute, 95–96; fairness and, 17, 91, 94–96, 106–7, 156 (*see also* fairness [Hampshire]); fallacy of false fixity, problem of, 98–99, 101; injustice, as an account of, 92; natural reverence for persuasion/debate and, 109; rational decision-making in, challenge to, 92–93; sufficiency threshold for procedures of, 94; ways of life/conventions that are not consistent with, problem of, 97–99

procedural justice, thick reading of (Hampshire): affective considerations raise concerns about Hampshire's wider thought, 107–11; prescriptive/affective considerations distinguished, 102–3; prescriptive considerations as inconsistent with Hampshire's wider thought, 103–7
procedural justice, thin reading of (Hampshire): concerns regarding, 100–102; critique of Rawls and, 96–97

rationality/reason: limits of (Berlin), 65; as a universal domain of thought (Hampshire), 75
Rawls, John: Berlin's view of, 194n18; choosing between values, disagreement with Berlin on necessity of, 52; "freestanding" political philosophy pursued by, 182–83n22; Hampshire's critique of, 96, 111; Hampshire's critique of, accuracy of, 199n4; "high liberalism" of, 143; justice as the first virtue of social institutions, 3; liberalism of, 150; as mainstream political philosopher, 1; as originator of debate between ideal and nonideal political theory, 183n32; philosophical abstraction, benefits of, 175–76; resolvable pluralism, 61–62; theory of justice as a structural model of political moralism, 9
realism/realists: correctives to moralistic political theory endorsed by, 9–11; as critical, oppositional, and constructive, 7, 12; as critique of and alternative to moralism/idealism (*see* moralist vs. realist approach to political theory/philosophy); "dry" and "wet" approaches, distinction between, 208n19; ethics and, 170–74; freestanding political theory, skepticism regarding, 183n22; Hampshire and, 71–72, 85, 87; ideal theory, rejection of, 11–12; international relations (IR), in the field of, 8; legitimacy, conception of (*see* legitimacy [Williams]); moral relativism and, question of, 21; nonideal theory not a variant of, 184–85n39; outstanding issues that need to be addressed by, 168–70; the politics of value pluralism and (Berlin), 57–63; positive of Berlin, Hampshire, and Williams, 174–76; "strong" and "weak" variation of, 170–72; Thucydidean, 9–10; value pluralism and (Berlin), 46
relativism. *See* moral relativism
resentment over political settlements, 60–61
resolvable pluralism, 61–62
Riley, Jonathan, 189n36, 191n56
Romanticism, 26–27, 41
Roosevelt, Franklin, 57, 195n31
Rorty, Richard, 134–35
Rossi, Enzo, 9, 170–71, 185n42

Sabl, Andrew, 7–8, 173–74, 208n19
Sagar, Paul, 162–63, 204n2, 206n47, 207n54

Sartre, Jean-Paul, 76
science: absolute conception of the world (Williams), 123; ethics and, difference between (Williams), 122–23
Scott, James, 206n47
sense of reality (Berlin), 55–56
Shklar, Judith: liberalism of fear, 67, 139, 154–56, 158; as realist political theorist, 7
Simmons, A. John, 141–42
Skinner, Quentin, 132–33
Skorupski, John, 125
slavery, Greek, 97
Sleat, Matt, 9, 144–46, 170–71, 185n42
Smith, Adam, 53
socialism, Hampshire's, 100
Sparta, Helot population of, 140, 144
Spinoza, Baruch, 85, 108–9, 198n8
Spragens, Tom, 200n12
Stears, Marc, 196n40
Stemplowska, Zofia, 183n32
Strauss, Leo, 30
Strawson, Galen, 16–17
subhumanity, belief in as false but intelligible (Berlin), 40–41, 190–91n52
Swift, Adam, 51

Talisse, Robert, 187n15
thick/thin concepts (Williams): characteristics of, 37, 190n46; ethical concepts and, 122–23; liberalism of fear as thin universals, 155
thick/thin readings (Hampshire), procedural justice and. See procedural justice, thick reading of (Hampshire); procedural justice, thin reading of (Hampshire)
thought, reason and imagination as two domains of (Hampshire), 75–76
Thucydides, 8
toleration (Williams), 150
tragedy as intrinsic to human life (Berlin), 25
truth (Williams): the "deniers," critique of, 163; historical narrative and, 163–64; virtues of, 132–33, 155

utilitarianism: as an enactment model of political moralism, 9; ethics of, rejection of (Hampshire), 77–78; ethics of, rejection of (Williams), 121–22
utopian thinking, rejection of (Berlin and Rawls), 52

value pluralism (Berlin): experience prioritized over theoretical parsimony, 27–28; impurity of political theory and, 47–52; levels at which plurality and conflict occurs, 24–25; moral particularism, relation to, 54; mutual dependence condition, outlooks and, 25, 42–43; negative liberty/liberalism and, 63–64; objectivity of morality, consistent with a belief in, 27; outlooks, implications of, 24–25, 187n8; pessimistic implications to, 44; philosophical justification of, reason for absence of, 27; politics and, 45, 57–63, 111; principal claim and implications of, 23–24; Rawlsian ideal theory and, 46, 52; reasons for, 26–28; resolvable pluralism and, 61–62; "theory" as guide to judgments, rejection of, 52–57; truth of, moral/political recommendations and, 45; value prioritization and, possibility of, 63–68; Williams on Berlin's, 202n12
value pluralism (Hampshire): absolute justification of values are unnecessary, 65; basic reasoning of, 73–77; moving beyond Berlin and Williams, three arguments for, 84–87; political implications of, 111
value pluralism (Williams), defense of, 54–55
value pluralism leads to moral relativism, denial of (Berlin), 28–30; empirical errors argument, 35–36; empirical errors defense of Berlin, 40–41; human horizon argument, 32–35; human horizon argument, analysis of, 37–40; minimum content of natural law argument, 30–32; minimum content of natural law argument, analysis of, 36–37, 39, 43–44; reasons to explore the possibility of, 21; trilemma facing Berlin, 43–44; values not outlooks defense of Berlin, 42–43; value-twisting defense of Berlin, 41–42
values: acceptance in good faith, criteria for (Williams), 133; choosing among (Berlin), 52, 186–87n4; Crowder's distinction between two types of, 41–42; historical progress, repudiation of pseudo-Hegelian view of (Berlin), 26; the human horizon and, 34 (see also human horizon [Berlin]); incommensurability of (Williams), 125–26; mind-independent, rejection of (Berlin), 27; objectivity of (see objectivity of values); plural intrinsic, conflict and incommensurability of (Berlin), 23–25, 27 (see also value pluralism [Berlin]); value judgments as descriptive propositions, Romantics and Kant deny, 27

Waldron, Jeremy, 14–15, 62, 181n6, 194n19
Waltz, Kenneth, 8
ways of life (Hampshire): content of and the "no-shopping principle," 25, 43; evolution and change in, 84; fallacy of false fixity in, 98–99; moral judgment and, 82–84; multiplicity of good, 73–77; procedural justice and, potential for conflict between, 97–98. See also outlooks (Berlin)
Weber, Max, 145
Wedeen, Lisa, 206n47
Weizmann, Chaim, 57, 195n30
Western political theory. See political theory/philosophy

Williams, Bernard: Greek slavery, discussion of, 97; Hume, changing opinion of, 209n21; introduction to, 3–7; political "moralism" and "realism," distinction between, 8–9; Rorty, critique of, 134–35; unsystematic nature of his moral philosophy, 117. *See also* Berlin-Hampshire-Williams

Williams, Shirley (née Shirley Brittain), 4
Wittgenstein, Ludwig, 31, 202n19
Wolf, Susan, 201n1
Woozley, A. D., 182n13

Zakaras, Alex, 190n42

www.ingramcontent.com/pod-product-compliance
Lightning Source LLC
Chambersburg PA
CBHW051355290426
44108CB00015B/2029